OVERLOADED
and UNDERPREPARED

Strategies for Stronger Schools
and Healthy, Successful Kids

By Denise Pope,
Maureen Brown
and Sarah Miles

CHALLENGE SUCCESS

JOSSEY-BASS
A Wiley Brand

Published by Jossey-Bass
A Wiley Brand
One Montgomery Street, Suite 1000, San Francisco, CA 94104-4594—www.josseybass.com

Jossey-Bass books and products are available through most bookstores. To contact Jossey-Bass directly call our Customer Care Department within the U.S. at 800-956-7739, outside the U.S. at 317-572-3986, or fax 317-572-4002.

Wiley publishes in a variety of print and electronic formats and by print-on-demand. Some material included with standard print versions of this book may not be included in e-books or in print-on-demand. If this book refers to media such as a CD or DVD that is not included in the version you purchased, you may download this material at http://booksupport.wiley.com. For more information about Wiley products, visit www.wiley.com.

Library of Congress Cataloging-in-Publication Data

Pope, Denise Clark, 1966- author.
   Overloaded and underprepared : strategies for stronger schools and healthy, successful kids / by Denise Pope, Maureen Brown, and Sarah Miles.
      pages cm
   Includes bibliographical references and index.
   ISBN 978-1-119-02244-2 (pbk.), ISBN 978-1-119-02256-5 (ePDF), 978-1-119-02246-6 (epub)
   1. School improvement programs–United States. 2. Educational change–United States. 3. Students–United States–Psychology. I. Brown, Maureen, 1959- author. II. Miles, Sarah B., author. III. Title.
   LB2822.82.P66 2015
   371.2'07–dc23

                                                                                            2015005827

Cover Design: Challenge Success
Cover image: ©narvikk/iStockphoto.com

Printed in the United States of America

FIRST EDITION

HB Printing 10 9 8 7 6 5 4 3 2 1

Contents

List of Tables, Figures, and Exhibits

Tables

Figures

Exhibits

*To schools that are making real and lasting changes
to improve their students' lives*

About the Authors

Denise Clark Pope, Ph.D. is a senior lecturer at the Stanford University Graduate School of Education and cofounder of Challenge Success. For the past sixteen years, she has specialized in student engagement, curriculum studies, qualitative research methods, and service learning. Challenge Success is an expanded version of the SOS: Stressed-Out Students project that Dr. Pope founded and directed from 2003–2008. She lectures nationally on parenting techniques and pedagogical strategies to increase student health, engagement with learning, and integrity. Her book, *"Doing School": How We Are Creating a Generation of Stressed-Out, Materialistic, and Miseducated Students* (Yale University Press, 2001) was awarded Notable Book in Education by the American School Board Journal, 2001. Dr. Pope is a three-time recipient of the Stanford University Graduate School of Education Outstanding Teacher and Mentor Award, and was honored with the 2012 Education Professor of the Year "Educators' Voice Award" from the Academy of Education Arts and Sciences. She has served as a trustee at several independent schools in the Bay Area. Prior to teaching at Stanford, Dr. Pope taught high school English in Fremont, California, and college composition and rhetoric courses at Santa Clara University.

Maureen Rutter Brown, MBA is executive director for Challenge Success, where she oversees daily operations as well as marketing, fundraising, and strategic planning. Ms. Brown comes to Challenge Success with over 20 years of consulting experience in health care, financial services, and technology. Prior to joining Challenge Success, Ms. Brown worked as an independent consultant and as a partner at APM, Incorporated, where she structured, sold, and managed strategic and operations improvement engagements for health care institutions, primarily university medical centers.

Ms. Brown has also worked in cash management for Philadelphia National Bank and Citibank. She has been on various boards at Georgetown University, and cofounded the Bay Area Georgetown Technology Alliance. She has also served as cochair of the Parents Committee and as an advisor to Duke University's Entrepreneurship Program, and she has been a board member at Woodside School.

Sarah Becket Miles, M.S.W., Ph.D. is a researcher with Challenge Success. She researches how schools and classrooms can best support student learning and engagement. She works with Challenge Success member schools to translate research into practice as well as presents at conferences and writes articles for education-related journals. She has also been a coach with two Challenge Success member schools and worked as a teaching and research assistant at Stanford University. Prior to receiving her doctoral degree, Dr. Miles taught fifth grade in Oakland, California, and worked as a clinical social worker in the Boston area.

About Challenge Success

Founded at the Stanford University Graduate School of Education, Challenge Success partners with schools and families to develop research-based strategies that provide kids with the academic, social, and emotional skills needed to succeed now and in the future. Through practical workshops, conferences, and presentations, Challenge Success offers parents the tools they need to raise healthy, motivated kids, and collaborates with educators to develop school and classroom policies that encourage students to engage with learning to reach their individual potential and find a more effective path to success. Success, after all, is measured not at the end of the semester, but over the course of a lifetime. For more information about this organization, visit challengesuccess.org.

Acknowledgments

We wrote this book because we believe that with a clear vision, sufficient resources, and ample support, schools and families can make real changes that will benefit our children. The same can be said for the writing of this book, and we are extremely grateful for the help we received from our many friends and colleagues.

Our Challenge Success Cofounders Madeline Levine and Jim Lobdell helped to launch Challenge Success and continue to spread our message in what has become a national movement. We are indebted to them for their vision, persistence, and commitment to helping every child thrive. Our core team, Margaret Dunlap, Samantha Spielman, Emeri Handler, and Genie Hyatt, picked up the slack and kept the organization working smoothly when we disappeared for days to write. Our work on this book would not have been possible without their flexibility and sense of humor. Thank you, too, to Shannon Davidson for stepping in to help us meet our deadline; your careful eye and attention to detail was invaluable.

To our incredible interns, Christopher Geary, Emily Breyer, and Julia Maggioncalda: We can't thank you enough for your dogged research efforts, skillful interviewing, and the detailed work you completed to help us get the book ready for publication. Your persistence in tracking down everything we asked for was impressive.

We are also thankful to Challenge Success coaches Alexandra Ballard and Paul Franz, and to Jerusha Conner and Karen Strobel for providing us with the extra help we needed in writing our chapters on project-based learning, alternative assessment, and a climate of care. Your clear thinking and valuable advice helped us frame those sections of the book.

Our Challenge Success Board of Directors, Advisory Board, and Research and Policy Advisors play a critical role in everything we do, and we are grateful for their guidance and insight. In particular, we would like to thank our board chair Charlene Margot for her tremendous leadership, along with our past chairs, Gabrielle Layton and Lisa Stone Pritzker; without their support and vision, we would not be where we are today.

We also want to thank the many Challenge Success volunteers, students, faculty members, and administrators who contributed directly to the book by allowing us to interview them and tell their stories in our case studies. Thank you to Lisa Babinet, Megan Boesiger. Patrick Burrows, Drew Ciancia, Shivani Dayal, Laura Docter, Mary Dowden, Elizabeth Fee, Ryan Fletcher, Kirk Greer, Karen Klapper, Thomas Lengel, Alex Lockett, Charlene Margot, Jessica Nella, Sharon Ofek, Dave Otten, Kristin Plant, Amy Richards, Anne Schaefer-Salinas, Pam Scott, Casey Sheehan, Richard Simon, Lisa Spengler, Karen Strobel, Patricia Tennant, Janice Toben, Alan Vann Gardner, Carola Wittmann, Susie Wolbe, and Matthew Zito.

Thank you to our publishers and editors at Jossey Bass/Wiley, especially Kate Bradford who was tremendously patient as she waited for us to find the right time to write this book. Thank you for giving us the nudge to move forward with this project and the support to complete it.

Finally we would like to thank our families. Thank you to our children for letting us "Challenge Success you to death," for being patient with us throughout this process, and for helping us realize that practicing what you preach isn't always easy or comfortable. Thank you to our parents for raising us to love learning and for giving us the encouragement to find jobs and careers that we love. And thank you to our fabulous husbands, Mike, Dave, and Kevin, who support all that we do at Challenge Success, and who remind us to prioritize PDF (playtime, downtime, family time), even amidst a busy project like this one. We love you guys, and are incredibly grateful to have you in our lives.

Introduction

- 6:15 A.M.: Wake up, get ready for school, and grab a quick breakfast
- 7:00 A.M.: Walk to bus stop to catch the 7:10 school bus
- 7:50 A.M. to 3:00 P.M.: School day that includes AP Calculus, AP U.S. History, AP English, Honors Spanish, Biology, Art History, and Physical Education. Also includes student council meeting during lunch.
- 3:00 P.M. to 3:45 P.M.: Service club meeting after school
- 4:00 P.M. to 6:15 P.M.: Swim team practice
- 6:45 P.M.: Arrive home, shower, dinner, and three to four hours of homework
- 11:30 P.M.: Bedtime, depending on homework load
- And then start this routine all over again the next day.

This is a fairly typical schedule for a high-achieving high school student. On top of seven hours of classes, some of which are honors or advanced levels, most students have sports practices after school, at least one other extracurricular activity—sometimes more—and several hours of homework. Other students may have fewer honors courses but have responsibilities at home or at after-school jobs that keep them just as busy. It is no wonder that these students are exhausted and stressed out. Our research at high-achieving schools has found that high school students get, on average, about six and a half hours of sleep each night (Galloway, Conner, & Pope, 2013), in spite of the fact that sleep experts recommend approximately nine hours of sleep for healthy development (Eaton et al., 2010). National research also shows that academics are the leading cause of stress for nine- to thirteen-year-olds and a top concern for high school students as well (National Association of Health Education Centers, 2005). In response to this stress, students are increasingly engaging in harmful behaviors, including overuse of stimulants such as Adderall and Ritalin, known as "study drugs," binge-drinking, and "cutting" or other self-harm practices (Feliz, 2013; Goldberg, 2012). In fact, 73 percent of high school students say that stress is the main reason they use drugs (Partnership for Drug-Free Kids, 2008). The effects of this unhealthy stress and overload reach beyond high school; nationwide, 50 percent of college students have felt overwhelming anxiety, and 30 percent reported that they felt so depressed it was difficult to function (American College Health Association, 2012). Many students and parents feel they have no choice but to continue day after day at this frantic pace. They believe the prospect of a good education and future employment and security are at risk if they don't.

Admittedly, many students in the United States have schedules that look nothing like the one at the start of this chapter. For a wide variety of reasons, these students may be struggling in remedial or basic level classes or on the verge of dropping out of school; they may spend very little time on homework or extracurricular activities and may have too much free time on their hands. For many of these kids, the current education system isn't working. But is it working well for the typical student who stays in school, strives to learn the material, earns good grades, and plans to go to college? In light of the mental and physical health concerns just outlined, along with reports of rampant cheating in high school and college (for a review, see Challenge Success, 2012a), and research showing that many students—even those at the top—lack sufficient critical thinking, communication, collaboration, creativity, and problem-solving skills (American Management Association, 2010; Casner-Lott & Barrington, 2006; Darling-Hammond & Conley, 2015; Lythcott-Haims, 2015), we question whether the current education system is preparing students well for college and future careers. At Challenge Success, we offer students, parents, and schools strategies for healthier and more productive pathways to success.

Challenge Success, a research-based project founded at Stanford University's Graduate School of Education, partners with schools and families to provide the information and tools needed to create a more balanced and academically fulfilling life for kids. Cofounders Denise Pope, Madeline Levine, and Jim Lobdell started Challenge Success because, as mental health and education-reform experts, they knew they had to speak out against an increasingly fast-paced world that was interfering with sound educational practices and harming kids physically and mentally. The program, which grew from Denise Pope's original work on Stressed-Out Students and celebrated a 10-year anniversary in 2013, has reached almost 800,000 students, faculty, administrators, and parents throughout the United States and across the globe. During our first decade we have learned what works and what doesn't when trying to make changes in schools and in homes. At the urging of those who have worked closely with us, we decided to write a book of best practices that we hope will be shared widely so that more schools and families can benefit from what we have learned.

While everything we do is based on research, our goal is to provide practical information and tools to effect change. We know that teachers, administrators, and parents can get overwhelmed by the research and jargon associated with school reform, and we are here to help. We review and synthesize the literature from the field, match those findings with knowledge from our own research and practice, and then help translate research into reality. We work with teams of educators, parents, and students at schools to identify problems and implement changes to school policies concerning curriculum, assessment, scheduling, and a healthy school climate. We provide support to parents by giving them the tools they need to help their children regain their balance, strengthen their sense of self, and learn how to deal effectively with the inevitable challenges of life. And we share our research findings widely via white papers, conferences, and webinars, so that the public can make informed decisions about educating children and advocating for changes in local communities.

OUR PHILOSOPHY

At Challenge Success, we know that every child has his or her own story and path to success. We believe that kids come with a wide variety of interests, skills, capacities, and talents. They need love, support, limits, and a safe environment to develop their full potential. This process of growing up is slow, deliberate, and often unpredictable, and therefore requires that kids have the time and energy needed to mature into resilient, caring, and engaged adults. Challenge Success recognizes that our current fast-paced, high-pressure culture works against much of what we know about healthy child development. The overemphasis on grades, test scores, and rote answers has stressed out some kids and marginalized many more. We all want our kids to do well in school and to master certain skills and concepts, but our largely singular focus on academic achievement has resulted in a lack of attention to other components of a successful life—the ability to be independent, adaptable, ethical, and engaged critical thinkers. These traits, frequently described as 21st century skills, have and will continue to serve students well into the next century. Our work helps to foster learners who are healthy, motivated, and skilled with these traits that will prepare them for the wide variety of tasks they will face as adults.

What have we learned over the last 10 years? Some policymakers and those in the media want us to believe that schools are broken, but our experience doesn't bear that out. The teachers we meet care about their students and work hard. Our team-based approach and in-depth professional development have shown that it is possible to make changes to further improve schools. By focusing on what works, like hands-on learning and alternative assessments, as well as educating students and parents about healthier ways to handle stress, we have positively impacted tens of thousands of kids. For instance, as seen in the table below, schools make changes even in their first few years working with Challenge Success.

How do we know if our work is making a difference? From our own evaluation following a small sample of schools over time, we found that when schools make substantive changes to practices and policies such as those in the table below, student engagement in school increases and student stress decreases. In addition, many students report they feel more supported in school, are less likely to cheat, and are getting more sleep (Challenge Success, 2014). Finally, schools report that these changes happen without negatively affecting students' academic achievement, college acceptance rates, or standardized test scores. We hope that compiling our lessons from the field and sharing best practices will allow more schools and families to make positive changes like these, so that all kids can succeed on their own terms and live healthier and more fulfilled lives.

Table I.1 Initiatives in Schools as a Result of Work with Challenge Success

	Percentage of schools accomplished or in progress by Year 2	Percentage of schools accomplished or in progress by Year 3	Examples of initiatives accomplished or in progress
Students' schedule and use of time	100%	100%	Revised exam or project calendars
			Changed homework policies
			Provided students with organizers
			Changed to a later start time
			Implemented new bell schedules
			Moved to modified block scheduling
			Revised athletics schedules
			Instituted homework-free vacations with finals before winter holiday

Table I.1 (*continued*)

	Percentage of schools accomplished or in progress by Year 2	Percentage of schools accomplished or in progress by Year 3	Examples of initiatives accomplished or in progress
			Used scheduling tools to prevent over- and underscheduling of AP/honors courses
Project-based learning	40%	50%	Added community-building school-wide projects
			Modified units to incorporate project-based learning
			Incorporated project-based learning into final assessments
Alternative assessment	80%	90%	Modified grading policy/weights
			Gave ungraded assignments in first quarter (comments only/no letter grade)
			Lowered significance of or eliminated mid-term and final exams and included more formative assessment practices
			Implemented "Revision & Redemption" policies
Climate of care	80%	100%	Added new advisory periods
			Initiated student mentorship programs
			Offered extra help periods/tutorials
			Established a Student Union
			Implemented wellness programs
			Conducted senior exit interviews
			Modified awards assemblies

(continued)

Table I.1 *(continued)*

	Percentage of schools accomplished or in progress by Year 2	Percentage of schools accomplished or in progress by Year 3	Examples of initiatives accomplished or in progress
Educating faculty, parents, and students about well-being	100%	100%	Organized parent book club discussion groups
			Held school-wide health fairs
			Offered faculty professional development on effective homework practices and teaching for engagement
			Created parent education programming
			Started student-run Challenge Success clubs

Chapter ONE

From Vision to Action: An Overview of the School Change Process

A CHEATING STORY

Megan was a high-performing student at an academically challenging parochial school—and she was frustrated. Everywhere she looked it seemed like her classmates were cheating. They copied each other's papers, wrote answers on their shoes, and forged notes to get extra time on tests; one student even created a custom water bottle label with test material embedded in it. Megan had never cheated. She wanted to do the right thing, but it felt like she was getting the short end of the stick. Why should everyone else get ahead by cheating, but not her? She couldn't help but think she was in a situation where you had to "cheat or be cheated." She considered approaching her faculty advisor about what she was observing, but that was complicated. She didn't want to get her friends in trouble, and besides, it seemed like some of the teachers knew what was going on and just looked the other way. So she decided not to do anything, and her frustration continued to build.

Megan wasn't the only one who noticed the cheating problem. A local newspaper ran a story on extensive cheating at her school when some high-profile incidents were leaked to the press. To their credit, the school leaders acknowledged that the school had a problem, and they came to Challenge Success for help. They formed a team of administrators, parents, teachers, and students that began to gather data to learn more about why students were cheating. By interviewing and surveying students and faculty, they learned that kids cheated for a number of reasons, such as having too much work to complete in the time available, feeling pressured to take too many high-level courses or to make a certain grade in a course, perceiving that the teachers didn't care about breaking the rules, and sometimes because they felt the whole system was unfair so cheating didn't really matter. The team collected and reported information on 38 incidents of general cheating, along with 50 incidences of plagiarism during the course of one school year, out of a total student body of approximately 1,600 students.

With data in hand, the team began a school-wide discussion on the importance of integrity. A panel of students spoke candidly to the faculty, sharing what was happening on campus and how concerned they were about the culture emerging at their school. As a result of these conversations, students and teachers together created an honor code to be used with every paper, quiz, test, project, and assessment. They also engaged in a massive educational effort to make sure that all parties — students, parents, faculty, and administrators — understood what this new honor code meant. All stakeholders signed the agreement, showing a commitment to solving the integrity problem together. The school made it clear that the honor code was in place to help students and faculty take responsibility for poor choices, not just to punish cheaters. The academic integrity task force clearly defined cheating practices and created a transparent process for reviewing infractions, including a student-run judicial board. The administration educated teachers on how and when to report violations, and because there was a consistent policy in place, the faculty felt supported in their efforts. In professional development sessions, teachers also learned to develop more "plagiarism-proof" assignments and alternative forms of assessment and to rotate exam materials to reduce the chances of cheating.

Integrity became as important as every other part of the curriculum, and teachers integrated the study of integrity into their subject areas when possible. For example, students were regularly asked to write journal entries on current events reflecting integrity or cheating behavior, and the principal wrote about positive integrity practices each month in her community newsletter. The faculty understood that adolescents make mistakes and that valuable lessons could be learned from a poor choice in order to prevent it from happening again. In parent education sessions, administrators addressed parents' fears of a blemish on their children's permanent record, and parents were coached on a case-by-case basis on how to respond appropriately at home when a student received a judicial infraction.

As a result of a community effort to fairly, transparently, and meaningfully address cheating, the school saw general infractions drop from 38 to 7, and plagiarism incidences drop from 50 to 11 during the next school year. Students and faculty reported feeling proud of their collective efforts to change the culture to one of community trust and integrity (Challenge Success, 2012b). As a result of their work with Challenge Success, the students on the team developed a catchphrase, "Find it, own it, live it." As one student explained, "Finding what integrity means to you and really owning that definition and living it out in academics, sports, extracurriculars, and even outside of school. This is something that you could apply to any aspect of your life."

This is just one example of how Challenge Success works with schools to make positive changes. Throughout this book, we will look at a number of examples of different kinds of changes in policy and practice that we think are relevant to schools nationwide. By sharing success stories and lessons learned, we hope to help educators consider the challenges their own schools are facing and how best to address the problems by creating an action plan for change. The next section describes the typical stages of this change process.

HOW DOES THIS WORK? PRINCIPLES FOR CHANGE

Our concept is straightforward: we believe that effective school change happens when all stakeholders—administrators, faculty, parents, counselors, and students—come together to identify problems and work on solutions. This is not a revolutionary concept, but how often have we seen reform efforts superimposed on schools with little student or teacher voice or input, and how often have we watched them fail? School reform experts agree: When schools work with a team of stakeholders in a focused way, they can make real progress toward improving policies and practice (Barth, 1991; for review, see Desimone, 2002).

At Challenge Success, we partner with suburban and urban public, charter, parochial, and independent schools. Schools involved in our program send full teams to attend an intensive conference in the fall, where they identify problems to be addressed at their school sites. In some cases, teams have a pretty good sense of what needs to be worked on when they arrive; in others, predetermined ideas are turned on their heads based on discussions and workshops at the conference. Our process allows schools to take the time to determine the root causes of student stress and disengagement at their particular site, and then we help the school design an individualized school plan for changes during the year to increase student engagement and well-being. We provide each school with a coach, who guides the team through this process every step of the way. This team-based, site-specific approach is key, and the coach helps to make sure schools stay on track and don't lose focus throughout the year. The coach serves as a primary facilitator and liaison who shares research-based approaches and best practices and helps schools to select and implement these at their sites. Finally, teams reconvene each spring to problem-solve challenges with other schools and to celebrate success stories. Many schools admit that without the helpful prodding from an experienced coach and without the built-in accountability that comes with attending the spring conference, they might not have made as much progress throughout the year.

We don't want "flash in the pan" results at Challenge Success schools; we want changes to stick. Too often schools enact the newest policies or practices du jour without thinking through how these changes fit with long-term goals and other initiatives going on at the school or district level. We know that in order to effect lasting change, several things need to happen: Everyone on the team needs to feel like he or she is a part of the process, and all voices need to be heard. You'd be surprised by how wise a sixth grader can be if you give her a chance to speak her mind. Our successful teams have a common vision for the long term, and they work with us to develop a roadmap to get to where they want to go. Team leaders take what they learn at our conferences back to their broader community to educate more students, teachers, and parents in order to earn their buy-in. When all of this work has been done thoughtfully, we see a culture of collaboration and trust form alongside a willingness to change that frequently doesn't develop with a top-down approach.

THE CHARACTERISTICS OF EFFECTIVE CHALLENGE SUCCESS TEAMS

Since the inception of our project in 2004, we have learned a lot about what makes an effective school team and the general progression that teams go through as they create changes to reduce student stress and increase health and engagement at their school sites. Figure 1.1 presents a visual depiction of typical stages in the process. While the change process varies from school to school based on the unique circumstances and needs of each, we have found some common characteristics of effective teams and the stages most teams go through as they create change.

An effective Challenge Success team has a clear leader or champion and a stable core team that may include the principal or other administrator, one or more teachers, one or more parents, two or more students, and one counselor or psychologist.

Figure 1.1 Typical Stages in the Challenge Success Change Process

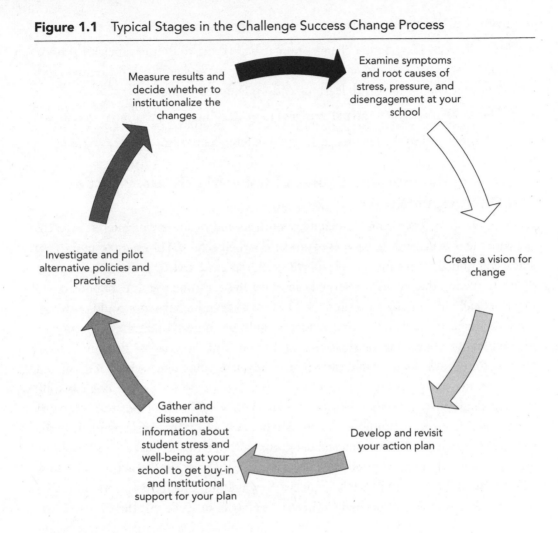

This team:

- Attends the Challenge Success fall conference and spring follow-up conference, and meets multiple times with the Challenge Success team coach at the school site.

- Regularly gathers and disseminates information to the school community about student health, engagement, and integrity, and encourages cross-stakeholder dialogue about this information.

- Has an action plan that reflects a vision for change and contains a clear but flexible schedule for moving forward.

- Holds meetings at least quarterly to review and push forward the action plan.

- Involves all stakeholders at each stage of the change process.

- Pilots discreet, incremental changes rather than trying to do too much all at once. Changes are based on the school community's needs and are known from research to improve engagement with learning and student well-being.

- Evaluates results of incremental changes before deciding to institutionalize reforms.

- Attends fall and spring Challenge Success conferences in future years as needed.

Identifying the Problem: Causes of Unhealthy Stress, Pressure, and Disengagement

Frequently school teams confuse symptoms of stress and/or student disinterest in learning with the root causes and sources of pressure at their school. For example, in the case study mentioned earlier, the school reported a widespread cheating problem among students. In theory, there could be several causes for the cheating: the student body could hypothetically be morally bankrupt; the pressure to get a higher score could outweigh the risk of getting caught cheating; students could be so bored that they lack interest in completing assignments on their own; and so on. You can imagine that solutions to curbing the cheating issue would vary significantly depending upon which of these root causes seemed most pervasive. One of the first things we do with our schools is walk them through an exercise that focuses on identifying what kinds of negative behaviors are happening on their campuses. Team members call out symptoms and identify the root causes as well as all of the stakeholder groups affected by these causes. In the cheating case, students were responding to certain cues at the school to act the way they did. The school discovered that students felt they had too much homework, unrealistic expectations from parents and teachers, and an overall sense that the climate at the school was based on a "survival of the fittest" mentality instead of a cohesive and supportive community. The teachers were also clearly affected and upset by the climate. Given the symptoms and causes the Challenge Success team identified, it seemed that the faculty would benefit from professional development on how to teach in a more engaging way, and that administrators needed help to implement policy changes to address cheating and provide more support to teachers. Parents also needed more education on why kids were cheating and what their role in the change process might look like. Since everyone seemed to be a part of the cheating problem at the school, everyone needed to be a part of the solution as well.

Figure 1.2 presents a sample of one school's "stress tree" exercise identifying symptoms and root causes. Note that we ask schools to consider symptoms and causes of

Figure 1.2 A Sample "Stress Tree"

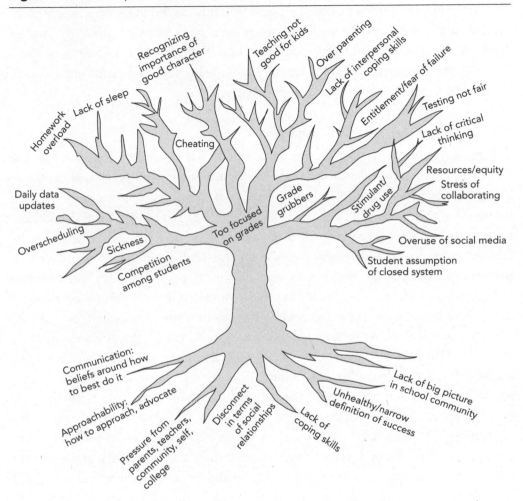

"unhealthy" stress when they create this tree. We know that some forms of stress (called "eustress") can be healthy and positive; for instance, when you are about to give a speech and you feel some butterflies in your stomach, this kind of short-term stress might provide energy and motivation to do well on the speech. When we refer to stress throughout this book, we are talking about an unhealthy, chronic form of stress, also known as "distress," that is associated with feelings of concern and anxiety and may lead to physical and mental health issues and poor performance on tasks. Different tasks or experiences can lead to distress for different students, especially if the students feel that they do not have the resources or ability to cope with the stressors.

Typically, we also recommend a school-wide survey or data gathering process to confirm the symptoms and root causes that surface in this tree exercise. Approximately 75 percent of all the schools we work with each year opt to take our Challenge Success survey as a way to gather preliminary data. Once the team identifies causes of stress and other negative behaviors at the school, and the team understands the impact on all stakeholders, we are ready to start creating a vision for change.

Moving (Slowly) Toward Change

In some ways identifying what is going on at schools is the easy part—students are not shy about telling the adults in the room what is really happening. Kids, after all, are living this day in and day out, and they have a lot to say about how things could be improved at their school. Students frequently lead the discussion on which problems are most important and help to guide teams as they agree on a vision for change at their school. Creating a vision statement seems straightforward, but many schools aren't used to thinking in these terms. They often struggle as we ask them to limit themselves to one or two root causes to address. Some team leaders want to take on multiple initiatives all at the same time. In our experience, schools are more likely to fail when they take on too much at one time. We make sure schools create a focused and feasible vision statement. The vision should address one or two root causes and should be something the school can actually accomplish. For example, the vision probably won't include changing college admission policies or abolishing the Common Core State Standards. We bring discipline to this part of the process and insist that schools start off slowly and with realistic goals. When schools are new and are starting from scratch—or when they want to start a new division or school-within-a-school where they overhaul many aspects of the original mission, curriculum, structure, and philosophy—we work with them for two to three years to carefully plan all the changes and hire faculty and staff who align with the new vision. For lasting change to occur at established schools, however, we recommend that they "turn their ship slowly" and stay aligned with a few root causes to address in a systematic way.

Of course, not all of our schools are working to solve the same problems. Our case study school, for instance, had a vision to foster a culture of integrity at its school. Other schools at our conference are working with different visions for change—perhaps a vision to increase critical thinking and creative problem solving for their students, or a vision to reduce workload without sacrificing rigor. Part of what we've learned over the past decade is that, although it would be terrific to have a one-size-fits-all approach to create change in schools (and in families for that matter), real change doesn't work that way. Though there are certainly common problems we see across schools—and some common practices to address these problems—schools need to examine their own issues and take their own paths toward implementing solutions. In other words, when you mandate a common approach, it tends not to work. Each school is unique, and understanding the nuanced culture and values at each site is critical to allow schools to design their own vision statements and action plans.

From Ideas to Action

Having a general idea and vision for change is one thing, but getting something done in a school environment is another. And, when you work with schools ranging from small private schools to large public systems, the expected rate of change differs from school to school. Some schools take much more time to analyze the problem and agree on a vision. But eventually they all get to the next stage in the process: making a plan for change.

Schools start by brainstorming potential strategies, and nothing is off the table, no matter how seemingly radical, bizarre, or impractical. Then they narrow their ideas down into specific actions that will support their vision. Back to our cheating example: The school wanted to instill a culture of integrity. Their action plan included the following:

We will ask all faculty and staff to have students reflect on the culture of integrity. Students will keep journal entries on times when they see conflicts of integrity in school and out.

Our theme for parent education this year will be integrity and the parents' role in helping to foster this.

We will ask all stakeholders to join in a process of creating and implementing an honor code and student-run judicial review process.

We will offer professional development sessions for faculty on creating more plagiarism-proof assignments.

We then ask schools to be clear on how these planned actions may lead to increased engagement and/or student well-being. For instance, our case study school wrote:

> A new honor code will help to engage students with learning as opposed to just "getting the grades."
>
> This, combined with the journal reflections, faculty professional development, and parent and student sessions on increasing integrity, should allow for a better school environment, which will promote student engagement and, ultimately, greater well-being.

Next, we ask schools to think about what resources may be needed to achieve their vision. For example, knowing that your school superintendent is on board may mean that he or she will fund needed professional development and parent education. We also ask schools to anticipate obstacles to realizing their vision and to devise strategies to overcome those obstacles. If the school suspects that parents and students will resist change (and they typically do resist change, as do the faculty), the school might schedule specific parent education sessions and faculty development workshops, and create a student task force to hear from a broader group of kids to achieve greater buy-in for the action plan.

We encourage our schools to be proactive when it comes to building institutional support; without the cooperation of all the various stakeholders, plans are not likely to move forward. Perhaps most important, we hold schools accountable for what they agree to do, and we benchmark their progress. We work with them to stay on schedule and to follow their action plans, and then help them to determine the effectiveness of the changes in policy or practice by implementing further surveys or research to see if the changes actually made a difference in alleviating the original problems.

WHAT YOU'LL FIND IN THIS BOOK

At Challenge Success we have organized our schools' best practices into a framework we call SPACE, as shown in Figure 1.3.

We based this framework on vision statements and action plans from Challenge Success schools in our early years of work, as well as on the research on best practices for

Figure 1.3 SPACE Framework

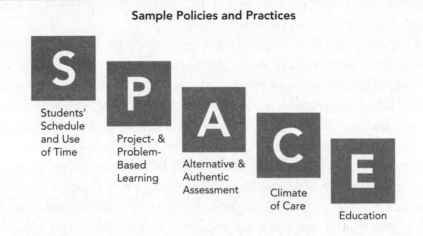

effective schools (for examples, see Darling-Hammond, 2001; the Whole Child Initiative; and the University of Chicago Consortium on Chicago School Research).

The remainder of the book is organized to cover each of these components, which we have identified as the main categories of change that we recommend to schools:

- Students' schedule and use of time

- Project- and problem-based learning

- Alternative and authentic assessment

- Climate of care

- Education for parents, students, and faculty

Additional chapters focus on homework and Advanced Placement courses, since these topics often impact several of the other components and tend to be particularly challenging for schools. We'll discuss how students spend time during the day and how that might be improved to allow more time for transitions, reflection, and deeper learning. We'll show how real, interdisciplinary, relevant projects enhance engagement and learning, and how different types of assessment can improve retention without sacrificing student well-being. We will also look at the importance of a caring, safe school environment, and how to educate all stakeholders to make lasting and effective change. Throughout the book we'll provide tools and templates you can use at your school site, and we offer case studies from Challenge Success schools that implemented changes aligned with the SPACE categories. We offer these very detailed descriptions and resources so you won't need to reinvent the wheel on your own and can learn from the experiences, mistakes, and successes of others.

This book is actually an example of what we mean by the E in SPACE: educating teachers, students, and parents about the importance of creating a school schedule, curriculum, and climate designed for every child to succeed. For schools that may already have some of these best practices and school components in place, this book offers ideas on how to extend and improve these practices at your site. We provide the latest research in each chapter, so you can explain the rationale behind your policies and beliefs to parents, students, and new faculty members. For schools that have not yet made some of these changes or that are in the midst of contemplating a new reform effort, this book can serve as a practical, step-by-step guide on how to enact effective policies and practices to increase student well-being and engagement with learning. We hope you will find each chapter and tool to be useful, and that you'll be inspired to try our suggestions in your communities—and let us know what happens.

Chapter TWO

A Saner Schedule

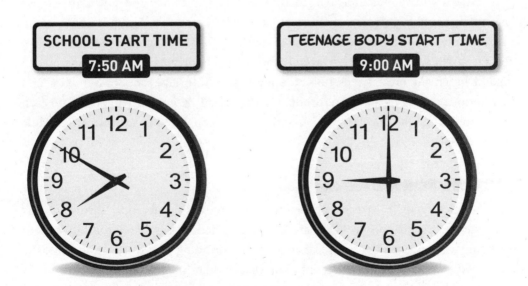

SCHOOL START TIME
7:50 AM

TEENAGE BODY START TIME
9:00 AM

School schedules aren't always a hot topic of conversation; the subject just isn't sexy enough to gain much attention. However, we have found that how a student's day and the school year are structured can have a substantial impact on engagement, teaching, and learning. Kids who run from class to class often struggle when it comes time to settle down and get to work. The research suggests that this may be because it takes time for the brain to transition (Cercone, 2006; Prince, 2005). It can be tricky to go from analyzing poetry in English class, then to the locker area and checking in with friends, then directly to math class and solving equations on the board. Students of all ages need times during the day to switch gears, take much-needed breaks, and refuel. This can be particularly difficult in middle school and high school when students take multiple classes from different teachers and need to walk to classrooms across campus during short passing periods. Teens also face an extra challenge during the early morning hours when schools typically start. Many teens come to school sleepwalking because their bodies' circadian rhythms are different from those of elementary students and most adults (Crowley & Carskadon, 2010). We have also found that the pace of the overall school year—from September to June, with holidays, exams, and multiple ramp-ups and wind-downs—can impact student stress levels and academic achievement. Finally, we have learned that changing a school's schedule is not a simple task; it takes ample time and a real commitment to professional development.

As schools think about alternate schedules for the school day and calendar year, we believe they should consider a number of factors: how traditional and modified block schedules affect time for engaged learning in middle and high school; the benefits of a later start to the school day for teenagers; the timing of midterms and exams; and how to schedule lunch and break times, homeroom/advisory/tutorials, school assemblies, and other periods during the day and throughout the year. This chapter will delve into each of these topics and provide case studies and tools you can use to create a saner schedule at your school.

STUDENT FOR A DAY

After completing their "stress tree" exercises at the fall conference, several of our Challenge Success schools realize that their daily schedule may be hindering student well-being and engagement with learning. Before deciding if and how to change the daily schedule, these schools often opt to participate in a "starter" exercise. They hire 5 to 20 substitute teachers to take over classes in order to allow several faculty members to participate as "student shadows" for a typical school day. The gist of Shadow Day is for a sampling of teachers to shadow individual students throughout the entire school day. (We offer step-by-step directions for this exercise in the Appendix.) Each "shadow teacher" will carry a backpack, use an assigned locker for the day, and attend all classes with the assigned student. Schools should aim for a diverse range of students for teachers to shadow in order to get a fair sense of what it is like to be a student going through the ups and downs and daily stressors of a full school day. One Challenge Success middle school shadow teacher told us that the exercise was eye-opening for her. She explains, "It was a really overwhelming day! The students have so many things they're trying to do every day, and it was just exhausting for the teachers to be the student for the day and try to follow. Just getting that perspective as a teacher [from the student's point of view] is so useful." Another teacher who shadowed students for a day at a different school said, "I was ready to go home after third period, and that was before hours of afterschool extracurriculars and homework! I never realized how hard it is to run from class to class and have to sit quietly and think hard and be on task 24/7. We expect a lot from our students, and the day doesn't offer nearly enough breaks or downtime." Starting with the shadow exercise allows faculty members to see the pros and cons of the daily schedule and ideally helps them to craft one that is more developmentally appropriate and much less hectic.

WHAT IS A BLOCK SCHEDULE?

A look at schools across the country reveals a variety of daily schedules, from traditional to modified block schedules to full block schedules and more. Before diving into the pros and cons of the length of class times, we want to define our terms:

In a **traditional schedule**, the school day is divided into six to eight periods of approximately equal length that meet daily over the course of a semester or a quarter. Class time typically runs for 45 to 55 minutes, with usually less than five minutes to transition from class to class.

In a **block schedule**, first introduced in the early 1990s, there are fewer periods each semester, trimester, or quarter, meeting for longer stretches of time, than those in a traditional schedule. One example of a block schedule is a 4x4 semester or quarter plan in which each school day is divided into four 90-minute periods, and students take four courses each semester or quarter. Some schools use block scheduling to teach a year-long class in a compressed period of time, such as a semester, in which the students focus only on one or two subject areas at a time and get credit for a full year. Another common schedule is an alternate day (A/B) schedule in which students and teachers meet every other day for longer periods rather than meeting every day for shorter periods. This is often called a **"modified" block schedule**. Many of the schools we work with use a combination of modified block and traditional class periods. For instance, some schools decide to have a couple of classes, such as science and history, meet in less frequent, longer periods while other classes, such as math and foreign languages, may meet in more frequent, shorter periods. See Exhibit 2.1 for a sample traditional schedule and a sample modified block schedule created by Burlingame Intermediate School as an outcome of our Challenge Success work.

Exhibit 2.1 Examples of a Traditional and a Block Schedule

Bell Schedules 2013–2014 (Traditional Example)

Burlingame Intermediate School

Regular Day Schedule—3:00 Dismissal—346 minutes

8:30–8:37	Homeroom	7 Minutes
8:41–9:26	Period 1	45 Minutes
9:30–10:15	Period 2	45 Minutes
10:15–10:24	**RECESS**	**9 Minutes**
10:27–11:12	Period 3	45 Minutes
11:16–12:01	Period 4	45 Minutes
12:01–12:34	**LUNCH (7th and 8th Grade)**	**33 Minutes**
12:37–1:22	Period 5 **(7th and 8th Grade)**	45 Minutes
12:05–12:50	Period 5 **(6th Grade)**	45 Minutes
12:50–1:23	**LUNCH (6th Grade)**	**33 Minutes**
1:26–2:11	Period 6	45 Minutes
2:15–3:00	Period 7	45 Minutes

Bell Schedules 2014–2015

Burlingame Intermediate School

Modified Block Schedule

Tuesday

8:30–9:52	Period 2	82 Minutes
9:52–10:05	**RECESS**	**13 Minutes**
10:05–11:25	Period 4	80 Minutes
11:25–12:00	**LUNCH**	**35 Minutes (all grades)**
12:05–1:25	Period 6	80 Minutes
1:30–2:00	Guided Study	30 Minutes

Wednesday

8:30–9:52	Period 1	82 Minutes
9:52–10:05	**RECESS**	**13 Minutes**
10:05–11:25	Period 3	80 Minutes
11:25–12:00	**LUNCH**	**35 Minutes (all grades)**
12:05–1:25	Period 5	80 Minutes
1:25–1:40	**BREAK**	**15 Minutes**
1:40–3:00	Period 7	80 Minutes

The Research on Block Scheduling

While we have seen the benefits for many schools and students when they change from a traditional to a block or a modified block schedule, the research is less clear on this subject depending on which student outcomes are being examined. For instance, the research comparing schools with traditional schedules and those with block schedules tends to focus mostly on differences in students' academic outcomes using standardized tests, and the results have been mixed (Gill, 2011; Harmston, Pliska, Ziomek, & Hackmann, 2001; Maltese, Dexter, Tai, & Sadler, 2007; Zepeda & Mayers, 2006). In fact, a meta-analysis of nine studies comparing student academic outcomes at schools with traditional and block schedules concluded that the findings of many of the studies reviewed turned out to be not significant, yielding no certain conclusions; of those that were significant, the size of the effects were so small that they were deemed to be inconsequential (Lewis, Winokur, Cobb, Gliner, & Schmidt, 2005).

While several studies look at differences in academic outcomes between schools with block and traditional schedules, few studies investigate differences in other important student outcomes, such as classroom and school climate, student engagement, and student stress. Of those we found that addressed these outcomes, one study found positive effects of a block schedule on student self-efficacy in mathematics as compared to those with a traditional schedule (Biesinger, Crippen, & Muis, 2008). Another study found that as many as 72 percent of high schools have implemented some version of a block schedule because these schools believe students with these alternate schedules benefit from an improved school climate, lighter daily homework load, and less disruption from transitions (Queen, 2009). Finally, we found some evidence that students and teachers may be able to form closer connections with one another in a block schedule as opposed to a traditional schedule (Deuel, 1999; Eineder & Bishop, 1997).

Unfortunately, many of the studies we reviewed did not look at differences in implementation, such as how teachers were trained to change their teaching practices in the new schedule. And, from what we have learned about changing from a traditional to a modified block schedule, implementation matters. For instance, just stringing together two traditional 45-minute lesson plans to fill a 90-minute block isn't necessarily going to improve student learning and certainly isn't taking advantage of what a block schedule might offer in terms of engaging pedagogy and curriculum. Teachers who learn to use blocks well know that they can engage students in more hands-on and extended learning activities that help students gain mastery of the material, as opposed to solely "telling" students information via class lectures due to tight time constraints to get through the material in a shorter period. Finally, the well-known *Prisoners of*

Time report, first published in 1994 and then again in 2005 by the National Education Commission on Time and Learning (NECTL), strongly recommended that schools think more creatively about scheduling. The Commission made a specific recommendation that schools shift to block or modified block scheduling to address the fixed time periods built into a traditional school schedule. The authors argued that these fixed and shorter periods tend to inhibit students from engaging in deep exploration and learning, whereas a more flexible schedule that includes longer periods allows for more individualized learning, the use of emerging technologies, collaboration among teachers, and the use of resources available in the community (National Education Commission on Time and Learning, 2005).

While the research may be mixed or lacking concerning the effects of changing to a block or modified block schedule, we have observed more of the benefits than the downsides of these changes. It may be that the schools we work with have transitioned to modified block schedules with more support than those presented in the published research. At Challenge Success, we have observed that making these kinds of shifts in the school schedule can fundamentally change the way teaching happens. Teachers we have observed aren't rushing to get the information out to their students before the bell rings; they are facilitating discussions and debates and are allowing time for students to form their own ideas and opinions. With the new schedule, teachers have more time for field trips, projects, and service learning experiences, and students have more time to grapple with the concepts and reflect on their learning. We also know that students in a modified or block schedule feel less harried because they have fewer classes each day, and they typically have a reduced homework load. After all, the students don't have to do homework for six or seven classes each night; instead they can focus on the three or four classes they have the next day. In fact, a recent survey of teachers, students, and parents at a Bay Area public middle school found significant positive results from making the switch to a modified block schedule. After one semester, they found that:

- Only 15% of students disapprove of the block schedule.
- 57% of students feel that the block schedule has made it easier to manage homework, with 21% feeling it is the same.
- 62% of students prefer days where only 4–5 classes meet rather than all 7 classes.
- 62% of teachers feel that they can go deeper into subjects because of the longer block periods.
- 73% of teachers feel more comfortable trying new instructional strategies due to the block schedule.

- 57% of teachers feel that the block schedule has increased their ability to collaborate with other teachers.

- 70% of teachers feel that the block schedule has increased the ability for students to collaborate as well as increased the ability for more student/teacher interaction.

- 70% of teachers feel that the block schedule has increased the ability for differentiation in the classroom. (Piedmont Middle School, 2014)

Of course, this can happen only when the transition takes place thoughtfully and with plenty of professional development opportunities. The following case study outlines how one Challenge Success high school spent three years making the change to a saner schedule.

Notre Dame High School, Belmont, California

When team members from Notre Dame High School, a parochial school in Northern California's Bay Area, first attended our schools conference, they felt that the existing schedule was contributing to student stress, and they were contemplating making changes. Working with a coach to examine symptoms and root causes of stress in their community reinforced their belief that their traditional seven-period day schedule was one factor leading to high student stress levels. Students didn't have time to learn material in depth during the short periods, so they weren't achieving their learning goals. The school wanted to find a way to improve student engagement, enhance student activities, balance time for student athletes, slow down the pace of the day, and provide opportunity for collaboration between teachers, between students, and between teachers and students. They recognized just how short a 50-minute period could be; after taking attendance and prayer at the start of class and kids getting ready to move at the end, they really had only 35 to 40 minutes of class time. Teachers frequently couldn't finish the work they had planned for the day, and students complained that the constant moving around was hectic, stressful, and not all that productive.

The school considered changing to a modified block schedule to allow teachers the time to facilitate longer discussions and hands-on labs and projects, and to give students the opportunity to reflect on their learning in class and collaborate with one another and with their teachers. Despite the perceived benefits, the decision to change the schedule was not an easy one. It involved creating three different committees (operations, planning, and policy) to think through the logistics, research best practices, and plan for the eventual implementation. Committee members knew the change to a new schedule might be controversial. Change is always hard, but this change in particular affected many stakeholders in a number of ways. Teachers would have to learn to teach differently; students would have to adjust to active learning during longer periods; and parents, students, and faculty members were all going to lose the early dismissal period every Friday that was a favorite part of the old, traditional schedule.

Once the committees agreed on a vision statement for a healthier and more engaging schedule, they began the second phase of their work—researching and marketing to the larger community. Teachers and students visited other local schools with different kinds of block schedules to experience what a full day felt like with fewer classes and more collaboration time between students and teachers. During several in-service days, experts, including teachers experienced with modified block schedules, worked with faculty and staff on how to adapt their curriculum, manage their instructional time with longer teaching periods, and use those block periods to go deeper and engage students in their learning. The school posted proposed schedules and curricular changes on a website where teachers, parents, and students could weigh in with their opinions and suggestions. Students presented findings from their school visits to parents at community meetings designed to create buy-in and calm any fears about the proposed changes, and the administration approved professional learning communities within departments to encourage continuing professional development beyond the initial in-service days.

After years of careful planning, the new schedule was finally in place, and the students immediately noted, in focus groups, the positive impact of the change: They had more time in their classes for learning and more time to get things done during a school day, and they felt the quality of their work improved because they were given more time to consult different resources and meet with teachers for help. As one student explained, teachers could plan fun lessons that involved hands-on work that they had never had time to do before, such as analyzing scenes from Hollywood movies for scientific errors: "We found a critical mistake in an Indiana Jones movie, which was really awesome and much more engaging than the typical 'This is the lesson; let's do it, let's get it done, and get on to the next.'"

(continued)

After a year with the new schedule, the administration planned one "tradition-al" day to incorporate a special school assembly without losing some instruc-tional time. After the students and faculty went through a full day of seven 50-minute periods with an added assembly period, they shook their heads in disbelief. As one vice principal explained, "We were completely exhausted after that traditional seven-period day; we couldn't believe that we did that for so many years, and we learned just how valuable that change to the new schedule was for us. Fifty-minute periods simply don't work, and we all need the breaks now incorporated in the new schedule. We will never go back!"

Implementation Tips for Changing the School Schedule

As illustrated in the case study, making changes to the schedule takes considerable time and effort. Here we summarize advice from various researchers and our Challenge Success schools as to the best practices for successfully implementing a change to block, modified block, or any kind of alternate schedule.

Involve all stakeholders in the change process, including teachers, students, and parents. Teachers are probably the most important constituency for the success of a schedule change, so their buy-in and understanding is particularly important. As Ullrich and Yeaman (1999) say: "It takes a huge effort by everyone to make [this] change. It requires more than rearranging minutes. It requires changing teaching techniques [and] philosophy about what teachers do and how students learn best" (p. 18).

Identify other local schools that use the model and go visit them. Interview those with firsthand experience revising their teaching practices for the new schedule, and ask about the challenges they faced during the change process.

Provide plenty of initial and ongoing professional development opportunities for teachers who are new to the field and/or the model, and recognize that many of these teachers will need to redesign most of their lesson plans to fit with the new schedule. This will take a lot of work and a lot of time, so it is important to provide ongoing support such as professional learning communities and mentoring throughout the first year and beyond. Researchers found that when staff development was provided, two-thirds of teachers increased the variety of strategies they used in their classrooms, such as more collaboration between students, case studies, simulations, Socratic seminars and discussions, and other active learning strategies to keep students engaged during the longer periods (Jenkins, Queen, & Algozzine, 2002; Queen, Algozzine, & Eaddy, 1997).

Consider team teaching and interdisciplinary courses that span block periods. Take advantage of the longer periods by encouraging teachers to work together to design more complex learning activities, and be sure to allow plenty of common planning time for these teachers as they collaborate. For example, many of our Challenge Success schools are using the long block periods to implement interdisciplinary STEM (science, technology, engineering, and math) units where students use the extra time to construct models, design programs, and practice real-world applications.

Not all courses need to be treated the same. Ideally, you will allot the same number of instructional minutes to courses of equal weight, but that doesn't mean you need to have a bell schedule where all courses meet for equal increments each day. Sometimes math and foreign language departments prefer more frequent, shorter periods, while humanities and science courses may prefer longer, less frequent periods. Consider the benefits of having some "skinny" and some extended periods throughout the week. Also consider rotating periods so that students don't have the same class at the same exact time each day. Teachers know that first period usually means sleepy students or more students who are late, and last period classes are usually the ones impacted most by the athletic game schedule. Changing the timing of when you meet with different period classes each day can prevent some of these "lost" minutes due to student absence or disengagement. Similarly, increasing the time and frequency for daily student breaks and lunch can help rejuvenate students so they are ready to learn each period (American Academy of Pediatrics, 2013; Ramstetter, Murray, & Garner, 2010). Lunch should be long enough for kids to make it through the lunch line and have some extra time for socializing or meeting with teachers.

Even if you do all of this, recognize that getting it right will take time. Don't rush to judgment in the first year if things aren't perfect—and be prepared to tinker some more. The first year is often the most difficult; for veteran teachers this may feel like being a new teacher all over again (Hackmann, 1995). As one expert notes, the block schedule works best if teachers become less disseminators of knowledge and more facilitators of learning (for review, see Queen, 2000). Lecturing for 90 minutes straight isn't going to work (but doesn't necessarily work in 45-minute periods either), so teachers will need to change their practices and allow for more student-centered, hands-on work. See Chapter Four on engagement and project-based learning for more ideas on how to do this effectively. Similarly, what works at one school won't necessarily work at another. For instance, one small private school with class sizes of about 15 to 17 kids found that they didn't need to have such long periods to experience the benefits of a modified block schedule. They found that, with the exception of some of the science lab periods, each student could participate in discussions and hands-on learning during a 65-minute period instead of needing a longer 90-minute period.

Many of our Challenge Success schools review the schedule every few years and decide to tweak the number of minutes in the block periods and change the way the periods rotate each week or how often classes meet. There is no magic algorithm to finding the best schedule, so devote the time and energy it takes to create one that works best for your school community.

A LATER START TIME

Along with changing the amount of time and frequency for each class during the day, you should examine whether your start time is impacting student health and engagement with learning.

The research on later start times centers mostly around the lack of congruence between adolescent sleep patterns and the time schools start in most districts. According to the National Sleep Foundation (2015) and other sleep experts, high school students need 8 to 10 hours of sleep each night, and middle school students may need up to 11 hours. This is not necessarily easy to achieve. Studies show that 80 percent of teenagers don't get the recommended amount of sleep (Eaton et al., 2010). At least 28 percent fall asleep in school, and 22 percent fall asleep doing homework (National Sleep Foundation, 2006). From our own research, we have found that, on average, high school students report getting about six and a half hours of sleep on a typical weekday—far below the recommendations for optimal health (Galloway et al., 2013). Kids who are sleep deprived tend to get sick more often, and it takes them longer to fight off the illnesses. They often have difficulty concentrating and remembering information, so they don't perform as well in school. Their decision-making ability and reflexes are slowed (making them more dangerous as drivers on the roads), and they can be much more irritable and crabby than they would be with adequate sleep. In short, we now know just how important sleep is for these kids, and we also know how hard it is for them to get the needed hours.

Part of the problem is that teenagers have a later release of the "sleep hormone" melatonin, which means they tend to not feel drowsy until around 11 P.M. That inclination can be further delayed by the stimulating blue light from electronic devices, which tricks the brain into sensing wakeful daylight, slowing the release of melatonin and the onset of sleep (Chang, Aeschbach, Duffy, & Czeisler, 2014; National Sleep Foundation, 2011).

Busy schedules, long commute times to school, hours of homework, stress, and the use of social media all can also contribute to later bedtimes.

Recent studies have shown that a later start to the school day can be beneficial in a variety of ways. For instance, researchers followed 9,000 socioeconomically diverse high school students across five school districts in three states before and after their schools changed school start times. They found that after the late start time was implemented there were increases in standardized test scores, attendance, and mental health (Wahlstrom, 2002, 2014). In another study, researchers looking at 10,000 high school students compared the rate of car accidents during the morning commute both before and after the school start time was moved from 8:30 A.M. to 9:00 A.M. They documented a significant decrease in teenage car accidents after school start times in the area were moved back 30 minutes (Danner & Phillips, 2008). Implementing a later school start time may also be related to increased motivation and engagement. For instance, in one study where researchers followed over 200 high school students in the Northeast before and after a late start time was implemented, they found that students got an average of 45 more minutes of sleep each night, and that students felt significantly less depressed and irritated. These students were also more motivated to engage in after-school activities such as sports and had more time to socialize and do homework after school (Owens, Belon, & Moss, 2010).

Lessons Learned from Changing to Later Start Times

Even though much of the evidence supports moving the school day to a later start time for middle and high schools, making this change can be complicated, and parents and schools wonder if it is worth the effort and disruption. They ask: What happens to kids who need to be dropped off early by parents on the way to work or kids who take an early school bus? What if the change doesn't meet teacher union rules or interferes with sports schedules and other extracurriculars at the end of the day? If kids get home later, doesn't that just mean they will start their homework later? How do we know kids won't just stay up even later now that they know school starts later?

We've seen schools address these worries from the community in a number of ways. When planning the change to a later start time, schools may want to consider many of the points highlighted in the earlier discussion of changing to a block schedule: They should involve all stakeholders—including students and parents—in the decision-making and change process; they should visit other schools that have made the change, and listen for tension points, pros, and cons; and they should allow ample time to make the transition.

Schools should also realize that there are different ways to implement a late start. Typically schools delay the daily start time by 15 to 30 and sometimes even 45 minutes, opting to start at 8 A.M. or 8:30 or even 9:00 A.M. in some cases. Many schools take advantage of the later start time to schedule faculty professional development or regular staff meetings, so the kids sleep in but the adults still get to school at the usual time and use it for collaboration. Some schools use a late start to allow for a regular proctored make-up period for tests and quizzes; kids who miss exams during the week can come in on Thursday morning before school starts to make up the test in a secure environment without unduly impacting the classroom teacher, who would otherwise need to find time during her busy week to offer the make-up exam. In some cases, staff members supervise morning study halls for kids whose parents still need to drop them off early or offer lounges where kids can sleep or eat breakfast before heading off to class. Most of our Challenge Success schools who make the change to a later start use the opportunity to rejigger the entire bell schedule instead of simply starting and ending later. They use modified block and creative scheduling to juggle instructional minutes without necessarily having school end 30 or 45 minutes later each day. Other schools opt for one or two later starts during the week instead of all five days. Kids at these schools agree that even one late start a week can have a big impact. As one student from Woodside Priory School, in Portola Valley, California, explains: "Once I had a really big social studies test, but because of late start day, I had time to wake up and just study — so I was a lot more confident for the test, and I did a lot better."

Menlo-Atherton High School, Atherton, California

Menlo-Atherton High School is a large public high school with a diverse student body. The transition to a later school start time from 7:55 A.M. to 8:45 A.M. (9:25 A.M. on Thursdays to allow for staff meetings) took two years of careful planning and education. The process began in 2007 when the school launched a program to educate students about the benefits of adolescents' getting nine hours of sleep per night. During the process, Menlo-Atherton PTA's newly appointed Sleep Team sponsored national sleep experts to speak to parents, faculty, and students about the need for increased sleep, and worked with Stanford University to create an award-winning program to teach teens about the value of sleep. Undergraduates from Stanford University's "Sleep and Dreams" course (Stanford Sleep and Dreams, 2010) trained Menlo-Atherton high school juniors—called "Sleep Ambassadors"—about the importance of teen sleep and best practices to use before bedtime. The high school students created a sleep curriculum to educate their peers. In addition, students offered sleep information in the school newspaper, made announcements over the PA system, and surveyed students to learn more about their sleep habits.

The late start change began with a mandate from the Sequoia Union High School District's Board of Trustees. Based on sleep research presented by Menlo-Atherton's Sleep Team, the board voted in 2009 to recommend a late start for all schools in the district. Once given the charge by senior leadership, Menlo-Atherton Principal Matthew Zito assembled a working subcommittee of the Shared Decision-Making Site Council to explore bell schedule options. Committee members, including administrators, parents, teachers, and students, spent many hours reading the sleep research and examining 15 different bell schedule options from other schools in the region. Principal Zito encouraged the committee to take a radical approach, one that would ensure an equitable schedule for all students. Menlo-Atherton's new schedule would require the majority of students to begin the school day no earlier than 8:25 A.M. and end the school day at the same time (3 P.M.), including those students who received extra academic support.

The transition at Menlo-Atherton was not easy, and the unwavering support of Principal Zito was critical to the success of the new late start schedule. Many faculty and staff members were upset about changes to their work schedules. Even though the total number of hours worked did not change, teachers had to stay later on certain days, and some faced longer commute times. Changes to the bus schedule caused some parents to complain, and sports practices and later game schedules had to be cleared with the school's athletic league. Parents who opposed the late start time for student athletes were appeased when Menlo-Atherton was able to secure new field lights for team sport practices. After several months of hearing students say they had no space on campus to hang out when working parents needed to drop them off before the start of school, Mr. Zito secured extra funds to open and staff the library during early morning hours. Despite these challenges—which eventually were resolved—district and school administrators agree that the change to a later start was worth it. The Sleep Ambassador program continues to be an effective resource at the school, and students appreciate the extra time to sleep, study, or hang out. As one student notes: "I'm finally eating breakfast; since the late start was implemented, I've eaten breakfast every single day—which is great!"

THE KIDS NEED A BREAK: MOVING SEMESTER EXAMS

Along with changing the bell schedule and implementing late start times, several of our Challenge Success schools have explored the benefits of eliminating or changing the timing of their semester exams. Typically, high schools operate on a semester schedule, where students start school around Labor Day, take a break over the December holidays, then come back, and a week or so later take end-of-semester exams. The second semester typically starts right after these exams, and then students finish sometime in June, depending on snow days. Most colleges and universities used to operate on similar schedules, but over the years they found that the students needed a real break in between semesters, so they shifted their yearly calendar to have first semester end before break, including end-of-semester exams. Instead of spending the break studying and cramming for the exams looming ahead, students had the opportunity to spend time with family and friends during the holidays and to return to campus refreshed and ready to face the academic rigor of the second semester.

Though we couldn't find any statistics on how many high schools have made similar changes to start school in August and offer semester exams before the winter break, and we could not find any solid evidence in the national research on the positive or negative effects on students associated with these changes, we have had very positive experiences with our Challenge Success schools that have made these shifts, and we have a few local studies to back this claim. In one of our schools, more than three-quarters of the students (77 percent of 10th graders and 76 percent of 11th graders) agreed that moving exams from after the winter break to before the break reduced their stress levels. At another school, seniors noted that this was the best policy the school had adopted during their four years there (Conner, Pope, & Galloway, 2009).

Even in a large public school district that debated this issue for almost five years, after the initial piloting of the change in 2013, the majority of parents, teachers, and students agreed that they preferred first semester finals to occur before winter break, despite some of the calendar compromises caused by moving the exams. The results were overwhelmingly positive after the pilot attempt. Of the more than 1,385 high-school students, 3,600 parents, and 520 teachers of all grade levels who returned the questionnaires, the majority said, "If I controlled the school calendar, I would want first-semester finals to occur before winter break"; this included over 85 percent of the high school students (see Kenrick, 2013). And although most parents, students, and teachers said they would prefer that school not start any earlier than the third week of August, most said that giving students a "schoolwork-free winter break" was the most important factor to consider when designing the yearly calendar. One parent who was initially upset about starting school earlier in August explained, "After seeing my junior daughter have a stress-free break, the calendar made sense. Also, looking forward to an early end to school in the spring has been a great motivator for the second semester" (Kenrick, 2013; Palo Alto Unified School District, 2013).

Tips for Implementing Exams Before Break: Responding to the Naysayers

Changing the school schedule may cause worry and tension for some families. Here we list the concerns we typically hear when schools consider making the shift to exams before break, and we offer our advice on how to address these.

Uneven semesters: Several schools are concerned that the semesters won't be exactly even in terms of instructional days. Teachers worry that kids in the first semester, which might be three to seven days shorter, will miss out on important material, and parents worry that teachers will simply try to cram the existing material into a shorter time frame. We like to point out that rarely are semesters exactly even. Schools have testing days and professional development days and holidays at various times throughout the year, and we advise schools—when they have some control—to schedule as many of these days as possible in the second semester to help even out the reduction caused by hosting exams in December. Most of our schools recognize that they offer very few "semester-long" courses and that the year-long courses aren't affected by uneven semesters because teachers adjust their exams and their units to take place either in December or January; they don't try to cram more in during November through December, as some parents fear.

Student stress during the holiday season: Parents and coaches are often concerned about the impact studying for exams might have on the winter season sports and the holiday music and dance productions, and whether moving exams earlier in the year actually increases student stress loads. Some people argue that students need time over winter break to catch up and to prepare for exams and that students are so busy during November and December that it is difficult to make time to study for these tests. We advise teachers to build in adequate time for review—just as they tend to do when exams are in January—and we point out that schools need to be careful not to schedule holiday concerts and sports practices during the exam period; but again, we find that the pros outweigh the cons here. Students admit that they need to cut back on extracurricular activities and that they often work hard during this time frame, but they truly appreciate a work-free vacation and time to regroup before the next semester (Palo Alto Unified School District, 2013).

Starting earlier in August: We know communities are not happy about schools starting earlier in August to even out the semester lengths, and we all want to preserve family time in the summer. Some schools start only a few days earlier and agree to have slightly uneven semesters. Others move the start date up by a week or so in August and let students out earlier in June, so the length of summer isn't shortened. As more schools start earlier in August, parents and students get used to the new schedule. Camps and other summer programs in these communities start up and wind down earlier, and more families adjust their vacation schedules accordingly. We have found that despite the change in timing, most stakeholders prefer the trade-off for a stress-free winter break (Palo Alto Unified School District, 2013).

Seniors and college admission: Senior year is busy, and we have heard concerns about seniors feeling pressure to take finals and complete college applications at the same time. However, the college counselors and school heads with whom we have spoken have actually found that students appreciate the vacation time, when they don't have to study for exams or catch up over break, to work on college applications. And college counselors have bumped up their internal due dates to accommodate students applying to universities with November and December due dates. As one student said happily, "It was the most amazing feeling to submit all of my college applications by January 1 and have nothing to worry about afterwards" (Kenrick, 2013).

Teacher workload: Some teachers are concerned that if exams are moved to before break, the kids will get a real vacation, but they won't. They worry that they will be expected to grade semester exams during the break and turn in grades when they return. We advise schools to allow teachers to have a real break too! Teachers can opt to use the downtime to grade exams at their leisure if they prefer, but they should be given ample time after break to grade as well. This practice does not impact the colleges, which are already accustomed to seeing seniors' grades in late January.

Final note: We also work with schools that have made the semester exams optional or eliminated them altogether. We know from research that more frequent, low-stakes or no-stakes quizzes may actually help students learn and retain material better than high-stakes cumulative exams, and we have found many benefits to midyear projects, unit exams (as opposed to cumulative exams), and alternative forms of assessment (see Chapter Five for more on this). If more teachers consider alternative forms of assessment in December and throughout the year, student stress levels may decrease even more, and engagement and achievement levels should rise.

AN IDEAL SCHEDULE?

We don't know that there is such a thing as a "perfect" schedule. Based on the research and our experiences with Challenge Success schools, we believe that some sort of block or modified block or other non-traditional schedule, which gives students and teachers more time for hands-on learning and collaboration, is preferable to a traditional schedule. In addition, ideally, teenage students should start schools later in the morning and should enjoy work-free breaks and plenty of time to transition between classes and between semesters. We believe that schools need to start with these basic tenets and tinker a bit to figure out what works best for their school community. The good news is that the hard work seems to pay off: We don't know a single school that has made these scheduling changes and then reverted back to a traditional schedule. Most of our schools find that the decrease in stress for students and faculty, the increase in engagement and time for deeper reflection, and the less frenetic pace are all worth the extra effort of modifying the school schedule.

Chapter THREE

The Homework Dilemma

"My daughter has too much homework. She never sees the light of day."

"My son is not doing nearly enough homework. His teacher needs to step it up and assign more, so he'll be ready for high school next year."

Sound familiar? We hear these types of comments all over the country, and the debates they cause are usually fraught with great emotion and angst. National movements have been dedicated to eliminating homework, and equally adamant efforts have been launched to preserve homework. So what's the right thing to do? At Challenge Success, we believe in talking less about whether students today have too much homework or not enough homework. Instead, we want to focus more on the quality of the assignments, the connections between homework and the broader curriculum, and the extent to which the homework assignments engage students in learning. If the homework discussions focus on these parameters, we think a great deal of the tension around homework will be reduced. But first, it may help to understand how we got here in the first place.

A BRIEF HISTORY OF HOMEWORK

Homework has been around for many years and has long been a source of contention, but why has the recent "war on homework" become such a controversial issue nationally? Here is a quick history behind the current homework debates (for more on the history of homework, see Gill & Schlossman, 2003, 2004; Kralovec & Buell, 2000; Vatterott, 2009). In 1983, the Department of Education commissioned a report on the state of schools in the United States. This well-known report was called "The Nation at Risk," and it said that the U.S. schools were "at risk" of falling behind, and that we were not where we should be academically compared to other industrialized nations (National Commission on Excellence in Education, 1983). This caused some panic and led to the eventual creation of state standards.

In the 1990s, almost every state moved to a standards-based curriculum. Each state identified content and learning standards that all kids needed to meet, and then asked educators to design curriculum based on those standards. Since individual states were allowed to decide what content to include and not include, some states ended up with over 180 standards per grade level—far more than most teachers could cover during the school year! Then, in the mid-1990s, the states began implementing high-stakes testing to hold students, teachers, and school districts accountable for ensuring that every student was meeting the required standards.

In 2001, with the passing of No Child Left Behind, the states were mandated to check each student's progress in reading and math in grades three through eight, and at least once in high school. That's a minimum of seven years of standardized testing, and some states went above and beyond the NCLB requirements and began testing students even earlier. This mandate put a lot of pressure on schools and districts because the stakes were high. If a school's scores didn't meet expectations, the school and district could be fined or put on probation. And because the stakes were so high, schools increasingly focused on improving test results—sometimes at the expense of focusing on learning as a process or real mastery of content. Because teachers had much more content to cover, some resorted to assigning more homework to meet the demands of the standards.

In 2010, the Common Core State Standards Initiative began as a state-led effort establishing a single set of clear educational standards for kindergarten through 12th grade in English language arts and mathematics. Different from some of the earlier state standards, the Common Core standards aim for depth over breadth, with students focusing on complex analysis, critical thinking, research skills, and application of learning. These Common Core standards are set to be assessed via different types of standardized tests that include more performance assessments wherein students "show what they know" and engage in genuine problem-solving. From what we have seen recently, the move to Common Core, similar to the standards movement earlier, has teachers assigning more work to their students in and out of class. As one teacher from a Challenge Success school (who wished to remain anonymous) explained,

> As a teacher, I feel a lot of pressure to cover the standards and prepare my students for the tests. The problem is that I am expected to teach much more content than I had to teach 20 years ago. This means I am assigning more homework, because I just can't cover everything in class. I know my students are really busy after school, and some aren't starting homework until late at night when they are tired. But the school district is counting on me to get these kids to pass the tests, and I can get in trouble if I don't teach all the content and prepare kids for the next level.

Given the similar comments we were hearing from a number of our teachers, and because homework came up over and over again as the number one stressor that students and parents listed on our surveys, the research team at Challenge Success decided to do an extensive review of the research on homework to determine how widespread the phenomenon seemed to be. Were teachers assigning more homework these days than in the past? And if this was indeed the case, was it doing any good?

THE RESEARCH ON HOMEWORK

In 2012, we reviewed over 20 landmark studies and homework meta-analyses from a variety of journals and books, focusing primarily on studies written in the past decade as well as those that we felt made significant contributions to the current discourse on homework. Much of the recent research on homework can be broken down into the following questions: (1) How much homework are students in the United States actually doing, and is it too much or too little? (2) Does homework help students or hurt them in the long run?

How Much Homework Are Students Doing?

Over the last 20 years, U.S. children between the ages of 6 and 17 have increased their time spent in school and doing schoolwork. U.S. children spend six to seven hours a day in school, depending on their age and level of schooling. Twenty years prior, data show that time spent in school ranged from five to six hours a day (Juster, Ono, & Stafford, 2004). While it seems clear that students spend more time in school these days, it is less clear whether they spend more time doing homework.

Two studies analyzing large datasets drew different conclusions about the time students spend on homework. The authors of one study found that the time spent studying after school has increased slightly for elementary school students since the 1980s and decreased for older students (Hofferth & Sandberg, 2001); however, the 2003 Brown Center Report found that the time spent on homework has been declining for most elementary school students and has remained stable for middle and high school students (Loveless, 2003). And some research suggests that children going to schools in which the majority of students are from middle- or upper-class homes are experiencing more homework than their low-income counterparts (Cooper, 2007). The differences among these studies may be explained by differences in the methodology used to collect the data (such as interviews versus surveys), the background of the students studied, and the types of schools included in the studies.

In our own research, in which we surveyed middle and high school students, we found that students in high-achieving public and private schools reported spending, on average, a little more than 3 hours on homework each night in high school and about 2.5 hours in middle school. We also found that only 20 to 30 percent of the students in the sample perceive the homework they do on a regular basis as "useful or meaningful" (Galloway et al., 2013; Pope & Galloway, 2006). Given how many hours the students are spending and how low a value they place on the work, we wanted to know whether homework was a help or a hindrance to student learning.

Does Homework Help Students?

Though the pros and cons of homework have been debated for more than 100 years, homework continues to be assigned to students, often because of a longstanding assumption that it is beneficial to them. Most of the arguments based on the faith that homework is good for kids go something like this: homework teaches kids to be responsible and develop a strong work ethic, and when students have a lot of homework, it is a sign of a rigorous curriculum and a good teacher. We also regularly hear that doing homework keeps kids out of trouble. If they didn't have to do homework after school, they might fill their time with other activities that adults don't want kids to pursue. In fact, some recent studies have suggested that time spent on homework may be related to a decrease in the amount of time kids spend reading for pleasure, participating in extracurricular activities, and enjoying time with family (Juster et al., 2004; Yankelovich, 2006), but, in our review, no research showed that homework kept kids from getting into trouble.

Even though these arguments have been around since the late 1800s, the assumption that homework is beneficial continues to garner attention in the media — witness the "Tiger mom" syndrome (Chua, 2011), but, in our review of the research on homework, we found no concrete evidence, beyond anecdotes, to support the views that homework is essential for a rigorous curriculum, a sign of a strong teacher, or an effective way to develop a good work ethic or responsibility in our youth.

Another common argument that supports the notion that more homework is a good thing is that the more time students spend on homework, the higher their grades and test scores will be. Some policymakers even argue — similar to the "Nation at Risk" report in the 1980s — that the United States is falling behind on international test scores because we don't assign kids enough homework. However, in a study comparing the standardized math scores across multiple countries, no positive link was found between student math achievement and the frequency or amount of homework given (Baker & LeTendre, 2005). Another study found that countries that gave students more math homework actually had lower overall math test scores than those that gave students less math homework (Mikki, 2006).

Harris Cooper has reviewed hundreds of homework studies and is often thought to be the leading researcher on homework (Cooper, 1989; Cooper & Valentine, 2001). While his earlier work made claims about the possible link between the time spent on homework and academic achievement, more recently Cooper and other authors have found that the association between time spent on homework and academic achievement is not as strong as they once concluded. They found no link for students in elementary school between the amount of time spent on homework and student achievement. In middle school, they found a moderate correlation, but after an hour spent on homework, this association fades. The authors found a correlation in high school, but this also fades after two hours spent on homework. Other studies have evidence that, even in middle and high school, the relationship between the time spent on homework and achievement may not be so straightforward. For instance, a study with over 5,000 15- and 16-year-olds of varying income levels and ethnic backgrounds found that the more time spent on math homework, the lower the math achievement scores across all ethnic groups (Kitsantas, Cheema, & Ware, 2011). Similarly, a 2002 study found that, while the frequency of math homework positively influenced math achievement in middle school, the amount of homework and length of time it took to complete it had no effect on achievement (Trautwein, Koller, Schmitz, & Baumert, 2002).

The results across the studies reviewed often depended on factors such as the grade level of the students in the study and how achievement was measured (such as grades versus standardized tests) and whether the homework was at an appropriate level for the child. The relationship between student grades and homework completed is further complicated because of the way teachers weigh homework as part of a student's overall grade in a course. Some students may be getting better grades merely for completing their homework and not necessarily for learning the material, so to conclude that completing homework leads to better grades can be misleading (Trautwein et al., 2002).

Does Homework Hurt Students?

Just as recent media attention has focused on the benefits of homework, there has also been a recent flurry of books and articles on the detriments of homework (Bennett & Kalish, 2006). Some studies have found that too much time spent on homework and academics, in general, can lead to health problems such as stress, exhaustion, and headaches as well as student disengagement (Galloway et al., 2013). And there may be a relationship between increased time spent on homework and decreased sleep on school nights, as well as between decreased sleep and increased feelings of anxiety, depression, and fatigue (Fuligni & Hardway, 2006).

What we have found is that the quality of the homework seems to matter quite a bit. If the homework is not seen as meaningful to the student or valuable to the teacher, it may turn students off from school and learning (Bempechat, Li, Neier, Gillis, & Holloway, 2011). In one study of low-income ninth and tenth graders, the authors found that when students were given homework but had few consequences for not completing it, students showed an increase in disengagement from school. The authors also found that, despite differences in achievement, the students they interviewed agreed that if they had to have homework, they would prefer homework that was more meaningful and relevant, and they wanted teachers to value the homework enough to monitor whether or not it was completed (Bempechat et al., 2011). Another study found that when students don't either understand the homework, feel it is necessary, or have adequate support for doing it, those who already have learning difficulties may be at an even greater disadvantage (Darling-Hammond & Ifill-Lynch, 2006). In contrast, students' confidence and identities as learners may be bolstered if students see the homework as feasible and manageable, in terms of both the time they spend and the content of the assignment (Sagor, 2002). And several studies have shown that when students have some choice over assignments, such as which topics to write about or which problems to do, they are more likely to be engaged in the work and complete it (Alpern, 2008).

Most of the studies also found quite a bit of individual variability in whether the amount of time spent on homework led to feeling fatigue — suggesting that some kids might be more or less vulnerable to feeling fatigued than others, regardless of time spent on homework. Thus, the research on whether homework load leads to disengagement and health problems is not conclusive, though our own studies and our work with schools and families point to a connection between too much time spent on homework and some health problems as well as issues with student engagement with learning.

What do we make of this? With all of the conflicting information, it's no wonder that educators, parents, and students are confused about the pros and cons of assigning homework. We think that the common arguments about homework should be viewed through a critical lens. First, it is difficult to isolate the effects of homework, as we cannot be sure how much achievement is due to homework versus classroom teaching versus prior knowledge (Trautwein et al., 2002). We also cannot be sure of the conditions under which homework was completed, and whether others helped the child with the homework or even did the homework for the student. For instance, we know anecdotally that many parents work with their children or hire tutors to help with homework, but a review of more than 50 studies on parent involvement in their children's homework found little evidence for any benefits to the children when parents were involved with the work (Hoover-Dempsey et al., 2001). Finally, the research on homework usually focuses on time instead of task and classes or groups of students versus individuals. So the real answer to whether homework helps or hinders is—it depends. It depends on the student, the teacher, the curriculum, the level of the stakes attached to the assignments, the developmental appropriateness of the tasks, and ultimately how meaningful and engaging the assignments might be.

The reality is that most teachers assign some amount of homework each night, and it doesn't seem to be going away any time soon. Given that, we have outlined several effective characteristics of meaningful homework assignments. We believe homework, especially in the middle and high school grades, can serve a purpose when it is clear, authentic, differentiated, and connects to the broader goals of the current unit.

EFFECTIVE HOMEWORK

Homework in middle and high school may serve as a review of what students have learned, a way to have students practice the skills that were taught in class that day, or as a preparation for the next class. For instance, students might need to read something to prepare for a class discussion or prep for a lab the next day. Homework can also serve as a way to assess an individual's skills. So a teacher may give homework to determine "Where is Michael in math compared to his classmates?" or "Where is he in math compared to last time?" Of course, if you don't know who is actually doing the homework each night—the student, the parent, the tutor, the best friend—then it might not be as effective to use homework as a means to assess individual learning.

One positive purpose of homework can be an occasional opportunity to involve the family in the schoolwork. When families are encouraged to participate in the assignment and get excited to help the kids complete the project, adults and kids alike might learn something new. The most effective family homework projects are those that are fun and interesting for everyone or assignments that couldn't be done without family involvement. For instance, teachers might assign an oral history of a grandparent or a career exploration and shadow assignment with a relative or neighbor. Once the purpose of the assignment is clear, the teacher should take care to incorporate the following recommendations for effective assignments.

Clear Directions

When high-quality homework is assigned, homework battles and homework stress can often be mitigated because students understand the purpose of the homework, perceive the value of the assignments, and can do the work on their own. One mandatory characteristic of effective homework, therefore, is that the directions for the assignments are clear. Try looking at the assignment as if you were a student who might not have been paying close attention in class when you explained the directions. Better yet, make sure the directions are clearly written at the top of the assignment, so that someone who wasn't in class that day might be able to complete the work. Ideally, the student will be able to do the homework without outside help from a parent, sibling, or tutor.

Student Choice and Voice

We also know from decades of research on student engagement that students do better when schoolwork allows for student voice and choice (Shernoff, Csikszentmihalyi, Schneider, & Shernoff, 2003). Try to structure assignments where the students get to pick which problems they do or which writing topics to choose. The more the students have a say over their learning and a choice to select from, the more engaged they will be with the homework and the more likely they will be to get it done.

Differentiated

We believe that homework should be developmentally appropriate and differentiated. In other words, not everyone should have to do 30 math problems—especially not the same 30 problems! Picture a kid who can zip through the math homework without much trouble at all. He probably hasn't learned much from that assignment. Now picture a kid who struggles with the first two problems and takes almost 20 minutes to complete them (and not necessarily correctly); that assignment isn't useful for that kid either. An effective homework assignment is differentiated for the needs of each student. Ideally the teacher would say, "Ok, Jessica, you need a little bit more help here. And, Sam, you need a little bit of help here. Why don't *you* do these problems, and why don't *you* do these other problems?" Of course, that means more work on the part of the teacher to assign different work to different students, but the alternative is that many students won't get the kinds of assignments that challenge them at the level they need. Technological advances, such as adaptive learning technology that can help to individualize instruction and provide immediate student feedback, may ultimately help save teachers some time as they strive to find the appropriate level of challenge for each individual student.

Authentic

Another characteristic of effective homework is that it is authentic. The more authentic you can make it—the more relevant and real—the better. Let's use the example of the oral history of the grandmother. This is a real person in the student's life, ideally someone she cares about and wants to know more about. That's an authentic assignment. The student may want to make sure she does justice to Grandma's life story. She may take extra care, both in forming the interview questions and writing up the report. And if the teacher assigns an authentic audience for the report, such as posting the report on the class website or compiling an oral history book for the parents in the grade, the student may be further motivated to revise and polish her writing for the readers. With this authentic assignment, the student may learn more than she would have if she just read the story of a stranger in a history book. When students feel like they are doing real tasks instead of busywork, tasks that will play some part in the real world and may have more than just the teacher as the audience, they tend to take the assignments more seriously.

Connected to the "Big Idea"

The most important characteristic, however, is that the homework connects to a big idea or key understanding from the unit. If you assign work, and the kids have no idea how it connects to what they are learning in class or the overall goals of the unit, the assignment will not be effective. It is one thing for *you* to know how an assignment connects, but it is also extremely important for the students to understand the connection as well. They need to see the value and meaning in the work assigned.

CREATING POLICIES FOR MORE EFFECTIVE HOMEWORK

Given what we know about the research on homework and the characteristics of effective assignments, how can schools help to educate their communities on best practices for homework policies? Some of our schools begin by surveying students, parents, and teachers to determine just how much homework students are actually doing. Some schools ask students to keep homework diaries for a few weeks where they write down the assignment to be completed and then track the amount of time (minus breaks) that it took to finish. Teachers keep diaries, too, recording how long they predict assignments will take, then comparing their predictions to the student diary responses. One administrator asked all faculty members to take one week in which they allowed students to do homework in their classes. The teachers and the students were surprised by the results. The students were surprised by how much they could get done when they were able to focus, when they weren't starting the homework late at night after a full day of activities, and without the distractions of social media. Some teachers noted that the homework took much longer (or in some cases much less time) than they had anticipated. When they allowed kids to do the work in class, teachers immediately saw when students were confused about homework instructions or when they didn't know the material well enough to be able to do the work by themselves.

As Drew Ciancia, a teacher at the Woodside Priory School, explains:

> Just like many of the other teachers here, I'm trying to get a better understanding of how long it takes our kids to do the homework. So from time to time, I'll have the kids do homework in class, so I can see how long it takes them to do it. I try to predict how long it might take, but you never really know unless you have the kid there. But I also like to see how they're going about doing their homework: Are they reading without distraction? Are they taking notes while they're reading? Are they marking in a book? [Doing homework in class every now and then] helps me to get a better understanding of how kids do their homework and how I can better help them with that.

In response to what Drew learned from having kids do their homework in class, he decided to experiment with a class without homework. He explains:

> Most of the classes are structured like workshops. Students are doing research in class and are posting their research up on a Google Doc. The impression I've got is that they come up with some great stuff when they learn together; they are able to

bounce stuff off each other, and they get different perspectives. It is a really creative environment, and their motivation is up. I've been really happy with the quality of work. I can see it all happening in the classroom. I can be on hand to answer their questions, so I've been happy with that.

Principal Sharon Ofek used another model when she realized that parents and students were extremely concerned about homework load at her public middle school.

Jane Lathrop Stanford Middle School, Palo Alto, California

Sharon Ofek, principal of JLS public middle school in Palo Alto, California, was hearing increasingly from parents and students about their concerns regarding homework. When she attended coffees and parent network meetings, she noticed that a lot of parents brought up the struggles with homework. "When it shows up one time, you think—'I'll look into it'; when it shows up another time, you think—'Huh, I wonder what this is about?' Then it shows up another time, and you think, 'Ok I have to get on this.'" She wanted to understand the basis of these concerns and to pinpoint exactly what the parents were concerned about. Through a series of intentional conversations, she heard that there was "a lot of stress in the community in general," and that parents wanted "more time for kids to be kids." Sharon agreed that kids needed more free time to play and to grow, and that kids needed to develop resiliency and an ability to make mistakes and learn from them. She wanted the new homework policy to reflect these values. She also realized that some parents wanted everything fixed immediately, and she knew this was not a realistic expectation.

Sharon worked with her team and Challenge Success to create a feasible plan. The first step was to host a Shadow Day exercise (described in Chapter Two) in which teachers could go through a full school day shadowing a student and then attempt to do the student's homework afterward. When teachers and administrators got together to discuss the Shadow Day exercise and reflection sheet, they noticed a trend that paralleled the parental concerns with homework. In the debrief session, shadow teachers were asked to reflect on whether or not they felt prepared to complete their homework for the day. Did they have a lot of homework? What was their experience like? Were the directions clear? Teachers admitted that they were often overwhelmed at the end of the

(continued)

shadow experience and that the school was asking a lot from the students each day.

The Shadow Day project created a willingness for the faculty to participate in a dialogue about homework, and it "allowed the student voice to grow strong, ironically through the mouths of faculty members [who were student shadows]." The administration responded with professional development on homework best practices; as a result, teachers felt supported and were encouraged to try new strategies in their classrooms. Elizabeth Fee, a teacher at the school, noted that teachers at JLS were given "total freedom to try whatever they want when it comes to homework," and that they were encouraged to experiment to see which strategies were most effective. In her eighth grade math class, Elizabeth decided not to grade homework, though she checks it every day and keeps track of what students did and didn't do. If a student doesn't do an assignment three days in a row, she sends a note home to the parents to let them know that their child isn't doing the homework, but she does not penalize the student in any way. Occasionally, Elizabeth finds that she has students who do fine in the class without doing their homework. In those rare cases, she observes the students and lets them go without completing the homework as long as they continue to understand the work and perform well. Most of her students, however, need to do the homework because they "need that practice time." Elizabeth has found that ungraded homework helps to promote engagement and practice without unnecessary stress. She said that the Shadow Day exercise made teachers much more aware of (1) the importance of assigning only meaningful homework and (2) the need to make good decisions regarding the amount they assigned each night.

As a result of teacher experimentation, professional development, and several parent education evenings, the school drafted new homework guidelines instead of a set policy. The guidelines included responsibilities for all stakeholders for homework best practices. Teachers agreed to assign meaningful and appropriate work; parents agreed to let the students do their own work and to provide the necessary resources, such as time and supplies, to help facilitate this; and students agreed to take their homework seriously and to communicate with their teachers if the homework load became unmanageable. An excerpt from the new guidelines is presented in Exhibit 3.1. The guidelines follow many of the suggestions listed at the end of this chapter and represent a positive step toward improving homework practices at the school.

Exhibit 3.1 Excerpt from JLS Middle School Homework Guidelines

Purpose of Homework

Homework is an essential part of the educational program at JLS and in the Palo Alto Unified School District.

Homework may serve many of the following purposes:

1. Provides important practice and refinement of skills and concepts taught in the classroom.

2. Preparation for a concept or preview of a unit that will be studied in the future.

3. Elaboration, enrichment, and/or extension of material learned in the classroom through inquiry and application.

4. Provides independent practice and reinforcement of proper study habits taught in school.

5. Provides opportunity for increasing self-direction, time-management, and independence.

6. Provides opportunity to integrate newly learned concepts and skills with what the student already knows.

Daily Homework Time Guidelines

6th Grade = Combined average of 45 to 90 minutes for all classes

7th Grade = Combined average of 60 to 120 minutes for all classes

8th Grade = Combined average of 60 to 120 minutes for all classes

Please recognize that the time a student spends on homework will vary based upon student preparedness, student focus and effort, learning/study habits, homework environment, etc.

General Guidelines

Homework and long-term projects will not be assigned over vacations, such as winter/spring breaks. No tests will be given, nor will long-term assignments be due, during the first week after such breaks.

Students may choose, as a time management strategy, to allocate break time to work on assignments and projects. This should not be seen as the teacher assigning homework, but as the student employing a valid time management technique.

Student Responsibilities
Students shall:

- Keep careful track of homework assignments by recording them in their binder reminder, by checking teacher websites, by viewing Infinite Campus, and/or by asking clarifying questions.

- Give maximum effort in completing and turning in assignments on time.

- Meet with teachers immediately after a planned or unplanned absence to arrange to make up all work that was missed by an agreed upon date.

- Meet/communicate with teachers prior to a planned absence to determine expectations and arrange for make-up of missed assignments.

- Communicate with their teachers and parents if homework appears to be excessive or too difficult, if directions/expectations are unclear, or if challenges arise.

- Make use of all school resources when support is needed by going to Homework Habitat, seeing teachers, by arrangement, before/after school or during lunch, and meeting with the school counselor.

Teacher Responsibilities
Teachers shall:

- Assign engaging and purposeful homework and/or projects and ensure that assignments/projects conform to the grade level time guidelines.

- Coordinate with team members to establish deadlines, due dates for projects/assignments, and tests in an effort to minimize student over-extension.

- Explicitly explain the directions, purpose and expectations that are appropriate for each homework assignment, project, or test preparation.

- Suggest and practice techniques to help increase efficiency, such as how to allocate time wisely, meet deadlines, and develop good study habits for each subject area. One example of this would be a focused use of the binder reminder as a communication tool between home and school.

- Differentiate assignments when it is determined that, despite appropriate effort and learning habits, a student is spending more than the expected time on homework.

- Clearly communicate to students and parents a homework monitoring process that may include checking teacher websites, recording assignments in student binder reminder, exchange of e-mails, and checking postings on Infinite Campus.

Parent Responsibilities
Parents will:

- Provide a quiet study area, appropriate materials, supplies, and sufficient time to enable students to complete homework.

- Facilitate and support the homework activity without solving problems or completing content for students.

- Support homework completion. This can include helping students clarify instructions, by acquiring resources, helping with time management/organization, discussing purpose, discussing effective learning habits, and/or reinforcing understanding of the task by checking teacher websites, viewing Infinite Campus, or reviewing student binder reminders.

- Encourage students to self-advocate and to communicate directly with teachers if the student is struggling with homework expectations.

- Monitor time spent on homework and communicate with the teacher if the student is consistently spending more than the time expected to complete homework.

RECOMMENDATIONS FOR TEACHERS

Based on our work with Challenge Success schools and the professional development work we do on making homework more effective, here is a summary of our top recommendations for teachers:

- Teachers should predict the amount of time homework may take. We know that the time homework takes will vary with the age and developmental stage and abilities of the students, so anticipating how long an assignment might take is not easy, especially given all the other things students tend to do while completing their homework, such as using social media and other distractions. Teachers might consider tracking actual homework task time (minus time spent taking breaks or being distracted) by having students do the assigned homework in class for a week, asking students and parents to keep homework diaries of actual time spent on work at home, and/or suggesting that students stop after a certain amount of time without penalty. These strategies all can help teachers gauge length and load of future assignments. Teachers of students in middle and high school should also take into account total homework time for students. If students spend an hour on homework for one class, that greatly impacts the overall homework time.

- Teachers should make sure homework is developmentally appropriate and differentiated, and not too difficult for students to complete independently. It is a challenge to design homework assignments that meet individual children's academic and developmental needs, but when homework is too hard or too easy, it may have a detrimental effect. Teachers should strive for the "just right" challenge for each student, and should ensure that homework is "doable" without the need for outside help from a parent, peer, or tutor. Having students get started on homework in class may help teachers assess whether or not it is doable and appropriate.

- Make sure students understand the purpose and value of the homework you assign. We encourage teachers to reflect on the purpose of a homework assignment and how it ties back to the enduring understandings or the big ideas of a given unit, and to make this clear to the students. When students perceive homework as busy work, meaningless, and of little value to the teacher, they may tend to be less interested in learning and in school in general. Some ways to increase the engagement factor are to allow students choice and voice in their homework assignments—let them choose which problems to do or which topics to write on, or allow them to stop when they believe they understand the concept.

- Use homework specifically for tasks that cannot be performed in class. Sometimes activities can't be done efficiently or effectively inside the classroom, particularly in middle and high school. It might make sense, for instance, for students to read a book outside of class, interview a community member, or collect backyard samples for a science experiment, since these are done more easily at home than in school.

- Determine whether homework should count toward student grades and, if so, to what extent. Teachers should consider whether students will receive a certain number of points for just completing the homework or for completing it correctly. Some teachers offer students opportunities to redo their homework and/or have lenient late policies. For some students, when homework is not completed, it may be due to organizational problems, task difficulty, or other legitimate reasons, and therefore penalizing the students may not be appropriate. Teachers might consider handing out homework packets that can be completed over time or homework "free passes" for students to use when the workload or home obligations are particularly heavy.

In the early grades, especially given the research noted earlier, we suggest that teachers consider not assigning homework other than free reading. Free or independent reading (with some guidance about the quality of the book) is often connected to higher achievement rates (Krashen, 2001; Topping, Samuels, & Paul, 2007) and might be a much better use of students' time after school. Teachers of older students might also consider adopting the "10-minute rule" established in 1996 by the National Parent Teacher Association and the National Education Association recommending that in third through sixth grades, homework should take students from 30 to 60 minutes per day to complete. If you extend this rule (homework should last about as long as 10 minutes multiplied by the students' grade level), middle school students would have no more than 80 minutes, and high school students would have no more than 120 minutes per night, which meets the rates associated with Cooper's research on correlations between homework and achievement cited earlier. Though this rule has been adopted by many schools, unfortunately this formula is not widely practiced (Kohn, 2006). Finally, teachers of older students should keep in mind that students are often doing homework from as many as five or six other classes on the same night. Students and teachers should work together to make sure that the overall load is manageable on a nightly basis. Some of our schools have had success implementing grade-level or school-wide homework and assessment calendars, so everyone in the community can see the average workload being assigned each week and can determine when to reschedule assignments or change test and project due dates to avoid student overload.

RECOMMENDATIONS FOR TEACHERS TO SUGGEST TO PARENTS

Homework is one of the few times when the worlds of school and home come together. Parents often view homework as a window into the kind of teaching and learning going on in their child's classroom, and finding the right balance can be just as tricky for parents as it is for teachers. We know it's hard to watch a child struggle, and the temptation for parents to jump in and "fix it" can be difficult to resist. We suggest that educators and parents work together to create effective homework policies, and we recommend that teachers educate parents about the rationale behind the homework assignments and the importance of students doing their homework by themselves. Educators should ask parents to try the following:

- Parents should act as cheerleaders and supporters, not homework police. Ideally, the child should be able to do the homework alone, without help from parents. Instead of checking, editing, or doing the work for the student, parents should provide necessary supplies and show an active interest in the content the student is learning, while allowing the teachers to intervene if the student fails to do the homework correctly or regularly.

- When scheduling after-school activities, keep in mind the student's homework load. Students who are overscheduled or exhausted will start homework later at night and will be less efficient. Work with your child to determine a healthy schedule of activities that will allow time to complete homework, work on projects, and study for tests — while still getting adequate sleep and time for play and a social life.

- Let children make mistakes and experience "successful failures." Recognize that a missed or poorly done homework assignment every now and then is not going to hurt a child in the long run. Parents can help students organize their time or prioritize assignments, but when parents deliver forgotten assignments to school or step in to rescue a child at the last minute, they may be denying the child the opportunity to develop resilience and fortitude.

A TOOL FOR EFFECTIVE HOMEWORK

Exhibit 3.2 presents a sample cover sheet that we use in our workshops with teachers to rate homework assignments and discuss strengths and weaknesses. It's best to use the cover sheet with real assignments from teachers at your school and to discuss these assignments with teachers from different subject areas and grade levels. You'd be surprised how many teachers disagree on the average amount of time an assignment might take a typical student to do, for instance, or how engaging an assignment might be for a student. We also recommend that teachers consider using a modified version of the cover sheet in their own classrooms. They can attach the cover sheet to their assignments and list the purpose of the assignment, the intended time limits, the level of parent involvement, if any (and ideally there shouldn't be any unless this is a family assignment), and how the work connects to the big idea of the unit. The cover sheet can help to ensure that the assigned homework is engaging, doable, and meaningful to all students.

Exhibit 3.2 Making Homework Work: Sample Cover Sheet

Assignment Sample # _____

Purpose of this assignment:

Expected time to complete the assignment (for a typical student):

_____

Less than 10 minutes   Over 60 minutes

Clarity of assignment:

_____

Not clear   Very clear

Level of parent involvement (for instance, parent discussion or action needed to complete work, help with the work, check the finished work, etc.):

_____

No parent involvement   High involvement

Student engagement level:

_____

Low   High

To what extent does this assignment support a big concept, central theme, or enduring understanding of the unit?

_____

Low support   High support

A SCHEDULING TOOL FOR COUNSELORS AND FAMILIES TO USE

A few of our schools have created scheduling tools for counselors and families to use when signing up for courses for the following school year. Miramonte High School, located in Orinda, California, for instance, asked all faculty members to estimate the approximate homework time required in each of their courses. They then compiled this information into a scheduling tool for students to use to estimate their workload (see Figure 3.1). The tool allows students to enter total homework time for all of their courses, along with estimated time for extracurricular activities and daily living activities, including sleep. The school asks that counselors, students, and parents sign the form so that everyone understands the expected time commitments the student may take on the following year. Counselors have said that using the tool has been a huge help, both for students (and their parents) to see that they probably shouldn't sign up for a load that will require them to do more than a 24-hour day, and for those students who might have some room in their schedule and would not otherwise have considered taking on a more challenging load or joining a school club or activity. Either way, it helps students to see on paper what they are signing up for and whether it is manageable.

Figure 3.1   Scheduling Tool

Time Management Activity
FILL THIS OUT FOR YOUR <u>BUSIEST</u> SEMESTER

School Activities	Average Hours/ Week
School (5 days × 7 hours)	35
Course Title	
English:	
Social Studies:	
Math:	
Science:	
Language:	
Electives:	
total school hours:	

Extra-Curricular Activities	Average Hours/ Week
Paid job	
Hobbies / Interests	
Community Service	
Sports	
Music / Performances	
total extra-curricular hours:	

Daily Living Activities	Average Hours/ Week
Sleep (7 days × 9 hours)	
Necessities (eating, showering, chores, etc.)	
Family Time	
Free Time (friends, TV, phone, Internet, video games, etc.)	
total daily living hours:	

Total Hours	Available Hours/ Week
School Hours = _____ Extra-Curricular Hours =_____ Daily Living Hours =_____ your total hours: [____] vs.	**Maximum Hours** **168**

(continued)

Source: Miramonte High School, Acalanes School District, Orinda, CA.

Figure 3.1 (continued)

These are estimations of how much time you will need to spend on homework each night

Use these guidelines to calculate your weekly time commitments

ENGLISH	min / night	nights / week	summer hw
English 1, 2, 3, 4*	30	4-5	
English Seminars*	30	4-5	
English 3 Honors*	60+	5-7	yes
English 4 AP*	60+	5-6	yes
Senior Project	1.5-2 hrs	5	
Creative Writing	30	2	
Public Speaking	10	3	

* expect a lot of reading!!!

SOCIAL STUDIES	min / night	nights / week	summer hw
World History*	30-40	4-5	
European History AP*	35+	6	yes
US History*	35-45	4-5	
US History AP*	45+	5-6	yes
Government / Econ*	30-40	3-4	
Comparative Gov AP*	45-60	4-5	yes

* expect a lot of reading!!!

WORLD LANG.	min / night	nights / week	summer hw
Level 1	20	5	
Level 2	20	5	
Level 3	30	5	
Level 4 Honours*	40	5	
Level 5 AP*	40	5	yes

* levels 4 & 5: expect major projects!!!

MATHEMATICS	min / night	nights / week
Pre-Algebra	30	5
Algebra A, 1	30	5
Geometry	30	5
Geometry Honors	30-45	5
Algebra 2	30	5
Algebra 2 / Trig	30-45	5
Algebra 2 / Trig Hnrs	45+	5
Math Analysis	30	5
Pre-Calculus	30+	5
Statistics AP	30-45	5
Calculus AB, BC AP	45+	5-6

SCIENCE	min / night	nights / week
Biology	30	4-5
Biology AP	1 hr	5-6
Biotechnology	30	2-3
Biotechnology Accel	30	3-4
Chemistry	30	4-5
Chemistry AP	30	4-5
Environmental Sci	20	2-3
Geology	30	2-3
Physics	30	5
Physics Honors	45	5
Physiology	45	5
Psychology	20	5
Sports Medicine	30	4-5

ELECTIVES	min / night	nights / week	other hw
Arch / Eng Des - CAD	0	0	
Art 1, 2	0	0	
Art Advanced	30	2	minor projects
Art Advanced Hnrs	45+	3	major projects
Art Studio AP	30	5	
Auto / Auto Adv	0	0	
Chamber Singers	20	5	concerts
Chorale, Wmn's Ens	10	5	concerts
Concert Band	30	5	4-6 events
Concert Choir	10	5	musical!!!
Design & Fabrication	10	1	
Digital Design	0	0	
Drama 1, 2, Adv	20	1	minor projects
Drama Prod: major role	1.5 hrs	5	3-4 shows
Drama Prod: minor role	1.5 hrs	1-3	3-4 shows
Jazz Ensemble	30	5	8-10 events
Leadership	2 hours /week		
Leadership Events	2-3 hrs	5	
Music Theory AP	30	4-5	
Orchestra	30	5	4-6 events
Photography	30+	1	
Symphonic Band	30	5	4-6 events
Video Production	10	1	
depending on job			

Journalism
  J1: 2-4 hrs / wk
  J2: 3-5 hrs / wk
  J3:* 4-8 hrs / wk
    *expect some wknds!!!

Yearbook
  Ph: 2-3 hrs / wk
  Wr: 1-2 hrs / wk
  Ed: 3-8 hrs / wk

Example: Biology AP: (60 min / night)(6 nights / week) = 360 minutes / week = 6 hours / week

Source: Miramonte High School, Acalanes School District, Orinda, CA.

Chapter FOUR

Engagement Matters: Backward Planning and Project-Based Learning

Figure 4.1 Science Fair Display

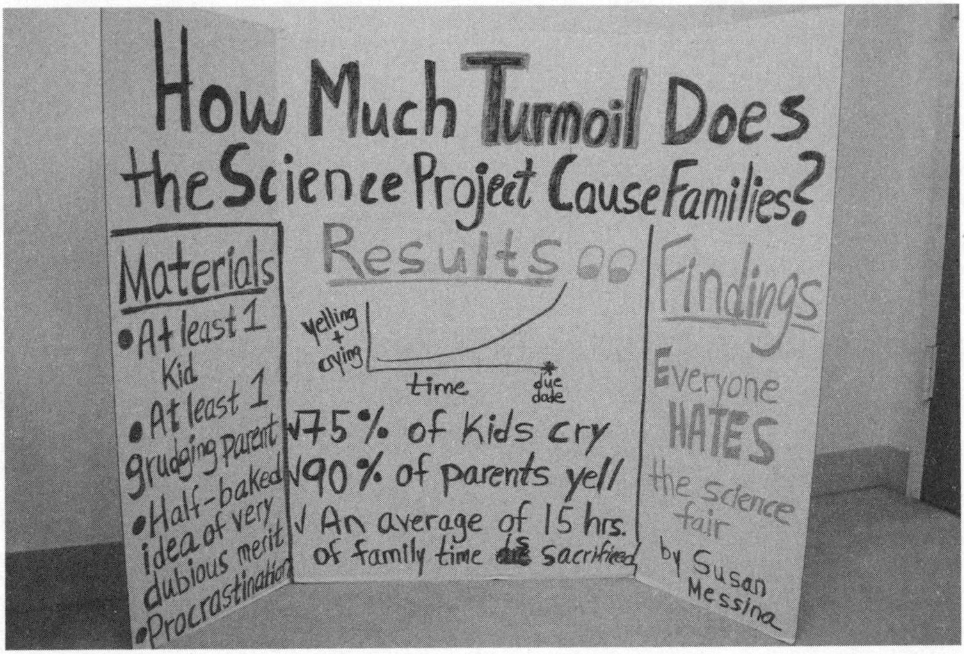

Over the years, we have heard parents, teachers, and students lament the lack of student engagement in school. Kids complain that what they are learning is not something they'll ever use in "real life." Parents and teachers worry about the emotional and intellectual futures of students who just go through the motions without really understanding or retaining the skills and knowledge they are supposed to acquire—or worse yet, kids who are so bored that they opt out or drop out of school. Consider this: across recent studies of high school students and college freshmen, approximately half or more of all students reported feeling disengaged and bored in class (Lambert, 2007; National Research Council, 2004; Sax et al., 2004; Yazzie-Mintz, 2010). Students listed many reasons for this lack of engagement, including uninteresting materials being used in the class, lack of interactions with teachers, and assignments that were not challenging (Yazzie-Mintz, 2010). This boredom can translate to a lack of attention, minimal effort, and incomplete work and tasks. Even students at schools with the most rigorous curricula can suffer from a lack of engagement, although in their cases their detachment is sometimes difficult to detect. These students often "do school"; they raise their hands, participate in discussions, and turn in assignments, but they get away with doing as little work as possible and don't necessarily enjoy or value what they are learning (Burkett, 2002; Pope, 2001). Kids who are not engaged or who are only "reluctantly engaged" cheat more frequently, earn the lowest GPAs, and show the most symptoms of stress (Conner & Pope, 2013b).

On the other hand, students who are truly engaged with learning benefit in a number of ways. Researchers show that engaged students are more likely to stay in school, take more advanced classes, cheat less, have fewer physical and mental symptoms of stress and less academic worry, and are less likely to abuse drugs and alcohol or suffer from emotional problems like depression (Conner & Pope, 2014; Henry, Knight, & Thornberry, 2012; Li & Lerner, 2011; Shochet, Dadds, Ham, & Montague, 2006).

WHAT DO WE MEAN BY ENGAGEMENT?

Clearly, engagement matters—but in order to increase engagement, we first must define it. Try this exercise for a moment. Think back to a time when you were truly engaged in learning something, either in school or outside of school. What made the task so engaging? When we pose this question to teachers in our workshops, we get many different answers. People fondly recall classes they took where they made a strong connection with the teacher or professor; they remember a particular assignment or author that challenged them to think differently or shook up their worldview; they talk about tasks that demanded learning new and important real-world skills, such as learning to play an instrument, fix a car, build a cabinet. People remember being so engaged with these learning tasks that they lost all track of time when doing them. They experienced the challenge of doing something difficult, but also the joy and satisfaction that came from completing a tough task. Csikszentmihalyi describes this feeling of full engagement as an experience of "flow" (Csikszentmihalyi, 1990; Shernoff, 2010). Flow is an experience of intense concentration or full absorption in an activity, and it is more likely to occur when the activity has a clear goal and when the person doing the task feels adequately challenged. The task should not be so difficult that the person can never achieve it, but not too easy either (Shernoff et al., 2003). These moments of "flow" come up again and again when we ask people to remember engaging learning experiences.

The examples from our workshops fit with what is known in engagement research as the ABC's. The A stands for **affective engagement,** when students are excited about the work and enjoy doing it. The B stands for **behavioral engagement,** when students show effort and work hard to complete the tasks, and the C stands for **cognitive engagement,** when students believe the work they are doing is valuable and meaning-ful (Fredericks, Blumenfeld, & Paris, 2004). When students experience all three aspects of engagement—the affective, behavioral, and cognitive—they are fully engaged and experience the benefits listed above: better mental and physical health, higher grades, and greater school achievement (Conner & Pope, 2014; Shochet et al., 2006).

BACKWARD PLANNING FOR ENGAGED LEARNING

Given the benefits of engagement, how specifically can we boost engagement in the classroom? To increase students' affective, behavioral, and cognitive engagement, we advocate a backward design approach (Wiggins & McTighe, 2005) to planning your courses, units, and lessons. Wiggins and McTighe coined this approach with their series of books titled *Understanding by Design*. We recommend that you read one of their books to learn the fine details of backward design, but we'll summarize the basics of this approach here and will expand on their backward design process to help make our point about creating engaging curricula.

Backward Design Approach

☐ Step 1—Identify desired results.

☐ Step 2—Determine acceptable evidence.

☐ Step 3—Plan learning experiences.

First, you will need to identify desired results. Ask yourself, "What do I want students to understand at the end of this curriculum unit?" Next, you should determine acceptable evidence: "How will I know the students understand this?" Then, once you have a good sense of the understanding goals and the acceptable evidence to show that students are reaching those goals, you should plan the most engaging learning experiences that will lead to those goals.

Wiggins and McTighe talk about "enduring understandings" as the main goals that students will achieve in a particular unit (see Figure 4.2). They distinguish this kind of understanding goal from other goals that concern student skills ("important to know and do"), and things that are simply worth being familiar with. Often, students spend way too much time studying and being tested on things that are only peripheral to the main goals of the unit, without focusing on the big picture or long-term goals. For instance, some teachers quiz students on facts but fail to show them the big picture of why they need to know the facts; sometimes teachers spend so much time teaching a particular skill that they forget to convey to the students how to apply this skill to the real world. Ideally, backward planning helps ensure that teachers and students keep the most important learning goals in mind so that all students understand why they are

Figure 4.2 Understanding by Design

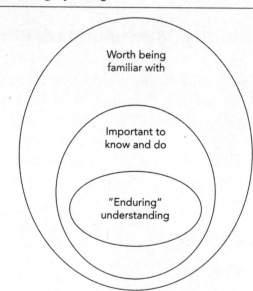

Worth being
familiar with

Important to
know and do

"Enduring"
understanding

Source: Reprinted with permission from Wiggins and McTighe (1998) *Understanding by Design®.*

learning what they are learning—thus avoiding some of the boredom that comes from being asked to memorize facts and figures that don't seem to make sense or have any utility in real life.

In the next section, Denise Pope uses an example from her curriculum construction course at Stanford's Graduate School of Education to help clarify how to use this approach and the concentric circles of Wiggins and McTighe in Figure 4.2.

Denise Pope's Curriculum Construction Course, Stanford, California

The main purpose of the course is to help my students—all of whom are educators—learn to construct effective curriculum units. I have students read books by John Dewey, Jerome Bruner, Nel Noddings, and Elliot Eisner, to name a few, but I don't expect students to memorize all the main ideas in these books. I characterize the ideas in these books as "worth being familiar with"—but it's really OK if my students forget what Bruner says long after the course is over. I also teach students how to design effective lesson plans and assessments. These are skills that are important to know and apply; however, my students need to learn more than just these skills. What is it that I truly want my students to understand and remember long after the course is over? They need to understand how and when to apply these skills to make an effective curriculum. In short, they need to know the big picture concerning curriculum development. I want students to understand that they can't design an effective curriculum in a vacuum. They need to know the context in which the curriculum will be implemented; they need to have a sense of the instructors and the learners and the materials available and the community in which the curriculum will take place. They need to know that their decisions as to what to teach and how to teach it are value-laden and often political and controversial. For instance, who ultimately decides the content of the curriculum? What subjects are traditionally ignored or marginalized in school? Who is benefitting or not from the teaching methods? These are ideas that Dewey, Bruner, Noddings, and Eisner each discuss in their texts, but I don't care so much that my students remember which author said what. I mostly care that my students understand the complexity involved in creating an effective and engaging curriculum. So I organize the class around these enduring understandings and a few essential questions concerning why, what, and how: Why this particular curriculum? What is its purpose? What content should be taught? And how should this content

(continued)

be delivered? Once I have crafted my enduring understandings, then I need to ask myself "How will I know the students can answer these essential questions and that they actually understand that curriculum construction is complex, value-laden, and contextual?"

What is the best way to ensure that students understand a complex concept? We will talk more in depth in the next chapter about evidence for understanding, but in my classroom, I ask students to work in small groups with a real site to create a real curriculum. Students choose a site and a curriculum topic that excites them and that meets a genuine need for the teacher with whom they are working. At the end of the course, they turn in the completed curriculum unit and a paper explaining what they learned as they went through the process of developing the unit. This represents step two in the backward-planning process, as the unit and the paper both allow students to show me what they know.

Once I knew what I wanted students to understand in depth from this unit, and once I had the end product in mind that would provide evidence of their understanding—that is, the curriculum itself and the paper explaining what they had learned—then I designed the learning experiences they would need to produce the final project and paper. In class, we studied curriculum theory, backward design, assessment techniques, pedagogical strategies, and more—all with the goal for students to apply these components as they designed the real-life curricula.

In short, this backward-planning process helps to align learning goals, assessments, and activities so that the teacher *and* the students are clear on what is expected and why they are doing what they are doing. And, ideally, the project (creating a curriculum for a real site) encourages a higher level of engagement in students than simply memorizing how to write an effective lesson plan or taking a test on curriculum theory. The real-life aspect of working in the field, interacting with teachers and kids, and working on a topic the students choose, makes this unit more engaging for my students and has a built-in authenticity that seems to encourage more dedication and deeper learning.

For instance, a group of my students working with a math and science team at a local public high school learned firsthand about the complexity of curriculum construction and the values and politics involved. The team was supposed to design a biology unit on health and nutrition. My students wanted to pick activities that would be authentic and truly engaging for the high school students. They looked for activities that were interesting and enjoyable (affective engagement), challenged students to put in effort (behavioral engagement), and had clear purpose and value (cognitive engagement). In one lab experiment they wanted to have students drink liquids with varying amount of sugar, sodium, and caffeine; study the nutrition labels on the beverages; and then test their urine and perform calculations to show how the body reacted to the different drinks. They were excited that kids would be learning about the digestion and urinary systems while also seeing how certain nutrients and chemicals affected their health.

The school pushed back and worried about the lab. They thought the experiment would be too controversial and upsetting to parents who might not want their kids to drink unhealthy beverages and wouldn't want the school to be testing their kids' urine. My students worked with administrators and teachers at the school to find a more acceptable way to do the lab and stay true to their intended engagement and learning goals. The school eventually allowed a few teen volunteers with parental consent to drink the controversial liquids and test their urine. They also agreed that all the students could drink a healthy vegetable drink and keep a log of how that made them feel compared to the volunteer students who drank the caffeinated and the sugary drinks. In their final papers for my course, my students admitted that they learned more about the "big picture," complex, value-laden, and contextual nature of curriculum construction (my enduring understandings for the course) from their real-life experience with the high school than they ever could have learned from reading books on curriculum design or writing a "pretend" curriculum as part of my course.

Of course, you can develop engaging curricula without using the backward design process, but we have found that the meaningful lessons and assessments that often result from effective backward design tend to align with the ABC characteristics of student engagement.

PROJECT-BASED LEARNING

Research shows that project-based learning (PBL), sometimes also called problem-based learning, when done well, is another method that can lead to effective student engagement. PBL's roots date back to John Dewey (1902, 1916), the progressive educator who believed that, "education...is a process of living and not a preparation for future living" (1897). Thus Dewey advocated for children to learn by doing. Several educators followed Dewey's advice through the years, but the idea gained further traction in the 1970s when a Canadian medical school professor pioneered the use of what he called "project-based learning" in the classrooms to try to reduce the deficit he saw between a medical student's education and actual practice. The method quickly spread to medical schools across the United States and started being used in high schools, particularly in math and science, eventually trickling down to elementary and middle schools as well (Barrows & Tamblyn, 1980).

When you walk into a well-run PBL classroom, the room buzzes with purpose (**cognitive engagement**), activity (**behavioral engagement**), and excitement (**affective engagement**). The students are working hard, and so is the teacher, as she or he provides clear goals and immediate feedback, student choice, scaffolding, and support. This structure in the classroom may not be apparent to the visitor right away, but is highly visible to the students in the room, who believe that what they are learning is relevant to their lives and therefore worthwhile. Who wouldn't want to be in a classroom like that?

How Does Project-Based Learning Work?

Project-based learning takes the idea of the traditional school project and turns it on its head. Take a moment to think back on the projects you did when you were a student in elementary, middle, or high school. How many projects were done mainly at home, alone, or in ill-trained groups? How many were assigned and then not talked about until the day they were due? How many were assigned as something fun to take up the last couple of weeks of the school year? How many were actually completed by a parent who swooped in to the rescue at the last minute? Chances are, quite a few.

A well-designed PBL unit, in contrast, begins with a driving question or problem that is a major part of the class curriculum for the duration of the project. Students must both collaborate and work independently to come up with an answer or solution, usually in the form of a product with an authentic, real-world application. Student work can take place both in the classroom and (sometimes) at home, and it is largely student-driven. What makes PBL especially intriguing is that often there is no right or wrong answer; students not only must come to their own conclusions based on their analysis, research, and knowledge, but also explain how they got there. In the earlier case study from Denise's classroom, we show two different examples of PBL. First, Denise's students engage in PBL when they work in groups to construct curricula for real sites and write process papers about their experiences, explaining how and why they made the curricular decisions throughout the project. The science lab is another example of PBL. The high school students engage in a real-life experiment as they track and are asked to explain how and why the human body reacts to the different liquids. In both examples, students participate in authentic activities to "solve" a problem or create a project in response to complex questions about how nutrition affects our health or what constitutes an effective curriculum.

The Research on Project-Based Learning

When learning about PBL for the first time, educators and parents sometimes ask, "If the class is focusing on one particular project for so long, how will the kids learn basic skills and other knowledge they'll need? What content, skills, or topics are they missing out on?" The good news is that much of the research has shown that PBL students, regardless of socioeconomic status, do just as well on standardized tests as students in more traditional classrooms and, depending on the study, they often do better. More important, they perform better on higher-order thinking skills and exhibit comparable or greater academic gains that last long after their PBL experience has ended (Chang, 2001; Geier et al., 2008; Hernandez-Ramos & De La Paz, 2009).

When students go into depth on a subject and have more opportunities for hands-on, personalized and group learning, several things happen. First, provided the teacher has done his or her job, the student feels motivated to learn more. Second, the chances of a student needing to activate, practice, and improve multidisciplinary skills—such as oral and written communication skills and critical thinking and analytical skills—increase in a PBL classroom. And third, the students often learn and practice skills they'll need to be successful in both their professional and personal lives, such as collaboration, problem-solving, and initiative.

Consider the following studies. In one, researchers created a PBL-based curriculum for an AP Government and Politics class and compared the exam results of students who took that course with students learning in more traditional, lecture-based classrooms. Students in high-achieving schools using the PBL-based curriculum had AP exam scores up to 30 percent higher than their lecture-based counterparts. The differences in moderately achieving and poverty-impacted schools were smaller, but still detectable (Parker et al., 2011). In addition to evidence that PBL can improve performance on exams, studies show that PBL can improve students' attitudes and approaches toward learning. In a study that compared PBL methods for teaching middle school social studies with traditional methods, the authors found that students using PBL methods gained a deeper understanding of the topic and engaged in more critical inquiry than those in the traditional classrooms. They also found that students in the PBL classes were more likely to have positive experiences and attitudes about the unit than those in the traditional classes and that these attitudes could influence their attitudes in future classes (Hernandez-Ramos & De La Paz, 2009).

Researchers from Stanford's Center for Opportunity Policy in Education found significant results in implementing a student-centered approach in high schools in which half or more students qualified for free or reduced lunch. These researchers found that when four urban schools implemented a curriculum that was rich and engaging to students; used a student-centered approach that focused on helping students learn collaboration, communication, and analytical skills; and fostered deeper connections between students and teachers, the students outperformed their peers in similar schools on state assessments, and the schools graduated more students and had more students who were eligible for college (Fridlander, Burns, Lewis-Charp, Cook-Harvey, & Darling-Hammond, 2014).

In another study, Kings College researcher Jo Boaler, now at Stanford, studied math students in two secondary schools in Great Britain. Both schools were composed of working-class students, and at least 75 percent of the students were testing below grade level in math. After two years of PBL instruction, the PBL students passed the exams at three times the rate of students in more traditional, textbook-taught classrooms (Boaler, 1997).

It is important to note that some studies have found that for short-term knowledge, traditional teaching methods have been shown to be slightly more effective. However, for higher-order thinking skills and long-term retention, PBL students test higher (Strobel & van Barneveld, 2009).

These higher-order thinking skills are emphasized in the Common Core State Standards and the initiatives supporting college and career readiness. The Common Core State Standards are not, as is widely assumed, complete curriculum units or content. Rather, they are a list of skills that experts believe our students need in order to be prepared for the modern workplace. The math standards require students to be able to problem-solve, communicate, make connections, reason, and provide proof for their reasoning. The English language arts and literacy standards require students to be able to read critically, to engage deeply with texts of all types, to reason, to use evidence to make decisions, and to analyze, discuss, write, speak, and listen. These critical thinking, analysis, communication, collaboration, and decision-making skills are often referred to as "21st century skills" that students need for life and careers (Partnership for 21st Century Skills, 2009) and can be found at the core of PBL. As teachers begin to implement the Common Core standards in their classrooms, they may want to consider PBL to convey these skills, especially given the research on the benefits of this method.

Though it is too early to cite research on Common Core and PBL, we did find research that confirms the advantages of using PBL for teaching 21st century skills. From 2008 to 2010, the West Virginia Department of Education, along with the Buck Institute, provided teachers with extensive training in PBL. In 2011, researchers administered a survey to learn the effects of that training. They found that teachers who were trained in PBL taught 21st century skills more frequently than those who were not. These numbers were not affected by the length of the teaching periods (block versus traditional, 50-minute periods) or by the achievement level of the students. Additionally, while not the ideal measure, students who were in the PBL classrooms did equally as well on high-stakes tests (Hixson, Ravitz, & Whisman, 2012).

In short, PBL can make teaching and learning exciting and can lead to long-term retention of material and foster important professional and personal skills. Students who participate in PBL-designed curriculum believe that what they are learning today will help them later in life, which increases motivation, effort, and interest in the subjects being taught.

PROJECT-BASED LEARNING IN ACTION

Laura Docter, a sixth grade history and social studies teacher at Castilleja School, uses PBL in all of her curriculum units. The following case study showcases PBL in action and highlights some of the benefits just mentioned.

Laura Docter's Classroom, Castilleja School, Palo Alto, California

Early in the school year, Laura Docter's students participated in a unit on Early Humans in which they used their "detective" research skills to identify and put four Hominid skulls in chronological order, spanning from 18,000 to 6 million years old. This early unit offered students a good sense of PBL, as they worked together in small groups, gathering evidence to support an argument concerning skull identification and dating. Laura also taught a unit on Ancient India and China in which students researched topics from that period of time and then

(continued)

made iMovies in which they pretended to be historic individuals and contemporary archaeologists and inventors. And Laura's students participated in a "mini" National History Day presentation for which they designed exhibition boards, with thesis statements, process papers, and annotated bibliographies on the ancient Maya. So by the time Laura was ready for the unit on Rome, her students had plenty of experience with PBL activities.

In each of these units, Laura touched on several of her main understanding goals and essential questions for the year, such as: How do we use evidence to construct an argument? How do we know which evidence is better? And how do we ask an authentic question? Laura also raised some essential questions about learning history in general, such as: How do we know what we know about the past? How does history relate to me? And she had some specific questions that related to studying ancient history in particular, such as: Who has power in the ancient world? What does it take to be a civilization? And what can we learn about an ancient society from studying its ruins?

These are all meaty questions with the potential to lead to deep understanding about the discipline of history and the process of constructing arguments. Keeping these questions in mind (and following the process for step two of the backward design process: determining acceptable evidence), Laura decided that one of the best ways for students to show that they understand how to ask an authentic question and construct an argument (her "desired results") would be to engage in an authentic research assignment. Laura wanted the students to be engaged in the lessons and not just go through the motions of picking a standard teacher-constructed research question that had a set answer from their textbooks or online sources. Instead, she wanted students to "do what real historians and archaeologists do" and study ancient ruins as a way to answer essential questions about power and the nature of civilization. Laura felt that one of the most engaging and effective ways to pursue answers to these essential questions was by participating in a type of archaeology lesson where the class simulated Roman ruins (the "learning experiences").

Classroom Snapshot: Introducing the Ruins

As the students sat in chairs in a circle, Laura navigated her way around five piles of small cardboard boxes and a few plastic Roman busts and statues that would be the ruins the students would study.

Laura explained to the students: "Imagine that you are an archaeologist and have come across this 2,000-year-old Roman ruin. You have an inquiring mind and are trying to figure out what this ruin was originally."

Laura continued, gesturing to the cardboard chaos in front of her. "If you were asked to interpret and understand this mess of stone blocks, what would you have to do before you could figure out what happened here?"

The students raised their hands and shared their thoughts.

"I would look around for specific artifacts," said one.

"I would look at the ruins and see if they were in a certain shape or what they were made of."

The students were excited. As Laura broke them into groups, she told them their task for the day: Research Roman architecture and try to make an educated guess about what these ruins might have originally been, then attempt to reconstruct them. The students were prepped; the night before, they'd read an article on the topic and clicked through an online photo gallery, compiled by Laura, of different examples of Roman structures. She'd also compiled a list of online resources for them to peruse during class.

Laura divided the students into five groups and set them loose on the cardboard ruins in front of them. They immediately got to work making claims and finding evidence to back them up.

A classroom community that supports learning and collaboration is essential in a PBL classroom, and Laura had worked since the first day of school to create a culture of respect, intellectual curiosity, and responsibility. She started her year by describing clear expectations for both academic achievement and being a solid community member, explicitly explaining not only what she expected but also what it looked like, and she had students work in small groups for a period of time almost every day. (See Chapter Seven for more on establishing an effective school climate.)

At the "ruin" site, students documented all their work in Google Docs, accessible to Laura at the end of the lesson. She used these docs to create a basic study guide for the class with 12 main questions, maps, notes, and vocabulary words that served as foundational knowledge for the unit. In earlier units, Laura provided this background information before introducing the project, but this time—due to an unavoidable scheduling change—Laura didn't have time to do her mini-lecture on Roman architecture before the students explored the ruins. As it turned out, this was an even more engaging strategy, since the

(continued)

students were excited to discover this information on their own through the analysis of the ruins.

Laura knew her subject matter and students well enough that she did not need to rely on traditional teaching methods whereby the teacher as expert tells the answers to the students. Instead, Laura worked hard to be a "guide on the side—but on the far, far side," asking lots of questions that prompted her students to go back and seek further information and evidence for their claims. She explained, "My goal is to help them reach their own understandings rather than simply giving them my understandings." She told her students, "It is far more important to ask a good question than to memorize someone else's answer." For instance, during the lesson, when group members based a decision that their pile of blocks had been an obelisk on a photo found on the Internet, Laura asked, "Do we have evidence that there was a fountain next to an obelisk in Rome? How could we find out? Did you find a picture? Is it a real place?" When they discovered the photo was of an obelisk in France, they were disappointed. Laura then asked, "Is there any way there could be Roman ruins in France?" The students brightened and went back to see if that might be plausible, using the sources that Laura had vetted ahead of time such as *National Geographic*, various online textbooks, and world history databases.

At the end of the lesson, the student groups didn't agree on the identification of the ruins. One group decided the ruins represented a road—in particular, the Appian Way. Another group disagreed and thought the ruins represented a part of the Arch of Constantine, near the Coliseum. Another group thought it was from a site in present-day Bosnia-Herzegovina; yet another thought it was the Triumphal Arch of Orange in France. They spent the next day defending their claims to the class, and it turned out that most of the claims were plausible. In fact, Laura hadn't chosen a particular site; instead, she had crafted boxes and statues that represented typical Roman styles.

After lessons that included returning to the cardboard ruins to look at how arches were constructed and how these were used in aqueducts to provide water to the towns, Laura dedicated one day each to a series of interactive mini-lectures that covered the following aspects of Roman history: Roman entertainment (gladiators and the theater), Roman politics, and empires. Although Laura provided some direct instruction during these lessons, the majority of the time was devoted to student-led investigations in each area via interactive electronic maps and other hands-on activities.

Once the students had a wide range of knowledge, they headed into their final activity. Each individual chose a topic of interest to research and then write up in a comprehensive paragraph for a roundtable presentation. Students could choose whatever question they wanted to explore, within reason. "The boundaries are wide," explained Laura, "divided by place and time. But they are there. You can't study unicorns, for example, and you have to meet the requirements of the assignment—including providing evidence as to how this topic contributed to the development, perpetuation, and/or ultimate demise of the Roman civilization." After a week of research and writing, the students presented their completed paragraphs at roundtables of eight students each, listening, taking notes, and asking good questions about each other's work.

Laura knew that not every student would learn the exact same thing in the unit, and this was OK. When she gave tests—which was rare, perhaps two or three per year—she did it to teach her sixth graders test-taking skills they would need in future years, such as completing multiple choice, matching, short-answer, and brief essay questions. For other assignments she used rubrics to assess the work, so students could receive feedback as to whether they were exhibiting the intended skills and showing evidence of understanding the key concepts. Some students, for example, learned more about a civilization's deities, and some learned more about trade, but that didn't bother Laura. She was teaching students how to be learners—how to ask an authentic question, find credible sources, and construct solid arguments about things they genuinely wanted to know more about. Similar to the two center circles in Figure 4.2, Laura focused her teaching on the skills and content that were "important to know and do" and that would help lead her students to enduring understandings.

And at the same time, Laura taught students how to work in groups, to collaborate and share resources, and to communicate effectively—all important 21st century skills. She explained, "So we see not only how Romans learned to live and interact and collaborate (or not) in ancient times, but also how modern day teenagers learn to interact and collaborate together as well to complete a task—and that's a very authentic way to study what it takes to be a civilization, then and now."

To learn more about how Laura constructed this PBL unit, see Exhibit 4.1 for a sample unit timeline, guiding questions, and instructions for the final individual project for the Rome roundtables.

Exhibit 4.1 Sample Materials from Laura Docter's Rome Project

Study Questions inspired by Roman Ruin Experience #1

Through their research, students collectively introduced each other to the following:

1. **Roman walls**. What is a Roman wall? When/where were they built? What was their purpose?

2. **Emperor Hadrian**. When did he live, and when did he rule? What was Hadrian's wall? What else was he known for?

3. **Triumphal arches**. What is a triumphal arch? When and where were they built? What was their purpose?

4. **Emperor Constantine**. When did he live, and when did he rule? What was the Arch of Constantine? What else was he known for?

5. **Roman armor/soldiers**. What type of armor did Roman soldiers wear? What types of weapons and protective gear did they have? With whom did they fight?

6. **Roman Aqueduct**. What is an aqueduct in general? What made those from ancient Rome special or interesting? What purpose did they serve? How were they built? Where were they?

7. **Appian Way.** What is the Appian Way? What does it look like? Where is it located? What purpose did it serve?

8. **Roman Coliseum**. What is a coliseum in general? And what is *the* Coliseum? What does it look like? Where is it located? What purpose did it serve?

9. **Roman Amphitheater**. What is an amphitheater in general? What was unique or special about ancient Roman amphitheaters? What purpose did they serve?

10. **Roman Forum**. What is a forum in general? What was the ancient Roman Forum? Where is it located? What could you find there today?

11. **Egyptian obelisks**. What is an obelisk? Why would there be an Egyptian obelisk in a Roman ruin? What was Rome's relationship with Egypt in ancient times and how did it change during the time of the Roman Republic and Empire?

12. Also mentioned in your notes, as possible men represented by the artifacts, were a) **Antoninus Pius** and b) **Caligula**. Who were they? When and where did they live? What were they known for?

Friday's Class Notes: Unpacking Roman Ruin Experience #1

In an effort to share insights across classes, I have compiled both sections below.

[The original maps that accompanied these notes are not shown here.]

The Tiger and Zebra classes think this may have been a ruin from **Dalmatia,** perhaps **Salona**, the capital city of a Roman province on the **Adriatic Sea** (Croatia and Bosnia-Herzegovina today). Romans lived there in approximately the early first century AD.

The Giraffe and Jaguar classes think this may have been a ruin in France, from when the Romans ruled there—probably **Orange,** where they have a wonderful triumphant arch. Please see World Heritage app for more information on the *Roman Theater and its Surroundings and the "Triumphal Arch" of Orange.*

The **Rhone Valley** is the low land around the Rhone River, which runs from the **Alps** of Switzerland south through France to the **Mediterranean Sea**. Orange is in the Rhone Valley and was once part of the Roman Empire.

Vocabulary that we encountered while researching questions related to the ruin:

emperor—ruler or king, sovereign ruler with great power and rank, especially one who rules an empire. For example, **Emperor Augustus** was the founder of the Roman Empire and its first Emperor, ruling from 27 B.C. until his death in 14 A.D.

cuirass—the armor that a warrior wore on his chest, breastplate and backplate fastened together.

coliseum—like stadium, scary sports often to the death, but also entertainment happens there, also sort of like a theater.

Pantheon (not to be confused with the Greeks' Parthenon)—in general, it means "all the gods together," but it is also a specific building in Rome that was a temple to all the gods during Emperor Augustus' reign. It was rebuilt during Hadrian's reign.

Triumphal Arch—from the word triumph—maybe because when they won a war they built an arch, it was a monumental structure in the shape of an archway with arched passageways (usually one or three) that often spans a roadway. We found there were triumphal arches all over, usually made for rulers, and that they were named after emperors (like Arch of Constantine in Rome, or Hadrian's Gate, Arches of Claudius, Arch of Titus, Triumphal Arch of Orange, etc.).

NOTE: These sources were provided to help interpret the "ruin": Everyone should look at Roman architecture on Artstor, preview ROMA app, look at these objects on BBC, and this photo gallery of Roman architecture and engineering on History.com.

My Roman Research Topic Worksheet

- **Homework Monday:** Write a sloppy copy of your paragraph based on your research in at least one library database.

- **In class Tues/Wed or Thur:** Do research in a book, and add additional information to your paragraph.

- **Homework Tues/Wed or Thur:** Rewrite your paragraph, fine-tune, and make it ready to read on Friday!

- **In school on Friday:** Present orally in round-table format at Festival.

- **Homework over the weekend:** Write up final draft of your paragraph.

Note about citing sources. You must use a minimum of two scholarly sources. They may be databases, encyclopedias, print books, or scholarly websites (*Wikipedia* and random websites or blogs do not count). At the end of the paragraph, you will list the sources consulted in full and proper MLA style.

Step 1: Define the Topic and Argument

You will need to **choose a topic related to ancient Rome**. It can be something from the Study Questions, something from the Galen book, something from *The Story of the World*, something you found in a library book or database, or something you wondered about as you dreamed of going to Rome. First brainstorm a short list of topics that especially interest you. Then choose a narrow and specific topic, as this will help you craft a more focused, engaging argument.

Once you've chosen your topic, answer the question: Why was this topic important in the development, perpetuation (how it stayed strong for so long), or demise (fall) of ancient Roman civilization? The answer will be your main argument. Come back and revise it often as you learn more and fine-tune your focus.

Define any complex words, but make a claim about your chosen topic that goes beyond the definition to touch on the development, purpose, relationship, or significance of your topic in ancient Rome. Use *Story of the World*, databases, library books, to gain information on your topic.

Step 2: Prove it with evidence and specific examples

In order to convince your colleagues that your argument is a valid interpretation of the past, you need to include evidence from respected scholarly sources. This could be a quote, a description of a visual, or a specific example that proves your point. This is the "meat" of your paragraph.

Make sure your overall argument is clear and thought-provoking. You may also need to provide *context* for the evidence—for example, letting us know when it takes place or briefly describing the people involved.

- Make your main points related to your topic clear.

- Provide evidence to support all your claims.

- Clearly explain how each piece of evidence supports your claims.

- Add a **concluding sentence** that mentions

  1. something about what else this relates to from History 6 and

  2. what it makes you want to research next (a question you have now).

Step 3: Proofread and Edit

Have a classmate read through your paragraph and note anything that is unclear or problematic. Revise for clarity, accuracy, and interest. Then have Dr. Docter "OK" your paragraph. Correct any problems. Practice reading your paragraph and see how long it takes. Think about what questions people might ask you or comments they might make after hearing your paragraph. Consider what you would like to ask your classmates related to your topic.

Please make a COPY of this, add your name, and put it in your history folder. Answer the questions and add images or explanations to the notes as you like. You may share ideas and help others, but each student is responsible to understand her answers.

Timeline for the Rome Project

6	7	8	9
Set up "museum" of Exhibit Boards and...	Welcome to ROME	Roman "ruin" activity	Class
HW: Prepare for the Investigation of the Ruin. In anticipation of having to interpret what you find in a Roman ruin, please research your section's topic. Everyone should look at Roman architecture on Artstor, preview ROMA app on iPad, look at these objects, and this photo gallery of Roman architecture and engineering.	Investigation of the "Ruin." In anticipation of having to interpret what you find in a Roman ruin, please research your section's topic. Everyone should look at Roman architecture on Artstor, preview ROMA app on iPad, look at these objects on BBC, and this photo gallery of Roman architecture and engineering on History.com.	Group doc for Tigers and Zebras	HW: Galen—see doc
		Group doc for Giraffes and Jaguars	Group doc for Tigers and Zebras
		HW: Finish Maya Boards and also add your thoughts to the Group document from class.	Group doc for Giraffes and Jaguars
	Archaeology Groups' Documents Linked here		
	HW: Finish Maya Boards (during study lab today and Thursday).		

Timeline for the Rome Project

12

1. Reflecting on Learning and Assessments

2. Questions and vocabulary—as a follow up to Roman Ruin Experience #1 and our notes in class, and in preparation for Roman Ruin Experience #2!

HW: continue to read, and write about, Galen 15 minute read/5 minute write: Do reading response #2.

13

Roman Ruin Experience #2 aqueducts

Fill out class survey

HW: continue to read, and write about, Galen—15 minute read/5 minute write: Do reading response #3.

14

More on Ancient Rome

J and G: complete study questions, read in SotW

HW: continue to read, and write about, Galen—15 minute read/5 minute write: Do reading response #4.

15

More on Ancient Rome —Empires

HW: continue to read, and write about, Galen Do reading response #4.

16

More on Ancient Rome

T and Z: complete study questions, read in SotW

J and G—Empires

HW: Finish Galen and do one last (#5) response. Begin thinking about: What you would like to write your paragraph about—see SotW, Study Questions, ROMA app, etc. for ideas.

19

Costumes and Culture Groups' Festival Slide Presentation

HW: Using at least one library database as a source, write a sloppy copy—(1st draft) of your research paragraph.

20

More on Ancient Rome

1. Work on your Study Questions (you have your own copy already).

2. More research paragraph writing—The Story of the World as a source.

3. Complete your Culture Group Slide.

HW: Finish any/all of the above and Galen responses.

21

More on Ancient Rome —"Roman Entertainment: Gladiators and Theater" FLEX—FOA prep

1. Write your research topic here

2. Procession Practice on the circle

3. Work with your group Culture Group Slide Decide on themes, colors, fonts, order, and complete the last two TOGETHER!

HW: Finish research paragraph, practice speaking it (3 minutes max), you MAY choose image(s) to accompany.

22

More on Ancient Rome —"Roman Politics: Emperors and Hereditary Rule" HW: Finish research paragraph

23

Festival of Antiquity

- Roman Round Table: Present research paragraph
- Olympics
- Slideshow Culture Group Slide
- Arts Performances

Homework: Write up the final draft (grammar, spelling, complete sentences, clear, title, name, bibliography with at least two scholarly sources, etc.) of the research paragraph you presented today.

Timeline for the Rome Project

26	27	28	29	30
Memorial Day NO Classes	1. More on Rome: J and G—Roman Politics: Emperors and hereditary rule T and Z—Roman Entertainment: Gladiators and Theater 2. The Legacy of Rome: Connecting what we learn about the past to our lives in the present and future. HW: Finish <u>Study Questions</u> (you have your own copy already)	Last day of history —Reflecting on the work of historians and links to our lives. HW: Make sure all of your Roman work is complete and your history folder is neatly organized! 1. <u>Research Paragraph</u> (presented orally at Festival) 2. <u>Study Questions</u> (you have your own copy) 3. <u>Galen Reading Responses</u> (you have your own copy)	Last day of history —Reflecting on the work of historians and links to our lives. HW: Make sure all of your Roman work is complete and your history folder is neatly organized! 1. <u>Research Paragraph</u> (presented orally at Festival) 2. <u>Study Questions</u> (you have your own copy) 3. <u>Galen Reading Responses</u> (you have your own copy)	Closing Day: Interdisciplinary Activities and Community Gratitude

Project-Based Learning and the Flexible Teacher

As exciting as PBL can be, it is also a method that takes time and effort to implement. We've found that teachers who use PBL are constantly learning and growing along with their students. Units and final products change from year to year based on what was learned from previous attempts. As a result, teachers must be all-in and willing to, in some cases, look at teaching in a whole new way.

Successful PBL requires teachers to constantly review and assess student needs— both academic and social. It necessitates daily instruction, scaffolding, and support. Students need deadlines, guidelines, and clear assessment tools. They need to be taught how to collaborate, how to function in a group, what roles group members need to fill, how to ask questions, how to research, how to interview sources for information, how to work independently, how to problem-solve, and a myriad of other skills that the teacher should model, instruct, coach, and facilitate.

Additionally, our teachers tell us that they have to be flexible and willing to change, tweak, or throw away lesson plans at a moment's notice depending on what their students need on that particular day. Sometimes that is the best thing that can happen to a teacher. Dave Otten from The Athenian School in Danville, California, told us, "My best teaching innovations have been accidents." He explained that these often come when he has to think on his feet in response to student need. Otten's prep time has undoubtedly grown more complicated, but he does the work happily. "I basically have to get up to speed on 20 kids' projects and hope to be a few steps ahead of each of them if I am lucky. It isn't my job to teach them what they are learning, but to help them if they get stuck. I try to remove the barriers for students to deconstruct their problems on their own. Every day is different and every year is different, which is a hard thing, but it is so much more rewarding."

And of course, classroom management is key. As Eric Isselhardt, Ph.D., chief academic officer at the Green Street Academy in Baltimore, Maryland, recently blogged on his school's experience transitioning the entire curriculum over to PBL, "We know that without excellent classroom management, project-based learning efforts devolve to classroom chaos." PBL teachers must prepare students for a different kind of learning environment—one that offers more time for students to work on their own and in small groups, and where the teacher spends much less time in the front of the classroom. Teachers have to help students learn to stay on task, work together, and let them know what to do when they experience a problem. Initially, it can take a lot of work to manage the PBL classroom, but we have found the payoffs to be well worth the effort. In addition to the academic benefits and life skills learned during PBL, we've seen students in elementary, middle, and high schools happily engaged in their work and full of pride when presenting their final products, eager to share the processes and steps they'd taken to get there.

Getting Started with Project-Based Learning

Transitioning to PBL can feel overwhelming at first, but once teachers experience success with PBL, they can't imagine their classrooms without it. To help you get started, we've compiled a checklist, based on our research, observation, experience, and conversations with PBL teachers.

Do your homework and plan backward. Most of the research we've read on PBL affirms that the effectiveness of a PBL unit depends on how well a teacher can execute it. PBL can be a great way to teach the Common Core standards; however, it is important to decide which standards you want to teach. Use the standards to choose your intended skills and enduring understandings, and then follow our earlier advice to backward-plan the unit goals, assessments, and learning activities. There are a multitude of resources that can help you to design, create, and plot out a PBL unit. A few popular sites include the Buck Institute and Edutopia.

Start small. Make your first project a manageable one. Professionals recommend starting with a project no more than two or three weeks long. Other experts recommend starting with a unit where only in-class research is required; leave the field research for your next project (Ertmer & Simons, 2005). Even teachers who work in schools that don't allow as much flexibility in curriculum planning can experiment with short PBL lessons that align with the required curriculum.

Prepare your students. Because so much of the project is student-oriented, it is essential that you are realistic about your students' strengths and weaknesses and that you prepare them for the tasks they need to complete for a successful project. For example, if your students haven't done a lot of small-group work, or if they have struggled to collaborate well in the past, you need to address this early on and plan specific lessons that will help them develop these skills (Barron, 2003). Similarly, students may need explicit lessons on how to ask a good question or how to use the library before they are ready to take on PBL. As Lisa Babinet from Waldorf School of the Peninsula in Los Altos, California, observes, "Trying to figure out how to meet all of the different ability levels in your class can be challenging." PBL can help you to differentiate your teaching to fit a wide range of learners, because not everyone in the class is expected to do the same thing. Still, Babinet suggests that teachers assign students to groups early on (instead of letting students choose their own groups initially) in order to assess and teach the skills necessary for successful partnerships and for kids with certain strengths in some areas to help those who may not be as strong. As students gain more experience working together, teachers can explore different group formations and can vary groups periodically, allowing kids to collaborate based on ability or on a common interest.

Provide structure and assess as you go. A successful PBL unit requires appropriate structure and scaffolding and constant assessment (Barron & Darling-Hammond, 2008). Teachers need to make sure they give enough direction and periodic feedback to students to keep them focused and to help them understand the learning goals and expectations, but not so much structure as to impede student freedom to discover answers on their own. To do this, provide students with rubrics and other assessment tools early in the process. Use these tools to assess students throughout the project (not just at the end), and offer lots of feedback for revision and improvement. Timelines, checklists, goals, and interim due dates, such as those used by Laura in the Rome unit, help scaffold the project and keep students on track.

Prepare your parents. We have found that parents can help or hinder the PBL process. Before you begin a new project, make sure that parents—along with the students—understand the timeline, the goals, and the reasoning behind the project, as well as the rules for work done at home. Explain to parents that students will do most of the work in the classroom, but on the rare occasion that students need to do some project work at home, that work is to be done by the students themselves. Too often we see parents who hijack the project at home (as in the science fair project that is usually done by the parent who is a professional engineer or architect). Parents can and should offer encouragement and support, but they should not touch the materials or engage in the research process for the students.

Be flexible. Research on effective PBL methods show that units can run longer than expected. If you go into the project knowing that sometimes lessons may have to be changed, new skills may have to be taught, or you may have to throw out everything you planned for the day to address an immediate need, it will be easier to deal with changes as they arise. Lisa Babinet advises teachers to help students learn to be flexible as well and to help them focus on what was learned in the process, even when the final product might not turn out. She explains: "One of my students used a fire spinner to explore conic sections. It didn't work. He was very upset, but he went on an earnest search and didn't find what he was looking for." Instead of having the student redo the project or choose a different topic, Babinet urged him to explain why the fire spinner didn't deliver the desired results, telling him, "I'd rather you explore, take risks, and make mistakes than just play it safe." (See the case study later in this chapter.) Sometimes the best lessons come from failed projects.

Enlist students for help in planning and assessing. Students are sometimes the very best resources for helping teachers plan the PBL units. They can be taught to self-assess and peer-assess projects, and they should be given ample time to discuss what is and isn't working in the project and to weigh in when needed. For instance, Dave Otten faced a quandary when one of his high school science projects was taking longer than in previous years. The project was a major component of his Applied Science and Engineering class, and the students were working hard on building micro controllers, but they needed more time. Dave had the option to either speed up the unit by cutting some corners, or cancel the final exam, or count the project as the final exam. To resolve the quandary, Dave did what he often does in this situation—he turned to the students.

Together, after thinking it through as a class, they decided to stay the course and stick with the micro controller unit and count it as the final exam.

Use technology when appropriate. Technology can be a useful tool for PBL, but only when it brings some added value to the project. Some schools build "maker labs"—similar to the shop classrooms of the past—where students learn to use the latest tools, gadgets, and technology to build or create products for their projects. Other schools invest in purchasing new apps and platforms or take advantage of free technology, such as Google Docs in Laura's course, to help students design and implement their projects. Whatever technology you decide to try, make sure that it adds particular value to your project. For instance, Google Docs can help students to collaborate more efficiently and track their thinking over time. Though a detailed look at educational technology is beyond the scope of this book, we recommend that you take the time to thoroughly research new technology and not be swayed by fancy bells and whistles or the newest fad. And of course, use your students as allies here. They often are more knowledgeable about and facile with the technology than many teachers.

Waldorf School of the Peninsula, Los Altos, California

When Lisa Babinet, a middle and high school math teacher at Waldorf School of the Peninsula, assigned a project requiring her students to explore conic sections, she let the students determine how they would explore the complicated subject. Her biggest criteria for choosing their project idea? Joy. She wanted her students to relate the material to a subject they were passionate about. As a result, one student built a model of the Archimedes Death Ray that had fascinated her on a popular television show. Another conducted agility training with dogs to see if they jump in parabolic shapes. And another explored whether or not BBs shot from an Airsoft gun arced in ellipses or parabolas.

Projects like these have taught Babinet as much as they've taught her students. Prior to arriving at Waldorf ten years ago, she'd taught for 20 years in more traditional classrooms. "I was used to giving out assignments and expecting people to do exactly what the instructions said. When I got to Waldorf, I had to let go of control. I got so many interpretations of the assignments I gave." At first, she said, it was unnerving. "I wanted ABC and got XYZ." But she quickly adjusted, and today she wouldn't have it any other way. "We are teaching students to think outside of the box; to think and process differently," she said, and, although she still has demanding criteria for every assignment, she has realized that "engagement and learning go up when students process material the way they think about it and not the way I am telling them to think about it. The ownership is higher."

Of course, with every new process comes a learning curve. Babinet quickly learned, "I had to be humble. I had to open up my creativity and flexibility." For her own sake, she said, she had "to figure out why it was so important to have it be exactly the way I wanted it." Once she did this, she found it easier to let go and lead her students toward the directions best for them.

Though some students might resist the responsibility that comes with PBL, once they are taught the skills and are given the proper scaffolding, most find the experience to be much more rewarding than the traditional lessons, in which knowledge tends to be more static as it is conveyed from the teacher to the learners. In PBL, the teachers and the students learn and explore real questions together and, in doing so, engage in authentic and meaningful work.

In this chapter, we discussed the backward design process and PBL as effective strategies to increase student engagement with learning. Teachers can boost student engagement in the classroom in a number of ways, including increasing student voice and choice over what and how the students learn; using varied pedagogical methods such as Socratic seminars, inquiry, simulations, and case studies; partnering with local community and businesses to establish internships, work-study models, and service learning experiences in which students can apply what they are learning; "flipping" the classroom to allow students more time in class for hands-on exploration; and using technology in various ways. Each of these strategies can be used individually or in conjunction with backward design and/or PBL. We encourage you to experiment with a variety of different engagement strategies and to use the tips listed in this chapter to help ensure that you are designing lessons and units that are aligned with your learning goals and that can engage students affectively, behaviorally, and cognitively.

Chapter FIVE

Authentic and Alternative Assessments

Everybody is a genius, but if you judge a fish by its ability to climb a tree, it will live its whole life believing that it is stupid.

—*Source unknown*

It is ridiculous to judge a fish by its ability to climb a tree, yet in many classrooms we see assessment practices that may be just as misaligned or ineffective. We hear teachers, parents, and students complain that current high-stakes tests are unfair and biased. We hear stories of kids who are over-tested and burned out from the rote practices that are often the result of "teaching to the test." And we know students who are so stressed about the tests that they vomit on the exam booklets, lose sleep, or suffer severe test anxiety despite "knowing" the material on which they are being assessed (Pope, 2001).

Imagine if, in the working world, your boss told you early in the week that you would have a test later that week. He couldn't tell you exactly what would be on the test, but it would definitely be timed, and you would not be allowed to use any of the typical resources on which you were used to relying, such as your working notes, your colleagues, the Internet, and so on. He would be the sole designer and assessor of this test; there would be no ability to ask questions or retake the test, and your score would greatly impact your next pay bonus. Sounds crazy, right? But in schools, this scenario may take place multiple times per week, and the students are suffering because of it. When teachers rely primarily on tests focused on memorization, students are more likely to cheat and are less likely to be motivated in school (Amrein & Berliner, 2002; Battistich, Watson, Solomon, Lewis, & Schaps, 1999; Harlen & Crick, 2003). For many students, the overreliance on tests can also mean more test anxiety and more stress (Cizek & Burg, 2006).

McTighe and Ferrara (1998), in their NEA publication, *Assessing Learning in the Classroom,* compare the assessment process to photography: A single test on any given day is like a snapshot. You have captured the student only in one moment in time when she might look beautiful or she might be exhausted, not ready for the camera; she might blink or move suddenly or be otherwise unprepared—and the photo doesn't do her justice. A series of photographs over time, such as a photo album, might be a more comprehensive way to represent the student, with the resulting montage more accurately capturing her essence. The same is true for assessments. One single snapshot may not provide accurate evidence of student understanding, but several different kinds of assessments, implemented over time, may reveal more accurate information. In fact, in two recent reviews of research on alternative assessment practices (Hardiman & Whitman, 2014; Shepard, 2010), the authors conclude that long-term engagement and motivation, metacognition, and retention of knowledge are best served by alternative assessment practices rather than traditional tests.

In this chapter we cannot cover every aspect of classroom assessment; there are scores of books written on this subject. Instead, we hope to use recent research and advice from assessment experts to convince you of the merits of multiple forms of assessment over time and, in particular, authentic and alternative forms of assessments, such as performance-based assessments, mastery exhibitions, and student self- and peer assessment processes. We present case studies from Challenge Success schools that are tackling the difficult task of how best to determine what exactly their students are learning and how best to design assessments and grading practices that inform multiple audiences and help students reach their learning goals without overloading or overwhelming them.

WHY ASSESS?

At the beginning of our assessment workshops, we pose the question: Why assess? We ask participants to consider the different purposes and audiences for assessing student learning. Answers vary. Some folks say they assess students in order to rank and sort them. "We have to assess students because the school/district/state requires us to test students and to post grades and scores, and then the community/real estate agents/colleges, etc., use these grades and test scores to determine admission decisions/housing prices/promotion and graduation decisions." Others concur: "Parents and students need to see how kids are doing in my class and how they compare to the other students." However, many teachers say they assess to determine what the students know and don't know—to help students and teachers understand the gaps in student knowledge and how to address these gaps. Notice the distinction between assessment for purposes of grading, ranking, and sorting, and assessment for purposes of improving teaching and helping students learn.

Back to Backward Design

To help understand the difference, let's review the process described in the previous chapter in our discussion of assessment as a driver of curriculum construction.

Backward Design Approach

☐ Step 1—Identify desired results.

☐ Step 2—Determine acceptable evidence.

☐ Step 3—Plan learning experiences.

This backward approach, developed by Grant Wiggins and Jay McTighe (2005), uses assessment as a way to determine exactly what teachers want students to learn, how they will learn this, and whether they have indeed learned what was intended over the course of a unit. In the case of Castilleja teacher Laura Docter (highlighted in the previous chapter), instead of waiting until the end of the unit on Rome to give a test of students' knowledge, she uses multiple forms of assessment throughout the unit to check student understanding, uncover gaps in their knowledge, motivate students to do further research, and provide feedback on student progress as they prepare their final products. Specifically, Laura uses all of the following forms of assessment in her unit:

- Laura asks questions throughout each lesson to assess student understanding and help them move forward in their thinking.
- Students write facts they discover on Google Docs, and Laura uses these to assess knowledge gaps.
- Students answer study questions based on the Google Docs information collected.
- Students present claims about their ruins and debate the plausibility of each claim.
- Students write paragraphs, citing at least two sources as evidence for their argument about a question or topic of their choice concerning the rise and fall of Rome.
- Students revise paragraphs based on teacher and peer feedback.
- Students present evidence from their paragraphs to small groups of students in roundtables.

Each of these assessments aligns with one or more of Laura's essential questions and understanding goals. For example, one of Laura's "desired results" for her students this year (and in this unit in particular) was that they be able to use solid evidence to construct an effective argument. They practice this skill when they present their claims about the ruins and again in the paragraphs and roundtable presentations. Laura also wanted students to learn to ask authentic questions and to consider "how we know what we know" about history, and she wanted them to think about how history relates to them specifically and to think about what it takes to be a civilization. The Roman ruins project—and the assessments that result from it—seem to be aligned with these goals. Students generate authentic questions about the ruins and about their Roman topics, and throughout the project they simulate what real historians do—gathering and synthesizing evidence from multiple sources and backing their claims. The project also allows Laura to work on other important skills for her students, such as collaboration and group work, public speaking, and written and oral communication skills. Had

Figure 5.1 Curriculum Priorities and Assessments

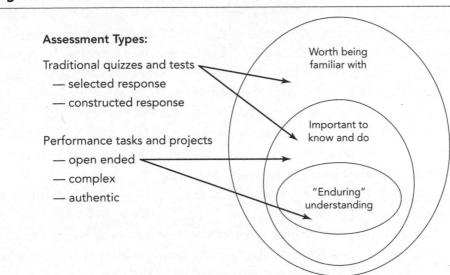

Source: Wiggins and McTighe (1998) *Understanding by Design®.*

Laura restricted her assessments solely to traditional quizzes and tests, she might not have been able to capture and show evidence of student learning in each of these areas.

Figure 5.1 depicts this well. Different forms of assessment are appropriate for capturing different kinds of student knowledge and depth of understanding.

Traditional Tests—Good or Bad for Students?

As shown by the concentric circles in Figure 5.1, traditional quizzes and tests, especially those with selected responses (for instance, multiple-choice answers), can show us only so much about what a student knows. When we use selected responses, students can guess or copy answers without actually understanding the material in depth. And if we don't ask students to show their work or explain their answers, teachers cannot know whether the wrong answer on a test or quiz represents a careless mathematical error or misreading of the question or signifies a larger gap in understanding. Shepard (2010) argues, for example, that students can easily be trained to pass multiple-choice tests without much retention or deep learning. And Black and Wiliam (2012) find that selected response assessments are problematic because they give no evidence of student reasoning and reveal little about how and what students actually understand. Some researchers have found that primarily relying on traditional tests that measure rote learning may actually impede student learning (for review, see Marzano, 2006).

Other researchers have been exploring the benefits of traditional testing when used in very specific ways. In the research we reviewed, Bangert-Drowns, Kulik, and Kulik (1991) found that low-stakes tests that were short and included questions aimed at understanding students' mastery of the material, rather than memorization, had a positive influence on student achievement and attitude towards the class. The authors, along with Hattie and Timperley (2007), emphasize that these effects hold when the feedback on these frequent and shorter tests is focused on student understanding, not judging of student performance. Studying for a short test or quiz by reviewing the information learned in class can help to cement certain kinds of information (Roediger & Karpicke, 2006); however, once the tests become cumulative or comprehensive rather than short, and once they start to factor into a student's overall grade, the negatives might outweigh the positives.

When assessments like these short, frequent, and low-stakes tests are used as an ongoing tool to help shape teaching and curriculum decisions and to help direct student learning, they are called "formative assessments." When an assessment is used as a cumulative demonstration of understanding and review of knowledge and skills gained, it is called a "summative assessment." Often summative assessments are implemented at the end of a unit and are used for purposes of ranking and sorting students and giving grades. Formative assessments may also be used for grading purposes; however, most formative assessments are designed to be used as a marker of what students know at a particular time during the unit, so that the teacher can plan lessons to address the gaps in knowledge. The key difference between formative and summative assessment is that summative assessment generally comes after the student is expected to have acquired the understanding necessary to move on in the curriculum. These assessments cover the sum of knowledge and skills already acquired, instead of the knowledge and skills still being formed. Whether or not a test or quiz can be considered effective depends on the purpose of the assessment (for instance, formative or summative), and how well the questions or tasks on the assessment connect to the desired learning results and allow students to show what they know.

PERFORMANCE ASSESSMENTS

For more accurate assessment of student knowledge or skills, especially when assessing essential questions or enduring understandings, teachers should consider using more performance-based assessments in which students construct their "answers" or show their knowledge via some kind of performance, product, or process, as illustrated in the chart in Figure 5.2.

Figure 5.2   Framework of Assessment Approaches and Methods

Framework of Assessment Approaches and Methods
How might we assess student learning in the classroom?

Selected-Response Format	Constructed-Response Format			
		Performance-Based Assessment		
	Brief Constructed Response	Product	Performance	Process-Focused Assessment

☐ Multiple choice
☐ True false
☐ Matching
☐ Enhanced multiple choice
	☐ Fill in the blank
	  • word(s)
	  • phrase(s)
	☐ Short answer
	  • sentences
	  • paragraphs
	☐ Label a diagram
	☐ "Show your work"
	☐ Visual representation
	  • web
	  • concept map
	  • flow chart
	  • graph/table
	  • illustration
		☐ Essay
		☐ Research paper
		☐ Story/play
		☐ Poem
		☐ Portfolio
		☐ Art exhibit
		☐ Science project
		☐ Model
		☐ Video/audiotape
		☐ Spreadsheet
		☐ Lab report
			☐ Oral presentation
			☐ Dance/movement
			☐ Science lab demonstration
			☐ Athletic skills performance
			☐ Dramatic reading
			☐ Enactment
			☐ Debate
			☐ Musical recital
			☐ Keyboarding
			☐ Teach-a-lesson
				☐ Oral questioning
				☐ Observation ("kid watching")
				☐ Interview
				☐ Conference
				☐ Process description
				☐ "Think aloud"
				☐ Learning log

Source: McTighe and Ferrara (1998).

This chart is useful, as it gives concrete examples of different performance assessments, such as student products, performances, and process-focused assessments. Performance assessments can be used as either formative assessments—to show what students know at a particular time and to address gaps, similar to how Laura used the study questions on the Google Docs—or they can be used as summative assessments to showcase student mastery at the end of unit, similar to the final paragraphs Laura assigned for the roundtables.

Process-focused performance assessments can be especially effective. Laura used process-focused assessments when she asked students questions and observed them as they explored the ruins. Sometimes oral questions, observations, or a simple "think aloud" can demonstrate far more about what a student knows and understands than could be determined by a selected-response quiz or test. However, using these process, product, and performance assessments isn't always easy. Teachers need to spend more time designing the assessment itself, build in time for students to prepare early drafts, respond to these early drafts or performances, and allow more time to view and offer feedback on student final presentations. Because these assessments do not have one right answer, it is not possible to use a Scantron machine to quickly calculate student scores. How should a teacher assess a student debate, for instance, or fairly assess students when the products and performances will likely vary widely?

When considering these different performance assessments, teachers need to ask: What would be sufficient and revealing evidence of student understanding? Against what criteria will I distinguish the work? Often, teachers construct rubrics or detailed checklists to help them prepare feedback and to help students understand what the teacher is looking for in a final performance or product. Transparency is the key here, as students and teachers—and other audiences as well, such as parents—need to see what is meant by "excellent work" in all the different assessment formats and how this will be determined. Teachers show students the rubric or checklist prior to having students do the work so that students know what kind of work is expected from them; after the work is completed, students and teachers use the rubrics and checklists to gauge how well they met expectations.

Though this kind of assessment work is more complicated and time-consuming, it gets closer to the root meaning of the word "assess." The Latin *assidere* means "to sit beside." Assessment is an opportunity to sit beside a student—literally or figuratively—to try to understand what he or she knows and can do. Assessment is an exercise in analysis, but also in empathy. Sitting beside our students, we put ourselves in their shoes and into their heads, trying to see what they do and don't understand and how we can best support their learning moving forward. Of course, when a teacher has over 150 students to assess, sitting beside each one may be nearly impossible. But when you use performance assessments as opposed to more traditional selected-response tests and quizzes, you are more likely to see evidence of the depth of understanding a student holds, and you will more likely be able to offer feedback that helps each individual make progress towards the learning goals.

"Voice, Choice, Revision, and Redemption"

One of the mantras Denise Pope teaches in her curriculum class at Stanford is "opportunities for voice, choice, revision, and redemption." To increase student engagement with learning, teachers should strive to offer students "choice and voice" whenever possible (Larson, 2000; Marks, 2000; Reeve, Jang, Carrell, Jeon, & Barch, 2004). One way to raise student engagement—and ultimately, the quality of the work that they do—is to allow students to have some say over the topic or type of performance assessment on which they will be evaluated. Laura Docter uses this strategy in the Roman ruins unit when students can choose their own topic for the Rome paragraphs, for instance. This strategy usually helps students to see the relevance of what they are learning and can increase motivation to do the work when students pick a topic or medium that truly interests them.

Quality of work also goes up when students are given opportunities for revision. In the workplace, it is extremely rare that a product or process works perfectly on the first try. Employees learn to collaborate, iterate, and improve upon the work each step of the way. Unfortunately, when teachers use traditional assessment strategies, opportunities for revision are rare. This seems counterintuitive. Even when large numbers of students don't excel on a final unit exam, teachers may feel pressure or feel that they are expected to move on to the next unit without offering chances for students to learn from their mistakes. At the very least, teachers should consider offering test revisions, corrections, or do-overs to ensure that students recognize their errors and learn the material well enough to succeed on future assessments on the topic. Experts recommend that teachers give students clear, specific, actionable, and timely feedback that helps to show students the gaps in their learning and what steps they need to take to improve (for example, see Wiggins, 2012).

This practice also fits with Carol Dweck's work on mindset. In her groundbreaking research, Dweck (2006) describes two modes of thinking about ability and intelligence:

(1) a "fixed" mindset and (2) a "growth" mindset. Someone with a fixed mindset believes that a person is born with a certain set of abilities and intelligence, and there is not much you can do to change what you have been given. Someone with a growth mindset believes that abilities and intelligence are malleable and are influenced by the amount of effort we exert. Dweck and her colleagues have found that our views about ability and intelligence can have a significant impact on learning and resilience. In multiple studies, Dweck's team found that people with a growth mindset are more likely to be intrinsically motivated, try new things, and persist when faced with challenges. In contrast, those with a fixed mindset are more likely to shy away from or give up on new and difficult tasks and are more extrinsically motivated (Grant & Dweck, 2003; Yeager & Dweck, 2012). When teachers offer chances for revision and redemption, they are helping to foster a growth mindset and to encourage students to persist as they strive to reach learning goals. By sending the message that work can be revisited and improved, teachers emphasize that intelligence and achievement are not fixed, and they allow all students to strive for mastery.

This raises issues around equity and other logistics for teachers. Where do I find time to offer all of this feedback? How can I possibly allow students to retest and then offer feedback for each revision? How do I grade students who master the material the first time versus those who take several tries to do so? Does this mean everyone should ultimately master every assessment? These are not easy questions to answer, and there is no one best way to address them, but the bottom line seems clear: if we truly want students to learn the material we teach, we need to build in the necessary time and structures and scaffolding to help them do so. The real world comes with real deadlines, and not everyone succeeds on every endeavor, but most of the time, people are given multiple opportunities to revise their work and redeem themselves. When students have the time and encouragement to master the material, they will likely be more prepared for the real-world tasks ahead, both because they have acquired the knowledge and skills necessary to complete future challenging tasks, and because they have practiced learning from mistakes and have gained the resilience that results from doing so.

In our work with Challenge Success schools, teachers have adopted different policies to handle the revision and redemption process. Many offer retest policies that give students up to one week to turn in test corrections and/or to retake an exam. Other Challenge Success educators build in room for revision via the use of portfolios: Students choose a handful of projects, papers, or other assessments to revise and turn in as a final portfolio of their learning. Some are exploring the use of "standards-based assessments": Students know the standards they must achieve in order to pass or excel in a class, and they have multiple opportunities to reach these standards. And some educators use "authentic assessment" strategies that typically have iteration and revision processes built into the assignments.

Authentic Assessments

Authentic assessments are those that "engage students in applying knowledge and skills in ways that they are used in the 'real world'" (McTighe & Ferrara, 1998, p. 15). Educators do not necessarily agree on what constitutes an authentic assessment. Some insist that an authentic assessment must be an actual task done in the real world, such as painting a mural to show understanding of the math concept of "scaling up," or presenting to city engineers a report on the chemistry of the local water source. These are tasks with which students demonstrate their knowledge for real audiences, and by doing the performance assessment, students leave a mark on their communities. Other educators may agree with the definition of McTighe and Ferrara—that when students simulate or mirror tasks typically done in the real world, the assessment is considered authentic. Examples here include some of Laura Docter's assessment tasks, in which students formulate, present, and debate claims based on evidence from the pretend Roman ruins. Even though these aren't actual ruins, the students are simulating the kind of tasks historians do in real life. Instead of reading about the ruins and how they demonstrate important concepts about Roman civilization, the students are constructing their own arguments based on pretend but fairly accurate historical "evidence." Either way, authentic assessments tend to motivate students to do better work; when students perform for real audiences, they are more likely to take the task seriously and work hard to revise and improve the performance. When they simulate activities done in the real world, they see the import and relevance of what they are learning and are more engaged (for review, see Fredricks, 2011).

IMPLEMENTING ALTERNATIVE ASSESSMENTS

Changing the assessment process at a school is not easy. Teachers need to backward plan their units and lessons to decide what exactly they want students to know and how they will determine if the students understand the concepts in depth. As with any change, the school needs to go slowly and offer plenty of time for discussion and debate among the faculty, along with professional development to help teachers learn to craft alternative assessments and the criteria—in the forms of rubrics or checklists, for example—to go along with these new assessments.

According to Black and Wiliam (2012), it is important for teachers to communicate with each other, particularly about what constitutes high-quality work, to ensure consistency for students and to promote learning for teachers. Finally, the school needs to agree on how to use these assessments for grading purposes and needs to educate parents, students, and other audiences, such as colleges, on the changes they have made to their assessment criteria and policies. At Challenge Success, we have several schools at different stages in this change process at any one time.

Forest Ridge School of the Sacred Heart, Bellevue, Washington

Forest Ridge School of the Sacred Heart, an independent all-girls school in the Catholic tradition in Washington state, is just starting to make significant changes to their assessment and grading policies. After developing a new, rotating seven-day modified block schedule based on work with Challenge Success in 2012, Dr. Carola Wittmann, the director of the high school, felt that changing the school's assessment policy was a natural next step to further increase student engagement with learning. Plus, this plan would dovetail nicely with other school goals, such as examining the role of homework, the possibility of a flipped lesson design, and the use of innovative technology in the classroom.

Carola and her team began by considering the school's grading system. Parents and students often approached Carola to express their concern that the current system put students at a disadvantage in the college admission process. While other Catholic, independent, and public schools in the area were grading on a consistent scale where, for example, a 90 was an A–, at Forest Ridge a score of 90 was a B. When Carola brought this to the attention of the faculty, some teachers informed her that they had already been using the more common grading scale. Realizing that parents, students, and many teachers viewed the current scale as unreasonable, Carola floated the idea of changing to the more prevalent scale. The response was immediately positive. Students and parents felt that the administration truly cared about what they had to say and seriously considered their feedback, and the faculty approved of the change as well. This positive change also allowed Carola and the Forest Ridge Challenge Success team to achieve some buy-in from the community to pursue other changes around grades and assessments at the school.

The change in grading scale led to more discussions with the faculty about the overall purpose of assessments. Guided by professional development sessions with Challenge Success staff, the Forest Ridge teachers began to consider making other changes to their assessment practices. Recognizing that most traditional exams at the school did not necessarily measure the depth of student understanding of the material, Carola encouraged teachers to consider alternative assessment processes discussed in the professional development sessions, such as other options besides exams, and to explore what would happen if they gave assignments with ample feedback but no grades. The school decided at this early stage not to enforce one consistent policy for assessment, but to leave it up to the teachers to decide if and how they wanted to incorporate alternative assessments into their curricula.

A few teachers in each department experimented with nongraded, formative assignments that focused on the process of learning, rather than on the grade as an end product. These assignments, in line with the research on best practices for assessment, occurred regularly, often at the beginning of a unit, and seemed to help students better understand the material without the pressure of grades. English teachers, for example, explained that typically, students skipped over the teachers' comments on their papers and just flipped to the back page to view their grade. When the teachers did not put a grade on the papers but still offered plenty of feedback, they were pleased to see how many students actually read the comments and incorporated these into their revised drafts.

Additionally, Forest Ridge started to question the purpose of final exams at the midterm and end of year. In the spring, teachers were asked about the value of finals. Some teachers weren't sure of their value, some admitted that they were just used to having them, and some stressed the importance of teaching students how to sit for an exam as an important skill for future years in college. They all agreed that the content of an exam should not be a surprise. And after meeting with department chairs, Carola and the chairs agreed that in order to ensure consistency and fairness, teachers in all departments would submit proposed final exams to their department chairs two weeks before they planned to administer them. The department chair then offered constructive feedback about the exam to the teacher and to the dean of faculty. This process allowed the school administration to address teachers' assessment practices on a one-on-one basis.

(continued)

Some teachers decided to pilot alternative assessments to see if they were more effective than traditional exams. For example, two teachers in the science department conducted interview assessments for each of their students at the end of the school year, and one teacher decided to replace the traditional exam with this interview format. A teacher in the math department held nongraded, one-on-one conferences with students to help them solve problems and observe their skills. The teacher found that this process gave her and the students a better sense of their strengths and areas for improvement than what might be seen on a graded assessment. Additionally, the English department chose that year to forgo finals for juniors and seniors. Instead, they asked all students to write in-class essays that were not considered exams; rather, they were meant as preparation for the handwritten essays students write for their International Baccalaureate exams. The goal was to mirror an exam setting and to alleviate the anxiety. Teachers then conducted one-on-one conferences with students after the "mock" exam to help students debrief the experience and learn how they might better prepare for the actual IB exams.

As this book went to press, Carola had a number of goals regarding assessment practices for the upcoming school year. Ideally, she wanted to see every teacher choose to replace traditional final exams with alternative forms of assessment. She hoped that the teachers would work on implementing more project-based assessments and consider how to assess multiple forms of intelligence and skills. Moreover, she wanted teachers to continue to consult with department chairs and the school's learning specialist to receive feedback on the quality of their assessments and to help put the focus on learning rather than on grades.

Ann and Nate Levine Academy, Dallas, Texas

When Susie Wolbe was the K–8 principal at Levine Academy, a Jewish Day School in Dallas, Texas, she and other administrators, teachers, parents, and students worked with Challenge Success to reduce student stress and increase student well-being and learning mastery. One of several successful strategies they implemented was providing alternative assessments to students. According to Susie, "Oral exams for those who had written language difficulties, or whose stress interfered with their ability to recall the information, proved quite beneficial. The same was true if a scribe was provided; it gave students, those with dysgraphia [difficulty with writing] and those without any diagnosis, the opportunity to think out loud without needing to also focus on writing." Teachers also experimented with offering the option of various performance assessments at the end of units instead of traditional tests, such as making videos, acting in self- or group-written skits, or creating art projects and corresponding explanations of how the projects exemplified the learning goals for the unit. As Susie explained, "Alternative assessments were a relief to everyone: students experiencing stress or who had diagnosed anxiety disorders, teachers who appreciated the additional creativity alternative assessments allowed, and students who desired, and deserved, a change from routine assessments."

Another strategy many students, parents, and teachers appreciated was the use of "show what you know" boxes on tests and quizzes. A few teachers started this practice after hearing a number of kids say, "I can't believe I studied that, and it wasn't even on the test!" Students were told they could choose one area they had studied that had not been represented on the test, and then demonstrate their understanding by writing about the topic or concept in the "show what you know" box. Students knew in advance how many points the information would be worth (anywhere from 2 to 5 points), and they had to stay within the confines of the box. This prevented kids from writing pages and pages of explanations or notes. And students didn't necessarily receive all the points offered; sometimes students thought they knew something well, but their explanations proved otherwise. Still, the students loved the boxes and were excited to share their knowledge.

The strategy became so popular that approximately half of the teachers in the school used the boxes regularly and allowed students to earn extra points. Even though the points scored were minimal, students said they felt more confident going into a test when they knew they would have this opportunity to demonstrate their understanding of the subject.

Del Mar Middle School, Tiburon, California

Dr. Alan Vann Gardner, principal of Del Mar Middle School, a public school in Tiburon, California, has been working with Challenge Success for over four years to design a vision of a an ideal graduate and to work with faculty and staff on a corresponding assessment protocol to facilitate this vision. The ideal Del Mar graduate is a motivated, self-directed, and creative problem-solver who takes

(continued)

risks, learns from mistakes, thinks critically, and applies knowledge and skills to real-life situations. He or she is an effective communicator and an engaged citizen who actively contributes to school, local, and global communities. The graduate also demonstrates empathy, integrity, and respect for self, others, and the environment. The school teachers and administrators spent ample time crafting, debating, and recrafting this vision; now they were grappling with how best to make it a reality. Through the process of developing the vision of the ideal graduate and figuring out how best to attain it, Alan and the Del Mar staff are redefining what they mean by student success as well as how to measure it.

Although Del Mar regularly devotes three to four days per year to professional development aimed at improving curriculum and assessment aligned to the new vision, Alan stressed that those days are not sufficient to produce school-wide change. He explains, "Much of the PD work and progress gets done within departments and in informal meetings between colleagues." For example, over the past few years, the departments have crafted "essential learnings" in each subject area that students need to know by the end of middle school. Teachers then use these essential learnings (similar to the enduring understandings and essential questions mentioned in the previous chapter) to map the curriculum by department and grade level and to make sure they are aligned with the Common Core State Standards.

Once the essential learnings and the vision seemed to be aligned, the school needed to design assessment protocols that would allow students to apply skills and knowledge in broader, more meaningful ways that aligned with these goals. Teachers worked to develop "summative prompts" (performance assessments) by department to assess the essential learnings, and they have designed rubrics to accompany the prompts to help ensure that teachers are on the same page in terms of assessment. See Exhibit 5.1, at the end of this case study, for an example of an authentic assessment from the social studies department: students write and present legislative bills based on social issue topics of their choice, followed by formal letters to politicians or lobbyists to advocate for their well-researched proposals and ideas.

Alan is excited to see the use of more rubrics and performance assessments throughout the school. He explains that the rubrics serve several purposes: they help teachers facilitate learning and align lessons to the standards, they serve to increase rigor as they describe and measure ambitious learning goals, and they serve as tools to help students learn to self-assess and peer-assess their work.

In addition to experimenting with rubrics and summative prompts, Del Mar teachers have begun to implement a system of digital portfolios for all students. The faculty wanted to enable students to tell a story of their learning over time in a way that is congruent with the school's vision. Digital portfolios allow students to collect evidence of achieving essential learnings each year and to build on areas that still need to be developed. Additionally, eighth grade students at Del Mar have been experimenting with showcase exhibitions, where they present evidence of their learning to teachers as well as to sixth and seventh grade students. This past year, eighth graders included evidence of achieving various aspects of the ideal vision of a Del Mar graduate, such as stories of overcoming obstacles, developing habits of motivated learners, creatively solving problems, and becoming effective communicators and engaged citizens.

Alan operates his school with a strategic mindset. To ensure the eventual achievement of long-term goals, he supports a collaborative environment and a system of "collective autonomy" that encourages individual teachers to be creative while staying focused and aligned with colleagues in regard to curriculum design and common assessment. To foster teacher buy-in as well as innovation, teachers have opportunities to pilot new programs or policies individually. Del Mar wants its teachers to feel like trusted professionals so that they can work collaboratively to advance student learning. This flexible system allows for teachers to have meaningful opportunities to revitalize their practices, and allows Del Mar to track the success of certain programs in small doses before committing to a school-wide change. Through opportunities like this, Del Mar staff have realized that they have a genuine voice in school decision-making. Additionally, Del Mar offers regular meetings and orientation information for parents, so that they too can give input and play an integral role in the process. These efforts have fostered teacher and parent buy-in for important changes over the past several years.

Alan expressed that, as a result of all of these changes, he now sees "students really owning their learning," in a way that was not previously realized.

(continued)

Furthermore, he has noticed astounding progress in student collaboration and ability to present their work to peers and adults, which he attributes at least partially to these new changes in curriculum design and assessment practices. However, Alan noted that Del Mar has to pay attention to the rigor and workload for the students. He acknowledged that having summative projects at the end of every trimester is a lot of work for 11- and 12-year-old kids, and since the caliber of work Del Mar is expecting is increasing, the school has to manage the workload carefully to mitigate potential student stress and overload.

This testimonial from a recent Del Mar graduate shows that the school has begun to make great strides in helping students achieve the vision of an ideal graduate:

> At Del Mar, we are inspired to stand out, flickering with qualities and a unique set of skills and tools. We're taught that simply memorizing information to regurgitate back and then forget the second we turn in the test isn't really learning. Yes, that might be what is classified as a good student, but it inspires me to question the difference between a good *student* and a great *learner*.
>
> We're taught to explore and analyze and dig deeper, beyond the information of a basic textbook. We learn to find primary sources and not believe everything we read, or hear, or see. Instead, we look at all perspectives and many lenses to make a decision, not just one. Del Mar has trained us to see the difference between being a student and a life-long learner, and how having those skills will push you farther than the average person, and make you *truly* a unique individual. [Anonymous student]

Schools that are experimenting with portfolios and exhibitions, such as Del Mar, are in line with research on the benefits of these practices. Exhibitions of mastery allow students to show what they have learned—their content knowledge—as well as their own initiative and process. For instance, students can represent how they came up with a problem, researched it, and solved or analyzed it, and how they created a public product or performance. Exhibitions take place in front of real audiences, often composed of experts from the field, so students are motivated to carefully prepare their presentation and do their best work (Wiggins, 1989).

Exhibit 5.1 Del Mar Prompt and Rubric

	Excellent (5)	Beginning (3)	Needs Improvement (1)
Format	The bill is properly formatted and contains all of the required elements including MLA citations.	The bill is mostly formatted correctly and contains most of the required elements including MLA citations.	The bill is not formatted correctly or does not contain the required legislative elements. MLA citations are missing.
Purpose	The purpose of the bill is clear and is related to a current issue in America. The author demonstrates extensive knowledge of the issue.	The purpose of the bill is generally clear and is related to a current issue in America. The author demonstrates a basic background knowledge of the issue.	The purpose of the bill is unclear or is unrelated to a current issue in America. The author demonstrates minimal background knowledge of the issue.
Originality	The bill offers an innovative solution to a problem (creative problem solver). Legislation is unique and wholly student-created.	The bill offers a reasonable solution to a problem. Legislation may have been offered by another individual or organization, or in prior legislation.	The bill offers a solution to the problem that is not significant, reasonable, or a new idea. Solution and related work is not student-created.
Content & Effectiveness	The bill demonstrates a depth of thought, analysis, and development of ideas. The proposal is constitutional and reasonable.	The bill demonstrates some depth of thought, analysis, and development of ideas. The proposal may be somewhat ineffective, unconstitutional, or unreasonable.	The bill demonstrates superficial thought, analysis, and development of ideas. The proposal is unreasonable, unconstitutional, or ineffective. The proposal may even be offensive or not presented in a serious manner.

PROMPT - Select a social ill in society and then use the power granted to our government under the Constitution to write a legislative bill that will effectively address the problem. Students will present legislative solutions to the class using the IGNITE presentation method.

ASSESSING 21ST CENTURY SKILLS

In the preceding case studies, the school leaders emphasize the importance of certain skills, such as communication, critical thinking, creative problem-solving, empathy, and collaboration. They know these skills are as important for kids to learn as content or discipline-based skills, but these 21st century skills can be difficult to measure. As one teacher in a Challenge Success workshop noted, "I know how to tell if a kid understands how to factor a polynomial, but I have no idea how to measure how well he collaborates with his group mates." If we want students to learn and practice and eventually demonstrate mastery over these important skills, how do we design assessments that will promote student growth in these areas? Castilleja School in Palo Alto, California, received a grant from the Edward E. Ford Foundation to pursue answers to this question.

Castilleja School, Palo Alto, California

Dr. Karen Strobel, the director of Partnership for 21st Century Assessment at Castilleja School, explained the three phases of the grant from Edward E. Ford that funds her position at the school. In the first phase, Karen works with the Castilleja faculty to create an inventory of assessments used at the school and to create assessment tools that best align with departmental learning goals. In phase two, the school plans to share and test these innovative assessment tools with similar private schools; they then will proceed to phase three, in which they plan to share the tools more broadly with private and public schools around the globe.

Before the school received the grant, the faculty was developing a curriculum framework in which department members articulated their philosophy, essential questions, and the knowledge, skills, and understanding to be developed within their discipline. As each department was thinking about discipline-specific skills, Karen conducted a listening tour within the school to learn about the skills that are valued and promoted across subject areas throughout the school. For three months, Karen had conversations with teachers from each department of the school. She spoke with veteran teachers, as well as those new to the school community, and asked: "What are the skills graduates leave here with, and what are the skills they need to build upon?" When Karen reported back to the faculty, they noticed patterns in the skills that were valued throughout the school that fell into three main categories, which they labeled initiative, agility, and purpose.

Initiative encompasses skills and attributes such as self-direction, curiosity, willingness to make mistakes, and the self-knowledge needed to pursue intellectual and social challenges. The second category, agility, refers to problem solving, flexibility, and creativity. The third category, purpose, includes traits such as empathy, collaboration, social consciousness, and communication skills, all of which are necessary for students to be able to effect change in the world.

Once they had agreement on the skills and traits they hoped to instill, the Castilleja faculty needed to figure out how exactly to measure these. Some of the traits seemed too intangible and subjective. As one teacher remarked, "I am comfortable giving feedback on student work in terms of writing and content skills, but when it comes to empathy, for example, how can I possibly be responsible for grading someone's soul?" This is exactly the point of the grant—to help teachers find ways to measure and give effective feedback on these difficult-to-measure skills and traits in order to promote student growth. And as Karen explained, many of the teachers were already teaching with these 21st century goals in mind—they just had never been asked to take stock of how they were doing it and how to track student progress in these areas over time.

Faculty members conducted assessment inventories in which each department listed all the forms of assessment they used to assess the learning goals outlined in the curriculum framework. Karen noted that many of the assessments in place at the school already effectively served to measure some of the 21st century learning goals. Her job was to help teachers recognize this and to help them develop tools to make this more explicit to the students.

For this first year, Karen decided to offer herself as a resource to any teacher who was interested in having her help design an assessment for an existing unit or project. Some teachers asked for help in tweaking an existing assessment; others asked for help in developing an appropriate assessment for a unit "from scratch." For example, in a computer programming class this past year, the teacher highlighted the need to assess communication skills, which falls under the "purpose" category. In this class, students were developing apps. As an authentic assessment, students had to develop an app and make a pitch to a panel of venture capitalists. Students were skilled in the development of the app, but many of them lacked practice in how to explain the app in a way that would entice the venture capitalists. Before their presentations, students were given a rubric that Karen and the teacher designed together to help students plan and prepare their remarks. The rubric was aligned with what the venture

(continued)

capitalists would want to know, as well as what the teacher wanted students to learn. For instance, students needed to consider why there was a need for this particular application. Were there other comparable apps out there? How exactly did their app work, and why should the venture capitalists consider funding it? Students had to think about the user's perspective and the venture capitalists' perspectives, and to consider providing screen shots and specific instructions and information to make their points. This assessment tool made students think about what was required in terms of communication skills in order to make their point to this specific audience, but the assessment also asked students to utilize empathy as well as problem-solving skills, creativity, and initiative—thus allowing the teacher to measure skills in all three focus areas of initiative, agility, and purpose. (See Exhibit 5.2 at the end of this case study for the rubric.)

The school uses rubrics as tools to encourage student self-reflection in all three areas, along with using student surveys and other tools to measure student attitudes and traits. Surveys, for instance, can ask students to reflect on how well they collaborated with others (purpose), how they felt when they faced a new and challenging task (agility), and how motivated they were to do the task (initiative). Other assessment tools, such as "design journals," create opportunities for students to document their thinking process and offer teachers insight into their students' idea development, problem-solving skills, and ability to learn from mistakes or mishaps. For instance, in an engineering class where students were asked to build a component for a cell phone, students were assessed based on their design journal, an authentic assessment tool that engineers and other designers typically use to explain the problem they are pursuing, track their ideas for solving or handling the problem, and explain the logic that led them to their final outcome. Students had to demonstrate their cell phone component prototype to their instructor, but they weren't graded on whether or not their prototype worked. Rather, they were graded on their design journals and their ability to document and explain why their prototype did or didn't work. In this way, a design journal can be thought of as a "think aloud" tool for students to show their work and the logic behind it.

Making these kinds of assessment changes uniformly will take time, willingness on the part of the faculty to experiment, and acceptance that not every idea will work. Teachers know intuitively what they want their students to learn, but these assessment tools require that teachers take the time to explicitly define and write down what particular skills look like, so that everything is transparent to students, parents, and other assessors of student work. Karen underscores the importance of teacher buy-in: "This process of changing assessments can't be top-down or mandated. The teachers themselves need to see the need for these performance assessments and need to see the value in using them. And many of the teachers are already using some form of these kinds of assessments in their classroom, but now they are learning how to explain them to the students and how to build rubrics or other tools that help them measure the skills consistently and help the students learn to assess these skills and improve upon them during the learning process."

Exhibit 5.2 Castilleja VC Pitch Rubric

	20 points Exceptional presentation	16 points Presentation needed more work	12 points Significant misunderstanding or lack of preparation	0 points Grossly unprepared
What is the problem?	Problem statement is clear and specific	Problem statement is vague or unclear	Problem statement includes the solution	Problem statement is missing
Who is your user?	Description of the app's users is clear and specific and demonstrates empathy (understanding of users' needs)	Description of the app's users is vague or unclear or lacks empathy (understanding of users' needs)	Description of the app's users is unconvincing or presents unfounded assumptions about users' needs	Description of the app's users is missing
How does it work?	Clearly demonstrates a working app and at least one central feature	Demonstrates a working app and only minor functionality	Presents screen shots, only	Display of app of any kind is missing

(continued)

Why is your idea better?	Provides at least one specific example of another similar app and clearly articulates how this app is superior	Description of a similar app or this app's superior characteristics is vague or unclear	Description of similar apps OR how this app is superior are missing	Description of similar apps AND how this app is superior are missing
Delivery	Within time limits and demonstrates excellent preparation (including a memorized script for a live pitch) and significant contributions by each team member	Within time limits, but needs more preparation or contribution by one or more team members	Within time limits, but demonstrates poor preparation or lack of contribution by one or more team members	Exceeds time limits or demonstrates poor preparation by all team members

The Partnership for 21st Century Skills recommends many of the assessment strategies that our case study schools are using to promote skills such as communication, critical thinking, creative problem-solving, and collaboration. Specifically, they recommend the following practices that sharpen students' skills in these areas:

- Giving students opportunities to select which kind of assessment task they want to do
- Allowing students to self-assess
- Providing detailed and specific rubrics
- Posing conceptually rich problems

- Returning to prior ideas and concepts in lessons and assessments throughout a course
- Building a collaborative learning environment and culture among students (Partnership for 21st Century Skills, P21.org).

As more schools use assessments as tools for improving teaching and learning and follow the suggestions included here, we'll likely see more engaged learners who are less anxious and stressed about assessments and who are mastering content skills along with the kinds of personal and professional skills we describe.

TO GRADE OR NOT TO GRADE?

In the beginning of this chapter we made the distinction between assessment for purposes of ranking and sorting, and assessment for purposes of feedback to foster better teaching and learning. Most secondary schools believe they need to use assessment for both purposes, but establishing effective grading policies can be extremely complex and difficult.

Why use grades? Grades can indicate or signify a level of achievement on an assignment or in a course, and they can be used to communicate that level to both internal audiences (students, teachers, others in the school) and external audiences (parents, other schools, colleges). Certainly, other forms of feedback can also signify achievement levels—for instance, when a teacher or student marks a specific column of a rubric—and schools and colleges find ways to accommodate students who do not have grade point averages or transcripts, such as students who are homeschooled or who attend the few high schools in the country that do not give grades. But for the most part, the A through F grade scale seems to be widely used to signify achievement in school.

The problem with this system is that students may believe that they are learning not for the sake of learning, but rather for the reward of a high grade or to avoid the punishment of a low grade. As several experts have noted, a reliance on the use of extrinsic rewards and punishments can often lead to several negative outcomes, such as losing interest in the subject matter and taking shortcuts or cheating to get the answers (for reviews, see Crooks, 1988; Lepper, 1983; Wigfield, Eccles, & Rodriguez, 1998). And, as Denise Pope found in her research in *Doing School* (2001), even the students who get the highest grades in school may not actually be learning or retaining the material when they become focused solely on achieving a top GPA.

In their review of research on motivation, testing, and grades, Harlen and Crick (2003) found that frequent, high-stakes tests that use grades without comments negatively influence students' motivation for learning. The authors write that assessments should emphasize and give feedback to students on their learning goals and should avoid comparisons with other students. Another study found that when middle school students were given narrative feedback on tasks they had completed, they were more motivated to continue working on more challenging tasks, as compared to students that received no feedback and students that received grades as the only form of feedback (Butler & Nisan, 1986). This matches the findings of the teachers at Forest Ridge when they decided to offer narrative feedback, but not grades, on student papers; they found that students were more likely to read and respond to the feedback. Several other secondary schools, colleges, and universities—for example, MIT and Brown—use a similar approach for their students: they do not give grades in the first semester (or at all in some of their courses), both (1) so the students can become comfortable in their new surroundings and (2) to encourage students to take risks, think outside the box, make mistakes, and learn from them, in a safe, nongraded environment. Eliminating grades can encourage students to reflect on their own learning and eventually learn to self-assess their work, a skill that is fundamental to success both in schools and in the workplace.

Standards-Based Grading

In light of the research on the common pitfalls of using grades, some schools have decided to use a system known as standards-based grading (SBG). The practice varies widely, but predominantly, in schools that use SBG, teachers assess and grade what students know, understand, and are able to do in relation to the identified learning targets as outlined by course objectives (see, for example, O'Connor, 2009). SBG typically doesn't use grades to reward homework completion or to punish late work. Grades are used only to signify meeting the learning targets. For example, in a traditional system, a student might take a test that covers several different learning targets. Let's assume the test has been well-designed and that it measures student mastery of several concepts in depth. Now let's say that the student does well on certain parts of the test but does not do well on others. In a traditional grading system, the student might receive a mediocre or even a low grade on the test overall, depending on how each section of the test is weighted. That single score will be recorded in a grade book and averaged in some way with other scores the student receives on past and future tests, quizzes, papers, labs, and so on. That score might also be averaged with a homework completion score or other grades that are not necessarily connected to showing mastery of a learning target. In a traditional system, for example, a student might get a C on the final but an A in the class by completing all the work; in contrast, a student might get an A on the final and a C in the class because he didn't do enough homework. This rewards completion, not mastery, and doesn't accurately represent what was or wasn't learned in the course.

In a SBG system, the teacher will give the student feedback and different grades or indicators of achievement for *each* of the different concepts covered in the test or paper or other assessment. The student can then retake parts of the test again or redo parts of the paper or project once he is ready to show mastery. In some SBG systems, students can retake tests or revise assessments until the end of the marking period. Instead of averaging the student's grades on assessments over time, the teacher may give the most weight to the most recent scores or grades, since they reflect what the student knows and can do after working hard throughout the semester. Thus, in SBG, grades measure mastery and are not used punitively.

Waldorf Schools have a long history of using alternative assessments and nontraditional grading practices. Waldorf High School of the Peninsula relies primarily on ungraded assignments and narrative assessments and rubrics, along with some elements of standards-based grading strategies to communicate feedback to students. Exhibit 5.3 shows a sample narrative report card for an English class at Waldorf High. Notice that the teacher offers narrative feedback along with specific feedback for each learning goal. Students can petition to revise work products based on this feedback, and can ask instructors for an estimation of a class grade at any time. According to the Waldorf High of the Peninsula Assessment Policy Summary (Babinet, 2013):

- Protocol is designed to help teachers assess student progress toward meeting specific learning goals rather than make subjective assessments about achievement and to keep the classroom environment free from competition between students.

- Grades are not given on any individual pieces of work assigned to students during a class, though a student may petition for an estimation of class grade at any time.

- Because the faculty recognizes that a number of colleges and universities, in particular the UC system, require a graded transcript for students to be eligible for the same evaluation in the application process as their peers at secondary schools where grades are given, teachers will assign grades for student transcripts after students have received final course assessments.

Even though Waldorf High teachers give ample feedback in the form of comments, rubrics, and checklists on individual assignments, they do not give the student a grade until the course is over. This system allows the school to use grades mainly for external purposes, and to put the focus of their assessment on learning and mastery.

Exhibit 5.3 Sample Waldorf Report Card

Spring
Course Description

The Grapes of Wrath by John Steinbeck chronicles both the plight and the flight of farmers displaced from their land during the "Dust Bowl"; it follows the shift to industrial practices in agriculture, where machines replaced humans and animals as the main labor force in food production. This shift, in combination with the "dust bowl," caused the beginning of the end of family farming as the primary way of life in this country. Many family farms failed during this time period, leaving the farmers unable to meet their mortgages. They had to leave their land. Thousands of families headed west to California hoping, in spite of no real certainty, to find employment. Both the journey and the inhospitable conditions they found upon their arrival resulted in extreme suffering and poverty for most. Many even starved to death. *The Grapes of Wrath* follows the fate of the Joad family as they leave Oklahoma and journey into the unknown. Many consider this novel to be one of the finest American literary works of the 20th century. It was a best seller in its time and received a Pulitzer Prize in 1940. Steinbeck's writing provides a model of clarity, power and poignancy for students to absorb. Its style contrasts dramatically with the novel studies in the ninth grade year. The students' task in this course is three-fold: first, to develop the ability to describe and identify powerful writing; second, to understand and discuss the major themes of Steinbeck's writing mentioned in the course's learning goals (see below); finally, to integrate their ability to effectively discuss key themes and the potent ways these themes are expressed in their own clearly written, analytical essays.

Comments:

[Name], you have burst onto the scene this year as part of the pack of sound and able readers. Your performance in this class would not lead one to suspect that you had ever had challenges with reading. Congratulations! Though you may not be a speed rocket just yet, the more you read the faster you will get.

In view of your ascent to the study of literature "big league," I would like to encourage you to invest yourself fully (more actively) in class. You listen well but should now be able to be a lead contributor to discussions. Your essay showed you are capable of sophisticated and persuasive analysis. Your art project was slightly disappointing in view of your deeply original work both in World Religions and your own song writing. I was a bit sad that you took images from online for your inspiration rather than from your own remarkable inner visioning. Otherwise, this year has shown you on the move in classes and the direction has been straight up. I hope you keep it up next year.

Student meets requirements for credit.

Learning Goals

Competently use essay elements: context, quotation, analysis and transition.	[Name] chooses strong quotations and writes really excellent analysis. She needs to practice her transition sentences and strengthen her capacity to provide succinct context quotations.
Explain impact of industrialization and corporatization on family farming.	[Name] can easily explain this.
Explain why they are powerful.	[Name] was able to explain how powerful writing functions for the reader in her self-reflection. I do not know if she would be able yet to explain it about any passage of writing thrown her way, but she will get there soon if she is not already there.
Identify examples of powerful writing.	[Name] did this excellently in her essay and also from time to time in class.
Identify instances in novel of author's view of industrialization.	[Name] grappled with this theme, whereas she was totally fluid with the human nobility theme. She evidences a basic understanding of this theme in what she says. She may have a better grasp of it than I observed.

(continued)

Identify instances in novel of what the author views as human nobility.	Ability shines through in her essay about Ma Joad.
Write clearly and persuasively in essay form (appropriate beginning, exposition and conclusion).	[Name] can write a masterful introduction and the "meat" of her essay is great. She is not yet adept at writing clear and forceful introductory sentences to main body paragraphs and tends to move her essay along with reference to the book's plot rather than her own thesis. This is an area for work next year.

The Case Against the Zero

However a school decides to use grades, several schools have been recognizing the inherent problem of using zeros as part of their marking systems. In his now-famous argument, Reeves (2004) makes the case that the current grading system, which places a zero grade on a 100-point range, is mathematically inaccurate and unfair to students. Teachers often think of a zero as similar to or as "bad" as a grade of F. This doesn't make sense; in the example in which the interval between grades is 10 points and the value of D is 60, then the mathematically accurate value of an F is 50 points. Students who receive a zero on an assignment receive 60 points less than a D grade on a 100-point grading scale. Reeves believes teachers should place the zero grade on a 4-point scale, which is mathematically correct, since it is one point less than a D, instead of 60 points.

Reeves mentions other problems with a zero grade as well. If the work is important enough to assign, why don't we hold students accountable for doing it—even if that means they will turn it in late? Once a student receives a few grades of zero, she may have no possible way to redeem her grade in the course, and worse, she is not completing important assignments. Reeves suggests that teachers require students to complete all work, and to assign study hall or other times to help the students do so.

Assessing students fairly and accurately in a way that increases student motivation and decreases stress and anxiety is not easy. We recommend that schools tackle this issue slowly and carefully, and that students, parents, and teachers are included in the dialogue on improving assessment and grading policies. In sum, we suggest the following:

- Educate all stakeholders on the purposes for assessing student learning.
- Clarify the distinction between assessing for learning and mastery versus assessing for ranking and sorting.
- Use a variety of assessment strategies, including formative assessments, constructed-response formats, and performance assessments. Aim for the photo album as opposed to the snapshot approach.
- Make sure your assessments are aligned with your enduring understandings and that they measure or showcase the concepts and skills that are "important to know and do."
- Use authentic assessments when possible; they can boost student engagement and typically allow you to check for understanding and mastery of several skills and concepts simultaneously.
- Offer opportunities for student voice, choice, revision, and redemption.
- Review grading practices and determine accurate, consistent, and fair ways to indicate student mastery.

Chapter SIX

The Advanced Placement Program – Benefits and Challenges

Many of our Challenge Success schools struggle with what to do about the College Board's Advanced Placement (AP) program. Some principals and heads of schools tell us that the AP program is considered by many to be the gold standard for a top-notch high school education. Aimed at making college level courses available to high school students, the AP program is often touted to hold the promise of effectuating college success, narrowing the achievement gap, and leveling the playing field for tradition-ally underserved high schools and students. Many parents demand that AP courses be offered at their schools so that their children are exposed to the "best" curricula and the brightest peers, and to ensure that their students remain competitive when they apply to college. On the other hand, some school leaders worry that the AP program has been oversold and distorted, and that real collateral damage is being wrought—straining schools; rewarding rigid, superficial memorization; and discouraging true intellectual curiosity in students.

As it has grown, particularly over the past decade, the AP program has become more controversial. In 2003, just over 1 million students were enrolled in AP courses.

A decade later, in 2013, more than 2.2 million students were enrolled in AP courses (College Board, 2013, 2014). In 2013, more than 30 percent of high school graduates took AP exams, whereas a decade earlier, less than 20 percent took them. With so many students taking AP courses, the stakes are high. Should schools be offering some of the 38 available AP courses, and if so, how many, and which ones? How do these courses fit into an already crowded school day? Are they really all they are cracked up to be? In other words, is there any value at all in offering AP courses?

To help our schools figure out how to answer these questions, we conducted a careful review of over 20 research studies on the topic (Challenge Success, 2013), including those presented by leading researchers in the comprehensive volume resulting from a 2007 research conference at Harvard University on the AP program (Sadler, Sonnert, Tai, & Klopfenstein, 2010). Here is what we found.

We found no conclusive data to suggest that taking AP courses makes students more likely to succeed in college, boosts students' chances of college admission, or makes college more affordable.

Champions of the AP program claim that students who take AP courses tend to earn better grades in college, take less time to graduate, and are more likely to succeed in college than are students who do not take AP courses. However, the research we reviewed suggests that although AP students, especially those who pass the exams, are more likely to experience more success in college than do those who did not take AP courses in high school, this success is probably not attributable to the AP program alone. Participation in the AP program in high school does not necessarily predict college success, nor does it appear to confer universal advantages on students beyond any they might have already had prior to enrolling in AP courses (Geiser & Santelices, 2004; Klopfenstein & Thomas, 2009). In other words, students who take AP courses in high school who then go on to be successful in college most likely would have been successful in college even had they not taken AP courses in high school.

There is some evidence that passing the AP exam, particularly in the sciences, may predict success in those classes in college. For instance, Sadler and Sonnert (2010) found that, after controlling for background factors — such as academic ability, prior coursework, and performance — students who passed the AP exam in biology, chemistry, or physics earned significantly higher grades in that same subject in college than did students who did not pass the AP exam in these subject areas. In spite of this finding, the authors caution that the advantage of passing an AP exam in the sciences was not so great that students didn't benefit by repeating the course in college. Overall, we believe more research needs to be done before we can verify the broad claim that taking AP courses makes students more likely to succeed in college.

Many students take AP courses because they think this will help them get into college. And while there is some research that indicates that students who are enrolled in AP courses in high school are more likely to enroll in a four-year college (Chajewski, Mattern, & Shaw, 2011), the way this information is used in admission decisions varies greatly from college to college. Some universities calculate students' high school grade point averages and give extra weight to AP courses; others simply factor in the AP courses a given applicant has taken as part of an overall assessment of the application (Geiser & Santelices, 2004; National Resource Council, 1999). College admission officers at more selective universities often tell future applicants to take a "challenging and rigorous course load" that includes honors and/or AP courses, but students are often left on their own to figure out exactly what that means and how many and which courses to take.

And while some proponents argue that AP courses make college more affordable by reducing the time it takes students to earn a degree, some research shows that after controlling for background variables between AP and non-AP students, taking AP courses has very little impact on the time to (and cost of) a degree (Klopfenstein, 2010). However, a study done by the College Board (2013) found that participation in the AP program was more likely to predict graduation from college compared to students who did not participate in the AP program in high school, even after controlling for student and institutional background factors. The contradictions in the research reviewed may stem in part from the different ways that colleges treat AP scores: some colleges allow students to earn college credit with a passing exam score (say a 4 or a 5), while others may advance students to the next level in a given subject but not award them any credit. And even among those students eligible to receive college credit, many opt to repeat the course instead of reducing their time to graduation (Sadler & Sonnert, 2010).

The AP program can help to narrow achievement gaps, but it doesn't always work that way.

The AP program has been hailed as a potential tool to narrow achievement gaps and promote educational equity for minority, disadvantaged, and historically underserved students. Unfortunately, expansion efforts in schools with historically underserved populations have been mostly unsuccessful, with the bulk of students not earning passing scores on AP exams and with little or no indication that the introduction of AP courses into the schools has improved the quality of learning or the caliber of education for students (Broad Foundation, 2013; Jeong, 2009; Klugman, 2013).

In cases in which the AP program does appear to be instrumental in improving the quality of education that students receive, we found that the AP program is only one part of a larger reform effort. For instance, as part of the Advanced Placement Initiative Program (APIP), a Texas-based program started in 1996, students receive extra tutoring and teachers receive professional development in conjunction with their participation in the AP program. The program implemented curriculum changes in earlier secondary school grade levels to equip and prepare students for college level AP coursework. The apparent success of this program resulted in its replication in several other states with grants from the National Math and Science Initiative (Mass Insight Education, 2012). The success of the NMSI is likely the result of many changes and factors including clear goals and metrics, buy-in from the participating schools, awards, funding, extra instruction for students, and extra training for teachers. Thus, while it is a laudable and worthwhile goal to ensure that all students have access to high-quality, challenging courses, the bottom line is that dropping AP programs into underperforming schools, where students and teachers often lack resources and the requisite preparation, and providing no additional support can be misguided and is often ineffective (Dougherty & Mellor, 2009). Using the AP program alone as a tool for narrowing the achievement gap is insufficient. If the AP program is to be used effectively to help narrow the achievement gap, it will need to be used as part of a broader initiative.

Some—but not all—AP courses can enrich students' high school experiences, but so can well-designed honors courses that handle topics in depth.

At its best, the AP program does what it was intended to do: make college-level study available to advanced high school students, and when done well, it can enhance students' high school experiences. Students get to study a subject with greater intensity, depth, and perspective. But not all AP classes are the same, and neither are all AP teachers. In general, teachers in AP classrooms tend to be more experienced, but even among AP teachers, there is great variance, and students' classroom experiences and consequent performances on the AP exams often depend on the teacher (Milewski & Gillie, 2002; Paek, Ponte, Sigel, Braun, & Powers, 2005). Simply enrolling in an AP course does not guarantee that you will have a teacher who is experienced and prepared to teach the demanding curriculum.

The practice of teaching to the test is another reason some fear that the AP program may detract from students' high school experiences. Critics of the AP program worry that in many subjects, the AP curriculum and exam are too superficial and broad, and that the breadth of the curriculum requires and rewards rote memorization over mastery of the subject. Teachers may feel the need to teach to the test instead of focusing on critical thinking and a deep understanding of the concepts in the course (National Research Council, 2002). In light of this criticism, the College Board is revamping the AP curriculum and exam in certain subjects.

The goal of the new curriculum and exam is to place more emphasis on performance tasks, application, and critical thinking. For example, new AP science courses aim to more closely reflect what goes on in the college science lab and the true process of science and inquiry, including hypothesis testing, experimentation, and analytic reasoning as opposed to memorization. In addition, the College Board launched a new course for 2014–2015, called AP Capstone (College Board, 2014), which is an AP program unlike any other that focuses on two courses over two years: AP Seminar and AP Research. AP Capstone allows for students to explore personal interests and research subjects of interest. It aims to train students in skills that are highly admired by colleges, such as independent research, collaborative teamwork, critical and creative thinking, and strong communication. Other changes are also in the works for several other Advanced Placement courses and exams that may allow for more in-depth teaching of concepts.

For all of these reasons, we qualify the claim that the AP program enriches students' high school experiences. Some students may have an engaging and challenging experience, while others may not. It depends on the teacher and the particular course and curriculum, and it depends on the students and their reasons for taking the courses, their overall workload, and how they handle the increased demands of a college-level class. Many students take AP classes to pad their resumes and college applications; they are not necessarily interested in the subject matter or engaged with the course (Pope, 2001). Other students enroll in too many AP courses, taking several at a time (sometimes more than a typical college student might take). Since AP courses tend to have more homework and require extra studying for the exams, students may find themselves overloaded. For instance, in a Challenge Success study, students who took five or more AP or honors courses reported doing significantly more homework each night (on average, approximately four hours nightly), than those students who were taking fewer AP or honors courses (Challenge Success, 2013). And students handle the stress associated with more challenging courses differently. Researchers found that students who took one AP or honors course had elevated levels of stress about academics similar to those of students who were taking multiple AP or honors courses (Challenge Success, 2013).

Schools with AP programs are not necessarily better than those without.

Many people construe a school's AP course offerings as an indicator of the school's quality. *Newsweek, U.S. News & World Report,* and other publications compile annual lists of top high schools across the nation, and schools' AP course offerings are a key factor in determining which schools make this list.

When implemented thoughtfully and effectively, the AP program may benefit certain students and allow for common assessments across schools and districts. And it may be a useful tool for colleges and outside evaluators in assessing school efficacy. However, the presence of an AP program in a high school is not necessarily a valid indicator of a school's quality. We found a number of reasons for this.

As noted earlier, AP courses and teachers can vary greatly from school to school. In some schools, students may get high grades in their AP courses, but many of these students are unable to pass the AP exams. In these cases, the value, content, and caliber of the course may be called into question. Could the content of the course be so watered down that the course itself is not deserving of an AP label? Or could more scaffolding be needed for the students or teachers to help them benefit from the AP experience? Or could the course content and exam need revision to align better with college-level expectations and subject matter goals?

Additionally, while some students may benefit from an AP program, several researchers note some hidden or opportunity costs involved in administering an AP program. Klopfenstein and Thomas (2010) offer three significant ways in which non-AP students at a school often pay the price for the AP program: they may receive lower instructional quality, as the best teachers are often siphoned off to teach AP students; they are in larger classes, as AP classes tend to be smaller than typical high school classes; and non-AP course offerings are reduced or limited in order to fund, staff, and expand AP course offerings. In these ways, the presence of the AP program can actually be a detriment to a school. In fact, some teachers and school staff worry so deeply about the negative impact of AP courses and feel so strongly that it thwarts their ability to develop deep thinkers and engaged learners that they've dropped their AP program in favor of homegrown honors/advanced courses that are not affiliated with AP testing (Hammond, 2005; Hu, 2008; Zhao, 2002).

WHAT'S A SCHOOL TO DO?

Schools have several options for how to handle the AP program dilemma. In some independent schools, AP courses are eliminated altogether and replaced by honors classes that allow the faculty more flexibility in covering material in depth. For instance, at Crystal Springs Upland School in Hillsborough, California, students in Advanced Topics science courses have more time to do authentic labs and experiments and are now free to spend more time on units the teachers believe will prepare them well for college science study. As Tom Woosnam, a physics teacher at the school, explains:

> [When I teach AP Physics], I teach to the test. That in itself is not necessarily a bad thing if the test is good. But the test to which I've been teaching is so broad that I constantly have to be putting off learning "the good stuff" because we have to stick to a bloated and out-of-date syllabus. In order to have my students do as well as possible, I have to resort to telling them they won't understand some material because we don't have enough time to study it. I have to tell them to memorize without understanding. In my book that is appalling pedagogy.

The school made a decision to eliminate all Advanced Placement courses in order to allow for more in-depth study. See Exhibit 6.1 for a sample of the FAQ document Crystal Springs sent to parents to communicate the rationale and address potential questions and concerns about this change.

Exhibit 6.1 Advanced Placement FAQ

What does this mean for your child's experience at CSUS? The program that our faculty envisions will continue to engage your child intellectually and personally. It will include many, if not most of the topics already encompassed by Advanced Placement courses, but the absence of the AP mantle will provide our teachers with the freedom to teach topics they don't currently have the time to explore. It will allow for more student-initiated projects and internships, investigative research and global experiences—all critically important for 21st century learners. Our teachers will have greater freedom to innovate, bring in new technologies, work together and across disciplines, and ensure that our programs are current.

You may still have questions about this change. We have attempted to anticipate some of those questions and have compiled them, along with responses, here.

Will my child be hurt in the college process by the absence of AP scores on his/her transcript? No. Every dean of admission we contacted, spoke to and read about was unanimous in their response to this question. Colleges and universities want assurance that the applicants have taken a rigorous academic program that has prepared them for the demands of higher education.

Don't students have to take AP exams as part of the college process? No. Unlike the SAT, AP scores are not required as part of the application process. AP scores are self-reported by students.

Will you still administer the Advanced Placement examinations? Will my child be provided the opportunity to sit for one or more of these examinations? Yes. We anticipate continuing to administer AP examinations, with time set aside during the two weeks in May when they are given.

Will my child need extra preparation for the AP exam most closely associated with a CSUS course? It depends. In courses like English, calculus, and foreign language (the courses where most of our graduates earn "advanced standing"), we anticipate the classroom experiences will continue to sufficiently prepare students for success on those AP examinations. However, it is possible that some additional preparation will be needed for success on other AP examinations, such as European History and Physics B, just as it is today.

In the wake of this decision, how do you envision the upper school program evolving? We have already developed new courses for next year. "Micro-economics and Finance," "Modern Middle-East Studies," "Engineering," and "Introduction to Computer Programming" are all new offerings for next year.

How will you assess the new courses and their ability to prepare CSUS students for college? We intend to employ some of the same techniques we currently use, techniques such as alumni surveys, course evaluations and the College and Work Readiness Assessment (CWRA). The Curriculum Committee also intends to devise a course assessment instrument that the Department Heads will use to evaluate the rigor of all courses (not exclusively the new courses).

Schools that eliminate AP courses in exchange for more in-depth courses carefully think through how to communicate the changes to students, parents, and college admission officers, and they typically see no dips in admissions to colleges or universities as a result of the change. Similarly, a number of our schools have reduced the number of AP courses offered, focusing only on those courses that they know they can offer at a high quality level. Other schools have had success when they combine AP and non-AP sections together in one classroom, with AP students doing supplemental reading, research, and writing and meeting a few additional times to prepare for the test. This way all students may benefit from increased rigor and better teaching, but not all students need to take on the full load of an AP course. Students who are not officially enrolled in AP courses can still sit for an AP exam on the topic of the course, and in these schools teachers explain what they will and won't cover in class so that students know which areas to focus on if they choose to do additional prep work for the AP exams.

In addition, several of our Challenge Success schools have used a scheduling tool (as seen in Chapter Three) so that students, their parents, and teachers understand what is really involved in taking a number of AP courses at one time. We know all AP courses are not "created equal" and that course content can vary widely by school. At one school, AP U.S. History may be a homework nightmare, while at another AP Calculus BC or AP Chemistry might have crazy workloads. By taking the time to work through with a teacher or counselor what is truly expected—both in and outside of class—for each AP course, a student can see, right there in black and white, what his or her workload will look like for the following year. Often it becomes clear that what sounds good to the student just isn't a manageable workload once the need for food and sleep are factored into the equation.

Haverford School, Haverford, Pennsylvania

In 2006, after nearly three years of evaluation, Thomas Lengel, head of upper school at the all-boys Haverford School, with support from Headmaster Joseph Cox, announced that the school would replace Advanced Placement courses with a "new advanced-level curriculum." He emphasized that "the new courses, designed by their teachers, would better teach the boys the critical thinking skills and in-depth, self-directed learning strategies necessary for college level study."

Why Ditch the AP Classes?

The Haverford School had been discussing concerns about the educational experience their upper school boys were having and how that didn't match what they hoped to achieve in the goals laid out in their Strategic Plan. Haverford created a task force to look at a number of issues, including what do about

(continued)

AP courses. Tom knew that a number of independent schools were wrestling with the same AP issues; in fact, just the year before he had participated in a well-attended workshop at the NAIS conference entitled, "The Future of the AP Program." Conversations with faculty revealed that many viewed AP classes as limiting, creating a "forced march" across an artificial curriculum designed by the College Board. The need, perceived or real, to cover a tremendous breadth of material, particularly in the sciences, was getting in the way of nurturing a love of learning. And many teachers worried about the impact of the load on the boys. Their April 2004 report noted: "We are taking our best and brightest students and lecturing at them, rather than engaging them in the material and/or allowing for self-directed learning and experimentation."

Further, extensive interviews and conversations with upward of 80 highly competitive colleges and universities revealed that dropping AP courses would not disadvantage their students relative to students from other schools who took AP courses.

How Did It Work?

After careful consideration, analysis, and communication with department chairs, the curriculum oversight committee, and faculty at large to ensure an understanding of the issue from all sides, the task force recommended unanimously to replace AP courses with rigorous electives. They further recommended that no grade "bump" be attached to the new advanced courses; they believed that their college applicants were being evaluated holistically—whereby colleges consider all aspects of a student's file, not just grades and test scores—and that abandoning the weighted GPA would allow students real choice in terms of courses to take, instead of having students (and parents) feel pressure to have students enroll only in courses with weighted grades. The school did acknowledge that some students would opt to take the AP exams on their own, and they asked teachers to develop supplementary materials for students to study on their own time to prepare for the tests.

What did Haverford do well? Perhaps most important, they aligned their core values with their daily decision-making and put the best interests of students first. They undertook an extensive process to make sure that there was consensus among faculty, and then they worked closely with college admission staff to make sure they wouldn't negatively impact their students. They communicated effectively with parents and developed materials that made their viewpoint easy to understand, including a series of communications from senior administrators and a well-thought-out FAQ and summary of the findings from the college survey. Finally, with the new policy in place, Haverford's college counselors created materials that clearly explained their choice and the new course offerings in the Haverford School profile.

SUGGESTIONS FOR EDUCATORS

The controversy around AP courses will no doubt continue, and not every school will follow the paths of Crystal Springs or Haverford. If you offer or are considering offering AP courses in your schools, we have the following suggestions for you:

- Consider the level of readiness and preparation of all involved. Do students and teachers have the background and support necessary to succeed? Are students in an AP program likely to thrive without the program being too big of a drain on the non-AP students? Take a hard look at the potential costs: teachers will require ongoing professional development, non-AP students will likely be in larger classes, non-AP course offerings may be reduced, and non-AP students may have less access to the best teachers in the school. Think carefully about whether it might be a better allocation of resources to invest in improving all existing classes and working with teachers to differentiate instruction for all learners.

- Know that in instances in which the AP program is being effectively used as a tool for school reform and increasing student achievement, the AP is only one part of a larger reform effort. Effective programs such as the National Math and Science Initiative not only provide access to and encourage enrollment in AP courses but also provide many supports such as funding, teacher training, and student tutoring, which are all crucial to the program's success.

- If you are assessing an existing AP program in your school, pay attention to how many students are passing the AP exam after taking any given AP course. If the majority of students are not earning passing scores on the exams, particularly if they are doing well in the class, something may need to change. Check both the rigor level of the course and whether the teachers and students are prepared for this type of course and assessment. Make sure that the course curriculum is adequate for cultivating a deep understanding of the subject matter. It could be that the curriculum is not well aligned with the test, or it could be that the AP curriculum and test are not well aligned with the needs of your students.

- Invite students (and their families) interested in AP courses to attend an AP information session that provides an overview of your school's AP program, course requirements and expectations, and a discussion of the commitment involved. Teachers from each department should be available to answer questions and provide information, including course syllabi and sample assignments (particularly any expectations of summer assignments). In an effort to make sure students have given serious and realistic thought to their obligations and time management, consider also requiring students to get permission and signatures from parents, counselors, and teachers for each AP course in which they wish to enroll. Consider using the scheduling tool from Chapter Three to help facilitate better course scheduling and time management.

- Establish an open enrollment policy, and make AP classes available to all students who have an interest in taking them, not just top tier students. Students can benefit from the AP for various reasons, including their passion for a topic, the need for a challenge, or the exposure to what it means to do college level coursework. However, along with open enrollment, consider creating a safety net for students who may need to be reassigned mid-semester, in the event that they get in over their heads, so that they have an option other than failing the course. The combined AP and non-AP courses mentioned earlier allow for a built-in safety net.

- Assuming your school has a good process for course enrollment in place that includes consultation with teachers and guidance counselors, and assuming you also have a safety net in place that allows for course reassignment midstream for students who need to transfer out of AP courses, don't cap or limit the number of AP classes in which students are permitted to enroll. Our experience shows that there is no magic number or formula for determining the optimal number of AP courses for students. The data from the Challenge Success survey mentioned earlier shows that stress levels in students are not necessarily correlated to the number of AP classes they take. Some students will be able to handle several AP courses at once; others will be unduly stressed by taking only one AP course.

- Don't confuse AP rigor with load. We have seen several successful teachers who can curb the homework load in their AP courses without sacrificing test scores. Just because a course is rigorous and offers college-level work does not mean that students need to complete hours and hours of homework each night to succeed. Students may benefit more from fewer assignments and a focus on deep understanding of concepts learned in class. Some teachers offer an AP course over two years instead of one, to make the load more manageable for students.

- Whatever your school decides about its AP policies and offerings, make sure that the School Profile that accompanies every college application accurately reflects your school's policies and most current offerings so that colleges will know how to interpret a student's choices.

Chapter $SEVEN$

Creating a Climate of Care

We know that students can't be engaged learners unless they feel safe, connected, and supported. In this chapter we focus on structures and tools that schools can use to create an environment where all students feel like they are part of a caring and cohesive community. We highlight the benefits of using small-group advisories, wellness programs, and strategies such as mindfulness, all of which have been implemented at Challenge Success schools to improve student-teacher relations and to create climates conducive to healthy and engaged learners. We know that in order to foster a more caring climate, some schools need to focus intensively on school safety—in particular, the physical safety of their students—and that some teachers need help improving classroom discipline strategies to make sure all students feel supported and part of a community of learners. While this chapter does not cover policies for physical safety or classroom discipline specifically, the tools provided here can help schools improve overall student behavior while promoting a caring climate in and out of the classroom.

WHAT IS A CLIMATE OF CARE, AND WHY DOES IT MATTER?

A climate of care is a broad concept with several different meanings in the education field. When we use the term "climate of care" in this book, we include the following: social and emotional learning (SEL), student-teacher relationships, student belonging, peer relationships, and school and classroom climates. Much of the literature on a climate of care in school stems from the framework developed by James Connell and colleagues, which suggests that for students to be successful in school and within classrooms, they need to feel that they belong or fit in, and they need to have supportive connections with others in those contexts (Connell, 1990; Connell & Wellborn, 1991). Several schools now focus on specific SEL skills such as "the capacity to recognize and manage emotions, solve problems effectively, and establish positive relationships with others" (Zins & Elias, 2007, p. 233), as a way to promote a caring climate.

Researchers tend to agree on the importance of fostering these skills in students of all ages as a way to improve student well-being, classroom behavior, and achievement and promote success in the workplace (Durlak, Weissberg, Dymnicki, Taylor, & Schellinger, 2011; for reviews, see Osterman, 2000, and Weissberg & Cascarino, 2013). For example, several researchers examining the effects of a climate of care on students' academic outcomes have concluded that students are more likely to achieve higher grades and test scores, are more motivated and more engaged in school, and are more likely to persevere in the face of difficulty when they feel connected with and supported by others in school (Farrington et al., 2012; Furrer & Skinner, 2003; Klem & Connell, 2004; Rivkin, Hanushek, & Kain, 2005; Wentzel, 1997). Several studies show that youth who are socioeconomically disadvantaged or in ethnic minorities, or who attend underresourced schools, reap considerable benefits when they feel supported by their teachers (Elias & Haynes, 2008; Olsson, 2009; Sanchez, Colon, & Esparza, 2005).

In addition to the academic benefits associated with a climate of care, studies also show positive benefits to students' social skills and mental and physical health. In a review of 75 studies on SEL programs, Sklad, Diekstra, De Ritter, Ben, and Gravesteijn (2012) found that when SEL programs were implemented effectively, students' social skills improved and antisocial behaviors decreased, their mental health improved, and they showed a decrease in substance abuse. Similarly, when students perceive that teachers support and care about them, they are less likely to try risky behaviors—such as smoking, drinking alcohol, and using marijuana—and are less likely to exhibit suicidal ideation and violence (McNeely & Falci, 2004). In a study of middle school students, researchers found that when students perceived teacher support, they were more likely to feel satisfied with life and less likely to experience symptoms of depression, anxiety, and aggression (Stewart & Suldo, 2011).

In our own studies with high-performing schools, we found that students who do *not* have at least one adult on campus to whom they can turn to with a personal problem, and those who feel connected to only a few teachers or none at all, were more likely to experience academic anxiety; more frequently felt depressed, hopeless, and sad; and claimed higher rates of physical problems often associated with stress, such as headaches and difficulty sleeping. Students in our study who felt supported and cared about by most or all teachers and who had at least one adult to confide in on campus fared much better. These students were less likely to feel sad and hopeless, had fewer physical health problems associated with stress, and experienced less academic worry (Conner, Pope, & Miles, 2014). These findings are consistent with previous research on the relationship between teacher support and students' mental health (Colarossi & Eccles, 2003; De Wit, Karioja, Rye, & Shain, 2011; Murray & Zvoch, 2011; Reddy, Rhodes, & Mulhall, 2003).

At a time when national estimates suggest that 20 to 25 percent of adolescents are experiencing symptoms of emotional distress, including depression, anxiety, self-mutilation, and substance abuse (Knopf, Park, & Mulye, 2008), the need to identify school and classroom-based practices that adolescents perceive as supportive and caring has become a matter of great urgency and importance.

MAKING IT HAPPEN: STRUCTURES THAT SUPPORT A CARING CLIMATE

In our work with schools, we often ask faculty members to describe qualities of a caring teacher. Some teachers answer that caring teachers greet students at the door at the beginning of class, learn all their students' names, have consistent discipline policies, and take the time to design effective lessons. When we ask the same question to students in our Challenge Success schools, their answers focus more on interpersonal qualities. They say that a caring teacher is accessible, listens to the students, is willing to explain concepts in depth, and understands that students have busy lives beyond the classroom. This matches the research on student perception of teacher care and climates of care. Students report that they know their teachers care about them when they solicit and value student opinions, when they treat all students fairly, when they resist comparing students to one another, when they hold high expectations for all students, and when they treat students with respect (McHugh, Horner, Colditz, & Wallace, 2013; Noddings, 1992).

We know that teachers care about their students, but that is only half of the equation. The students themselves need to perceive a caring teacher, and different students may define these characteristics differently. Some students may prefer that a teacher ask about their lives outside of school; attend their music, drama, or sports events; and occasionally eat lunch with them. Other students may not want this kind of personal attention but may crave more attention in terms of academic help, as when a teacher offers to stay after school to help with homework or to change the date of a test because it conflicts with too many other major assessments that week. Given that our students may perceive a caring teacher in different ways (Phillippo, 2012), what can teachers do to promote a caring climate in their classrooms and in their schools? Our Challenge Success schools have been experimenting with various ways to promote stronger teacher-student relationships that support a climate of care.

The Jared Project: The Wheatley School, Old Westbury, New York

At Wheatley, a public school serving approximately 800 students in grades 8 through 12 in New York, faculty and students were concerned when a student named Jared was on the verge of failing out of school. Jared's situation was puzzling because originally no one at the school saw any warning signs of a student in distress until the grade reports were posted. As more information emerged, Richard Simon, who was Wheatley's principal at the time, realized that no one on the faculty knew Jared well or had made any personal connection with the student. Richard wanted to do whatever he could to prevent this situation from recurring. He wanted to change the culture of the school so that students would feel more connected to faculty members. To increase student-teacher relationships at Wheatley, he created something called the Jared Project, based on an idea he read about in an Association for Supervision and Curriculum Development (ASCD) journal article. At the start of the school year, Wheatley staff members created index cards with pictures of every incoming eighth grade student. Richard asked teachers to go through the cards and mark a student's name once they had made a strong connection with that student and felt they had formed an emerging relationship. At the end of several weeks of circulating the cards, any student who didn't have a mark by his or her name was assigned a teacher to help forge some kind of connection, and students with only one mark were often assigned a teacher as well. Richard and his staff looked at the student's schedule and identified a teacher that they thought would make a good match, and then asked the teacher to reach out. The school had recently transitioned to a common lunch period for all students and staff, so that was a natural time for students and faculty members to interact. By the end of the semester every student had at least one mark by his or her name.

Was this system foolproof? Not necessarily. Even if a teacher felt connected to a student, the student might not feel the same way. Further, it wasn't entirely clear what a "strong connection" meant to merit a mark next to the student's name, but the project was a way to remind teachers and students of the importance of student-teacher relationships, and to help adults identify possible kids who might be slipping through the cracks in the system. We know from our own research and that of others (Conner et al., 2014; McNeely & Falci, 2004) that students who have at least one adult at the school to whom they can turn with a personal problem fare better in terms of academics and well-being than those who do not have an adult confidant. The Jared Project is one way to help kids find that one adult.

Advisory

Another way schools can foster greater personalization, whereby teachers create long-term and meaningful connections with small groups of students, is by setting up advisory systems (Darling-Hammond, 2002; Phillippo, 2013; Yonezawa, McClure & Jones, 2012).

In a typical school advisory, one adult at the school meets regularly with small groups of students throughout the school year to offer academic and nonacademic support (Darling-Hammond, 2002; Phillippo, 2013; Poliner & Miller Lieber, 2004). Typically these groups have a ratio of one adult for every 10 to 20 kids and can meet as often as once a day, once or twice a week, or once or twice a month, depending on the model the school is using. The advisor is the one person who typically sees the "whole child" on a regular basis, and, although most advisors are not trained counselors and do not replace counselors at the school, they often free up the counseling staff to focus on priority cases. In general, an advisor may serve a variety of roles in a student's life:

- Act as a liaison between the student, the school, and the family
- Monitor academic progress
- Offer academic counseling—that is, which courses to take and where and when to get extra help or enrichment activities
- Help to individualize the learning path for each student
- Provide college and career advice and write letters of recommendation
- Help students handle academic and some nonacademic problems
- Serve as a "first responder" in noticing physical and mental health problems and social and emotional issues, such as a problem with a peer or family member
- Teach students about wellness and positive coping strategies
- Create a community of learners by promoting a safe and nurturing place for group bonding and peer-to-peer and student-teacher connections

Although many secondary schools now use advisory periods (Poliner & Miller Lieber, 2004; Yonezawa et al., 2012), there are few comprehensive studies that examine the effects of advisory programs on students. In a small study of one urban high school, researchers found that, compared to other similar schools, students in the school with an advisory program had better attendance, lower suspension rates, and higher achievement scores (Gewertz, 2007). Results from two different studies of advisory programs also found that students reported better overall relationships with their teachers, including increased trust and belonging (Totten & Nielson, 1994; Ziegler

& Mulhall, 1994). And in a nationwide survey of principals, those with advisory programs in middle schools reported a smoother transition for those students into high school (Mac Iver & Epstein, 1991). However, another study found that, while a more personalized approach with high school students surveyed was positively related to student achievement, advisory, specifically, was inversely related to student achievement, such that positive feelings about advisory were associated with lower test scores (McClure, Yonezawa, & Jones, 2010). One reason for this could be that the advisory programs at the 14 schools studied were not implemented well. In fact, at least one study we reviewed concluded that, when advisory programs fail, it is usually because teachers have not been effectively trained to lead advisory (Mac Iver, 1990). Given the positive effects shown in the research on personalizing learning and promoting more effective teacher-student relationships, along with the studies on effective advisory programs already noted, a well-conceived and well-implemented advisory system has great potential to enhance students' school experience. So how can a school set up a successful advisory system?

We know from our own work with schools that several components need to be in place for a successful advisory system. All advisors need a training component to learn more about adolescent development and to understand their roles as advisors and how they differ from school counselors. Advisors need to know, for example, how to notice signs of student distress and when they should refer a student to see a school counselor. Advisors also need some sort of curriculum to follow. The curriculum can be flexible; for instance, not every advisor has to teach a specific lesson during each advisory period, but the curriculum should provide core topics and activities to be covered over the course of a month or quarter/semester. We have seen advisory topics range from improving organization and study skills to college and career readiness, positive coping mechanisms, diversity education, and even yoga instruction. Finally, schools should strive to ensure a good fit between advisors and students. How schools do this may vary greatly. Some schools allow students to rank their top choices for advisors; others do not allow student choice. Some schools keep the same advisory groupings for several years; others allow students to switch advisories each year or every other year. Some group advisories by grade; others group kids together from multiple grades. Regardless of how the groups are formed, the purpose of advisory needs to be made clear to all stakeholders, and the school needs to put benchmarks in place to measure the success of the program. If these components aren't in place, advisory period may become just another study hall or home room—a vehicle for taking attendance and not much more.

University High School, San Francisco, California

After receiving a clear mandate to improve the existing advising program, Alex Lockett, dean of students at University High School in San Francisco (UHS), reimagined the school's student support program with a team of teachers and program directors. Although the school had an advisory program in place, teachers, students, administrators, and parents all felt that the program wasn't fully realizing its potential to provide comprehensive student support. Results from the Challenge Success survey confirmed that, while students felt academically engaged in their classrooms, they didn't feel as much support in terms of social and emotional well-being, and student stress levels were high. UHS faculty and administrators believed that if they could increase student-teacher connections at the school, then they could not only improve student well-being but also create an integrated learning opportunity whereby teachers could serve as mentors for students and further enrich student learning and growth.

Before deciding on what the new and improved program should look like, the team had to make some key decisions. Should the school adopt an "off the shelf" SEL program? What would training for teachers look like? What should the content of the program look like? How would it differ for different grades? Would mentors or advisors be released from class time, and if so, who would fill in for them and how would it be paid for? What schedule would be optimal to accommodate these changes? How would its impact be measured? And how would they communicate all of this to the parents?

After exhaustive research of external programs and internal needs, the school decided to design a completely new mentoring program that focused equally on the needs of students and of the faculty who would be serving as their mentors. UHS decided to focus the program intensively on ninth grade students to set them up with the skills, attitudes, and relationships that are foundational to future success within the school. Additionally, ninth graders would have the benefit of having mentors for all four years of their high school experience, allowing administrators the chance to track student growth over time as well as the opportunity to design the program year by year. Finally, because this program started as a pilot, the school felt that this major shift in approach would be easiest to test on a group of students new to the school.

A major design constraint that UHS faced was figuring out how to provide teachers with adequate time and resources to address the collective and individual needs of the students they would mentor. The robust and integrated program would require significant training and coaching of mentors to help them (1) form strong relationships with their mentees, (2) be accessible to their mentees on a regular basis, (3) lead sessions with their mentor groups three times per week, (4) spend time each week processing with other mentors, and (5) interact with parents or guardians in a timely and comprehensive manner.

Reframing this role of mentor as one equivalent to teaching a class was a major turning point in the program design. Consequently, the school committed to providing course release time for seven teacher mentors and a mentor coach, resulting in the cost equivalent of two full-time positions. While resource intensive, the school felt that devoting this amount of time and resources to training mentors would ultimately be a tremendous investment in providing each student with customized and complete support.

After much research into existing advisory curricula, UHS administrators and teachers agreed that instead of a specific "scripted" set of lesson plans, mentors would engage in weekly routines with students that would focus on building relationships and skills. Mentor groups (14 students, 1 mentor) meet regularly for three sessions a week: two one-hour sessions and one 40-minute session. During the longer Monday and Wednesday sessions, mentors lead a check-in with their mentees as a group, talk about homework and time-management/study skills, and in the remaining time meet with students one-on-one while the other mentees start homework. During the shorter Friday session, mentor groups engage in a fun and playful activity to build group connections. Additionally, mentors occasionally attend human development classes where program directors lead sessions about health and wellness, metacognition, cultural competency, and community service learning. Beyond these structured weekly meeting times, mentors and mentees set up one-on-one meetings to address specific academic, social, and emotional needs as they arise. One important goal is for the relationship between mentor and mentee to be solid enough that students feel safe and comfortable seeking their mentor's help if they have a problem.

One of the mantras of the program is that "mentors receive as much support as they are expected to give." From day one, mentors are enveloped in support from their mentor coach and from the dean of students. Beginning with a comprehensive week-long training in August, mentors are coached on everything from active listening skills, to how to teach kids better organizational systems

(continued)

and note-taking skills, to how to help students with emotional problems. The mentor coach (a teacher and mentor at UHS) is responsible for working with the group to address needs in a weekly hour-long mentor meeting as well as to work individually with mentors to ensure that they are given space to reflect, learn, and grow from their experience. Because of this intensive support and focus on growth, mentors cite this program as one of the most profound professional development experiences of their career.

The program is now in its third year, and the feedback from research, surveys, and informal observation is overwhelmingly positive. Students report feeling more connected to each other, to teachers, and to the school. As Alex Lockett notes: "There is a lack of cliquishness, and we see more reaching out to adults and asking for help. Seeking out support is now a norm, whereas before it was seen as a sign of weakness." Ninth graders are more involved in sports, theater productions, and clubs on campus than in previous years. Students gravitate toward mentor teachers at the school, drawn by their reputations as student-centered advocates and allies. Teachers report that students are more active in the classroom, more comfortable asking for help, and less anxious about assessments, thereby creating a healthier and more productive learning environment. Overall, UHS students are missing less school, getting more sleep, and feeling more supported by each other and faculty. Parents are calmer and happier with the school and feel more connected, thanks to more contact with their child's mentor.

There are some downsides, however. While the majority of faculty and parents supported the new program, some felt threatened by the change and worried about its impact on school culture. Some faculty members worried: if they didn't have the skills to participate as mentors, would they be less relevant to the school? The program is also resource intensive. Until the program is fully developed after four years, each year requires the mentor coach and administrators to design the next phase of the program. The school will also need to strategically address long-term sustainability to support mentors and the full program over time.

Based on the UHS experience, Alex advises schools to involve as many different constituents as possible to make the case for why mentoring matters, and to offer plenty of support, training, and mentoring for the mentors themselves.

Alex continues, "While the focus of this program is on supporting the students, there are secondary benefits that we didn't count on. Faculty members have new, stronger relationships outside of their department, and parents feel that they finally have an advocate within the school that truly knows their child, allowing them to trust the school more fully." While there are real costs of time, money, space, and shifting culture, Alex believes the investment in the program is making even more of an impact than originally intended, and the entire UHS community is benefitting from the focus on student support and well-being.

Tutorial Time

Challenge Success schools that don't have the immediate time or resources to create full advisory systems sometimes implement a weekly tutorial time—a type of modified school-wide study hall. During tutorial time, all students are expected to be in a classroom with a teacher. Students can use tutorial time as they wish; they can work on homework, take a make-up test or quiz, schedule a brief conference with a teacher, take a nap, or listen to music quietly at their desks. Students can choose which classroom to attend for tutorial time, though some popular teachers need to set a limit on the number of students they let in each week. It should be noted that tutorial time is not a substitute for an advisory system. Teachers are not conducting lessons or discussions such as those that take place in advisory, and they aren't working with one consistent small group of students over time. We see tutorial time as a benefit to students: it offers a chance to catch up on work or sleep and an informal opportunity to interact more with staff members. But for schools that want to strengthen student-teacher connections, we advocate for more formal structures with clear goals, benchmarks, and teacher training.

Wellness Programs

In addition to creating time and space for small groups of students and teachers to meet regularly in advisories, some of our Challenge Success schools have been developing specific wellness programs and curricula for their students. Some schools create wellness centers on campus, complete with opportunities for students to receive free, confidential counseling. The wellness center in the Piedmont Unified School District, for example, aims to provide resources for prevention, early detection, and education for students and their families on a wide range of topics including, stress, relationships, grief/loss, substance abuse, anxiety, depression, parent/child communication, and self-advocacy (for more information, see Piedmont High Campus Life Wellness Center). In addition to in-house counselors, they offer training for students on peer mediation techniques, as well as middle and high school peer advisors who teach mini-units in physical education classes on topics such as drinking and driving and improved decision-making.

Schools that do not have the resources to build wellness centers can still offer wellness programs to their communities. Several of our Challenge Success schools implement peer mediation programs, for instance, and peer counseling programs. Others host semi-annual wellness fairs, often planned by students, with lunchtime activities for the school community, including hands-on mini-lessons and booths that educate youth on positive coping strategies such as yoga, mindfulness, and meditation. Students enjoy the fun activities these fairs provide, including healthy snacks and back massages, but they also tell us that they learn a lot from the experts hosting the booths and from the guest speakers who offer presentations during lunch and assembly times during wellness weeks. After learning about the advantages of yoga at one of the school's health fairs, several students at one of our Challenge Success schools even decided to form a yoga club that meets every Monday during recess. And some of our schools take this one step further and develop wellness curricula that are implemented throughout the year in PE and Health classes. The case of Castilleja School that follows describes the process used to design and implement a comprehensive wellness program at the school.

Castilleja School, Palo Alto, California

In 2006, when Nanci Kauffman (assistant head of Castilleja School at the time and now head of the school) wanted to expand the school's traditional Physical Education program, she visited schools across the country to learn how effective wellness programs were being implemented. Nanci, along with other members of the administration, wanted a wellness program that went beyond California's PE requirements and would help prepare students for "the world they live in now." The team knew from experience and from Challenge Success survey data that students and adults were stressed and pressed for time in a fast-paced world, and they aimed to develop a comprehensive curriculum to prepare students to face the challenges of growing up in a media-driven, results-driven culture.

Since the original fitness program seemed to be working well, the team decided that the fitness faculty, along with two new wellness teachers, would teach fitness and wellness components together in required PE courses in grades 6 through 10 at the school. Fitness classes take place throughout the year and dovetail with four to six wellness units, each about a month long, as part of the required curriculum. During a wellness unit, students typically have two fitness classes and two wellness classes each week. The fitness and wellness curricula are designed to overlap to reinforce concepts and skills for each grade, based on the most relevant topics. Sixth graders, for example, need to learn about forming new relationships—how to make new friends, how to resolve conflicts, and to form healthy habits such as getting adequate sleep, nutrition, and exercise, so those topics are covered in sixth grade wellness units. At the same time, the fitness instructors explain how being active can help students be effective and efficient in many areas of their lives and include relaxation strategies, like yoga and breath awareness, in their sixth grade fitness classes. The seventh grade curriculum includes units on digital citizenship, diversity and tolerance, self-esteem, and body image, while the eighth grade "balanced mind and body" unit provides students with strategies to manage their responsibilities and stressors. The program in the ninth and tenth grades addresses similar but also more developmentally advanced subjects, such as substance abuse prevention, teen safety, and romantic relationships, and again the fitness components are coordinated when applicable with the wellness topics; for instance, students learn self-defense during the safety unit.

Faculty, parents, and students are supportive of the wellness curriculum, and the school did not encounter much resistance during the transition because the program is developmentally appropriate and integrated into existing curriculum rather than added on. The teachers especially are pleased with the wellness curriculum because, according to Patrick Burrows, middle school athletic director, "They see what the girls need and what they are going through, and they know the units we teach address the whole student." According to annual feedback surveys, the middle school students seem to find the program "very engaging and useful," but the upper school students have been less receptive at times. As of this writing, the administration was trying to readjust the curriculum to increase engagement for the high school students. They had also hired a new director for SEL at the school to work with the fitness and wellness instructors to weave new SEL components into the curriculum.

(continued)

While UHS and Castilleja both decided to design their own advisory and wellness models, many schools adopt SEL programs and packages that have been around for many years and have been validated by outside vendors. The Collaborative for Academic, Social and Emotional Learning (see CASEL), for instance, offers one of the most comprehensive clearinghouses for evidenced-based SEL programs for schools. Their website curates research on the advantages of using SEL in schools and offers considerable resources for teachers and parents interested in learning more. Another resource is the Institute for Social and Emotional Learning, founded in 2009 by several teachers from The Nueva School in Hillsborough, California.

The Nueva School, Hillsborough, California, and The Institute for Social and Emotional Learning

Nueva School founder Karen Stone McCown believed that affective education was a critical component for Nueva, and when Janice Toben arrived at the Nueva School in the 1980s, she was surrounded by a vibrant educational philosophy that embraced the notion of "learn by caring, learn by doing." In this dynamic school setting, Janice recognized the need to proactively focus on student well-being and to continue with the tradition of developing *intra*personal and *inter*personal skills. From 1990 to 2009, she synthesized many principles from best practices in conflict resolution, creativity, and group and personal awareness to set in motion at Nueva a full-scale SEL program that was experientially appropriate for the different age groups, first grade through eighth grade. Janice's approach included a wide reach—facilitating agreements young students would make and strive to uphold as they played at recess and as they ventured out on week-long camping trips, needing strategies for resiliency and sensitivity to each other's needs.

Drawing upon SEL research and many of the competencies described by CASEL, she focused on building specific skills and tools with students for self-awareness and self-regulation, as well as positive communication skills and personal decision-making that would promote ethical, empathic behavior, in and out of the classroom.

In 2009, Janice and a few Nueva SEL teachers wanted to share their insights and ideas for promoting SEL with other teachers outside of the Nueva community, so they started the Institute for Social and Emotional Learning.

The Institute's mission is "to empower educators and young people with the tools and training to transform their organizations into caring and inclusive communities." Janice and her team knew that bringing their work to private and public school teachers would not be simple. They understood that a "one size fits all" model would not work with the many different schools they hoped to impact. Instead, the team created a model for teacher professional development that focused on interdisciplinary and experiential learning, teacher personal renewal, and intentional reflection to inspire social and emotional learning. At the Institute, teachers do many of the exercises they will eventually use in their own classrooms with students. They have breakout sessions called "Make It Happen" where they mull over how to bring their insights back to their schools. They focus on methods for activating social and emotional skills. These include:

1. Inter- and Intrapersonal Questioning Strategies. For example, after doing a cooperative building exercise or an improvisational game, they are asked critical questions such as: How did you feel at the beginning of that exercise, in the middle, and at the end? Did you feel different? Why? What did you notice about the way you worked with others in that experience?

(continued)

Creating a Climate of Care   149

2. Centering and Focusing exercises begin each day and model how teachers and students benefit when they deepen attention and mindfulness.

3. Teachers come to understand and engage in the use of rituals for community building with their students and with each other, such as adding an Appreciation Circle, where members share words of gratitude and acknowledgment about each other and their behaviors that day.

One of the most popular tools learned at the Institute for Social and Emotional Learning is The Open Session, created by Janice after years of facilitating groups with middle school students and parents at Nueva. She explains: "In The Open Session, classmates respond to student-generated issues through an intentional, supportive exchange of listening and ideas. This opportunity, when held consistently within a middle or high school community, allows students to offer their personal wisdom, advice, or clarification to guide their peers to a healthy resolution to everyday problems in a safe environment." Janice developed The Open Session because she knew that students have "valuable insights and information to share about life experiences and need an opportunity to express themselves." She believed that students could work together to help solve real, daily personal challenges and social struggles and that doing so would create strong listening and communication skills and reflection and analytical skills, along with greater empathy and resilience for each member of the group.

How does it work? The sessions, typically 45 to 55 minutes, take place with small groups of students—ideally 12 to 25—sitting in a circle. Led by either trained teachers or counselors, the session begins with a check-in and reminder about ground rules, followed by asking the students to write down on index cards any worry, concern, or upcoming decision that is stressful for them, or a joy that they would like to share with the group. The facilitator's primary role is to unfold responses from the group, not to lead the discussion or to solve the students' problems, and the students work within the framework of offering socially and emotionally sound practices of "clarification, support, and encouragement, or wisdom, ideas, and solutions."

More specifically, after the check-in time, every student turns in a card, some anonymously, and the facilitator reads the card. Students offer clarification—anything that would help better understand the scope of the issue. For example, students might say: "I'm thinking about what the person meant by _____?" or "I wonder if there are some assumptions the person is making about_____" and "I'm thinking about whether the person has spoken to anyone else about this issue?"

Or students might offer support and encouragement: "I hope this person knows that they have people around who really care" or "I hope things get better for that person," or "I am sorry that this person is feeling that way." The group also contributes some possible solutions and specific actions the student might take to improve the situation. They might suggest, "In my experience it helps to_____and then _____" or "Maybe there are new ways to look at this . . . ."

Most of the problems the students share relate to daily life issues and decisions, though some students also bring up stress over family issues. Here's an example from a recent session. The index card from the student reads: "For the last few months, I have had trouble staying asleep. I wake up in the middle of the night and my mind starts racing, and I can't get back to sleep." The empathic, collective wondering begins, and students then might offer support and clarification, saying that they have the same problem, especially around exam time, and wonder if worrying about school and grades might be causing the inability to sleep. Some students might offer wisdom from their experience and suggest that other stressors can cause sleep problems. And then students offer solutions such as: "I've read that darkening the room and turning off technology can help . . . or keeping a pad of paper beside your bed to write down your ideas . . . That way you won't be kept awake because you are afraid you will forget in the morning . . . ."

Other examples of student cards include:

- I'm really worried about a friend who is bulimic and she's not getting help.
- I've never been to a funeral and am nervous about it.
- I'm being laughed at in front of the boys this week at lunch, and I'm sick of it.
- My parents constantly ask me about my grades. I'm working really hard, but nothing I say or do seems to be enough for them. It's really getting me down.

Occasionally the facilitator may read a card that expresses self-harm or shows that a student may face serious stress. When this happens, facilitators use their

(continued)

judgment about whether to read the card aloud or not; they might say: "I have a tough card here. I don't know who it belongs to, but I hope that this person comes to talk to me or another adult, so I can help him or her and discuss resources at school or elsewhere." Sometimes the facilitator expresses that a card is difficult and decides to read the card so that students get the chance to share what they would do under this kind of stress and how they wish to support the anonymous classmate.

This group process of "collective wondering" creates a tremendous feeling of support as students work together to solve their own problems. The sessions allow students to practice positive communication and active listening skills as they become more aware of the challenges facing members of their community. They can build confidence and resilience as they learn to cope with personal, social, and academic conflicts and stressors. As one student explains, "I really like Open Session because it helps me to be able to get advice without anyone knowing that it is me asking for help. Sometimes, asking a friend for advice is helpful, but Open Session is better because I can get a variety of different ideas and suggestions. It's like a basket full of choice, and I can use the one that I like the best. I also like sharing because if I have had a problem that is the same or similar to the anonymous person, I can give them advice."

Relaxation and Stress-relief Practices

Many of our Challenge Success schools have discovered the benefits of teaching students to use relaxation and stress-relief practices during the school day and at home. Schools work with kids to practice mindfulness, meditation, yoga, and a variety of other breathing and calming techniques to improve student health and well-being, build resilience, and help foster a more caring climate. The terms "mindfulness" and "meditation" are sometimes used interchangeably and, although they are related in that they are both specific ways of paying attention, they are different practices. While we are not going to go into detail in this book about the definitions of these practices, it might be helpful to know that meditation is the practice of sitting comfortably, often with the eyes closed, focusing on breathing. And mindfulness is the practice of purposefully bringing your attention and tuning your senses to your present experience. (For more information on these practices, do a browser search on "transcendental meditation" and visit the websites of the David Lynch Foundation, the Greater Good Science Center, and the

Hawn Foundation.) The mention of these activities used to elicit eye-rolling and smirks from those not familiar with the practices, but that's not the case anymore—at least it shouldn't be.

We found quite a bit of evidence about the benefits of mindfulness and meditation in schools. For instance, meditation practices have been found to reduce stress and increase coping skills in adolescents (Black, Milam, & Sussman, 2009; Nidich et al., 2009), and another study found that incorporating meditation practices into a middle school increased students' self-control as well as their test scores (Rosaen & Benn, 2006). Similarly, mindfulness practices have been found to reduce stress in students as well as to help students gain focus, empathy, self-control, and insight (Frank, Jennings, & Greenberg, 2013; Greenberg & Harris, 2011; Meiklejohn et al., 2012). For instance, a randomized control study of almost 1,000 elementary students showed that just four hours a week of mindfulness practices increased students' ability to pay attention, get along with others, and show empathy and care toward others in their classrooms as compared to students who did not receive the mindfulness curriculum (Mindful Schools, 2013). In addition, Broderick and Metz (2009) studied the effects of a mindfulness program on the emotional well-being of high school females and found that the girls who were part of the mindfulness program were more calm and less stressed than those who did not receive the mindfulness lessons. In another study, teachers reported that the pre- and early adolescent students who participated in a mindfulness program were more optimistic and got along better with their peers after the program than those who did not participate in the program (Schonert-Reichl & Lawlor, 2010).

Mindfulness and meditation practices offer benefits for educators as well. In a randomized control study with teachers, those who received mindfulness training were less likely to experience burnout and stress and were able to offer a more supportive environment to their students than those teachers who were not given the mindfulness training (Jennings, Frank, Snowberg, Coccia, & Greenberg, 2013). Similarly, another study found that the use of meditation practices with teachers in a school for children with behavioral problems reduced teachers' stress, depression, and burnout (Elder, Nidich, Moriarty, & Nidich, 2014).

Though fewer studies focus specifically on the use of yoga in schools, we found two randomized controlled studies about the effects of yoga in a high school that indicated that students who took yoga, compared to those who didn't take yoga and had regular PE classes, had less stress and anxiety and had improved body images (Conboy, Noggle, Frey, Kudesia, & Khalsa, 2013; Khalsa, Hickey-Schultz, Cohen, Steiner, & Cope, 2012).

The Challenge Success schools that have incorporated relaxation and stress-relief strategies have noted similar positive benefits for their students.

Katherine Delmar Burke School, San Francisco, California

Lisa Spengler, the assistant director of the Upper School for Student Life and Leadership at Katherine Delmar Burke School (Burke's, as it is commonly known) in San Francisco and a member of the Challenge Success Advisory Board, explains how the school's work with Challenge Success led to the implementation of a school-wide mindfulness program. After the Challenge Success survey revealed an undercurrent of student and adult stress at the school, the Burke's Challenge Success team decided to create a more comprehensive health and wellness program using mindfulness as the cornerstone. After a spirited conversation among the head of school, division heads, and Challenge Success team leaders on what the mindfulness program should look like, and whether it should be a full school rollout or a pilot program within a single division, the head of school ultimately decided that in order to "do it right," Burke's should commit the entire school to the program, and she allocated the necessary funding to do so.

Burke's selected Mindful Schools, an organization based in nearby Oakland, to help them implement the program in all of their grades (K–8). At the end of that spring, the Mindful Schools executive director explained to the Burke's faculty and staff what they expected to accomplish over the following school year, and together they set implementation plans in place. Mindful Schools returned for further teacher training in August during opening faculty-staff meetings. School administrators decided it was important to let teachers and students settle into the school year before launching the student training, in order to ensure a trusting and safe environment. At the end of October of that year, the school embarked on a multimonth training program that included Mindful Schools instructors teaching 15-minute lessons to students twice per week; these included specific exercises on breathing, focus, and attention. Instructors worked with each grade level and individually with teachers. Scheduling the sessions was a challenge, but classroom teachers were mostly cooperative in giving up instructional time. Though a few teachers initially resisted the program, primarily because of concerns about the time it would take to implement in class, overall the teachers were receptive and embraced the short training sessions.

Because of the broad commitment, when the school eventually rolled out the full program, faculty members were "all doing the same thing on the same day at the same time." As a result, the faculty and staff could talk about their experiences and what was and wasn't working. The two Mindful Schools instructors listened carefully to the feedback from the Burke's teachers and formed a positive, trusting relationship with the faculty. According to Lisa, the instructors could really "read kids, classes, and teachers," and they knew exactly how to support and "work with teachers who were resistant to draw them in."

A big part of the program's success can be credited to the full support of the administration, the eventual buy-in of nearly all teachers, and the thoughtful implementation plan. For the first three years of the program, each school year started with a two-hour professional development session for faculty led by a mindfulness instructor. Faculty and staff members are also encouraged to take opportunities for additional professional development on mindfulness training at conferences and local workshops. An openness to mindfulness practices has become an important part of the hiring process for new teachers as well. In addition, quite a few teachers have developed personal mindfulness practices that have allowed them to not only reduce their own stress, but also to enrich their classroom-based mindfulness experience and address the underlying stress that led to the all-school adoption.

Parent education was also important to the success of the program. During the first year, the school-wide Tuesday e-newsletter explained what Burke's was doing with mindfulness and why. The school held two parent education sessions, albeit with somewhat disappointing attendance, and addressed head-on some issues that emerged, explaining what mindfulness really looked like for those who misunderstood it as a new age or specifically religious practice.

During the second year of the rollout, the faculty and staff were assigned *The Mindful Child* by Susan Kaiser Greenland (2010) for summer reading, and the head of school's parent book club also read the book. Susan was the featured parent education speaker in February, when she spent a day at Burke's speaking with parents and faculty, spending time in classrooms, and doing an extended mindfulness exercise with the entire Upper School. Burke's has also committed to bring in other professionals to talk about mindfulness and continue to strengthen the program. Many parents now consider mindfulness along with the overall SEL program at Burke's as a major benefit of the school.

(continued)

They want their children to have an excellent educational experience while acquiring tools to become more thoughtful, balanced young adults.

Finally, the majority of students really like practicing mindfulness. While at first some students pushed back because it "wasn't cool," those who had actually tried to practice mindfulness during their class sessions intervened to say, "Hey, you really need to try this." Now students frequently ask for mindfulness time before assessments. Kids and parents both report that kids are using mindfulness at home to help them fall asleep or destress while doing homework, and as a means to refocus during sports competitions. Teachers, counselors and administrators regularly refer to mindfulness as a tool when helping students problem-solve around both academic and social-emotional challenges.

The program is now integrated into both Lower and Upper Schools at Burke's. Mindfulness is part of the balanced approach that has become integral to the school as part of its work with Challenge Success. As Lisa explains, "it has been a five-year journey for us with Challenge Success" to enhance student well-being.

PLANNING FOR A CLIMATE OF CARE

In this chapter we have discussed a wide range of strategies to foster a more caring climate, including advisories, wellness programs, and specific strategies such as Open Session and mindfulness. Regardless of the particular strategy or program a school adopts, all teachers, parents, and students should be made aware of the research on the benefits of a caring climate and the power of positive student-teacher relations to improve student health and achievement. Remember that for these benefits to occur, the students themselves must perceive that their teachers care about them. Thus, an important first step toward a more caring climate is to initiate dialogue between students and teachers as to what a caring teacher and a caring climate might look like.

Latin School of Chicago included students in these kinds of conversations as they developed their new strategic plan. As Kirk Greer, Upper School history and social studies chair and cochair of the Strategic Planning Process, explained, "We included student voice in the process of formulating our most recent strategic plan. Students identified stress and hypercompetitiveness as problems. From their collective concerns, we were able to persuade key stakeholders with more traditional understandings of rigor that there was no tradeoff between a school attentive to the social-emotional effects of its curriculum and academic achievement." In fact, "Wellness as a Foundation for Education" is one of four key strategic priorities in Latin's new plan, which includes educational excellence, community engagement, and inclusive and supportive community. In the first year of enacting the strategic plan, the school formed a 15-member wellness committee that included all directors and representation from all divisions (junior kindergarten through grade 12), and conducted over 20 shadow days following students from grades 4 through 12 to get a better sense of the students' experiences and needs and to help shape next steps and recommendations. An excerpt from Latin's Strategic Plan can be found in Exhibit 7.1. Notice the focus not only on students, but also on faculty and staff well-being as a priority; the entire Latin community — students, parents, and all adults at the school — are included in the overall plan for a healthier school climate.

Exhibit 7.1 Excerpt from Latin School of Chicago Strategic Plan 2013–2018

Priority II: Wellness as a Foundation for Education

Our students will gain the most from our challenging educational program, and be happier, when they are physically and emotionally well. Research and experience conclusively indicate that higher-order thinking, creativity, performance, and engagement all rely on student energy and self-confidence. We will strengthen practices that encourage students to reflect on their choices, develop skills that preserve health, and build a community that values the wellness and self-confidence of each member. In pursuing this priority, we will engage our parent community in a dialogue about how best to promote our children's academic development and happiness.

We are also committed to promoting the wellbeing of our faculty and staff and will encourage adults in our community to meet their own needs as they fulfill their responsibilities.

A. Wellness

Integrate the objective of promoting student and adult wellness into all aspects of the school.

1A. **Health and Wellness for Students**: Build a healthy school climate that promotes student wellness, wise decision-making, and reflection.

Conduct further self-study, as informed by existing data on Latin student health and wellness practices, and make recommendations to improve the student experience. Recommendations may consider:

- Impact of workload expectations and curricular changes.
- Heightened attention to executive functioning and time-management skills in our digital age.
- Organization of the school day and calendar.
- Use of outdoor play, physical education, and athletics programs to support health and wellness objectives.
- Use of homerooms and advisories.
- Integration of affective education and Roundtable with age-appropriate peer-to-peer strategies to improve student health.
- Establish forum for parents and school to discuss patterns in student behavior, share experiences and research, and formulate strategies to strengthen commitment to student health.

2A. **Wellness for Faculty and Staff**: Build a professional community in which each member contributes to Latin's excellence in a sustainable manner.

- Conduct self-study of schedule and time use to create improved opportunities for faculty and staff to reflect, collaborate, and plan.
- Examine distribution of co-curricular and committee participation among faculty and staff.
- Ensure that faculty and staff are provided with opportunities, including time, to engage in professional development.
- Include the promotion of balance as a theme in the faculty evaluation process.

Schools may want to consider building a wellness component into their strategic planning or accreditation process, similar to the one that Latin developed, or they may want to begin by reviewing teaching standards such as the California Standards for the Teaching Profession, excerpted in Exhibit 7.2, to help teachers reflect on practices for more caring classroom communities. We like these standards in particular because of the use of questions as a way to prompt self-reflection. The standards ask teachers to consider a variety of questions to help promote positive student-teacher relationships, peer interactions, parent connections, and behaviors that help to "establish and maintain learning environments that are physically, intellectually, and emotionally safe" (Commission on Teacher Credentialing, 2009). As more teachers and schools focus on establishing and improving student support structures, SEL curricula, and wellness strategies, the more likely it is for all students to experience the positive benefits of a climate of care.

Exhibit 7.2 Excerpt from California Standards for the Teaching Profession

Standard 1. Engaging and Supporting All Students in Learning

Teachers know and care about their students in order to engage them in learning. They connect learning to students' prior knowledge, backgrounds, life experiences, and interests. They connect subject matter to meaningful, real-life contexts. Teachers use a variety of instructional strategies, resources, and technologies to meet the diverse learning needs of students. They promote critical thinking through inquiry, problem solving, and reflection. They monitor student learning and adjust instruction while teaching.

1.1 Using knowledge of students to engage them in learning

As teachers develop, they may ask, "How do I…" or "Why do I…"

- know my students as people and as learners?
- understand reasons for behavior?
- recognize atypical behavior in students?
- build trust with students and foster relationships so that students can thrive academically?
- adapt my teaching to reflect knowledge of my students?
- differentiate instruction based on what I know about my students' strengths, interests, and needs?
- get to know parents and connect with the community where I teach?

Standard 2. Creating and Maintaining Effective Environments for Student Learning

Teachers promote social development and responsibility within a caring community where each student is treated fairly and respectfully. They create physical or virtual learning environments that promote student learning, reflect diversity, and encourage constructive and productive interactions among students. They establish and maintain learning environments that are physically, intellectually, and emotionally safe. Teachers create a rigorous learning environment with high expectations and appropriate support for all students. Teachers develop, communicate, and maintain high standards for individual and group behavior. They employ classroom routines, procedures, norms, and supports for positive behavior to ensure a climate in which all students can learn. They use instructional time to optimize learning.

2.1 Promoting social development and responsibility within a caring community where each student is treated fairly and respectfully.

As teachers develop, they may ask, "How do I..." or "Why do I..."

- model and promote fairness, equity, and respect in a classroom atmosphere that values all individuals and cultures?
- help all students accept and respect diversity in terms of cultural, religious, linguistic, and economic backgrounds; learning differences and ability; gender and gender identity; family structure and sexual orientation; and other aspects of humankind?
- engage students in shared problem-solving and conflict resolution?
- provide learning opportunities that encourage student-to-student communication with empathy and understanding?
- develop students' leadership skills and provide opportunities to apply them?
- create a classroom culture where students feel a sense of responsibility to and for one another?
- help students to appreciate their own identities and to view themselves as valued contributors to society?
- develop activities that support positive interactions among students and that help students get to know each other?

2.3 Establishing and maintaining learning environments that are physically, intellectually, and emotionally safe

As teachers develop, they may ask, "How do I…" or "Why do I…"

- arrange the learning environment to facilitate positive and productive classroom interactions?
- encourage, support, and recognize the achievements and contributions of all students?
- encourage students to take risks and to express thoughtful and respectful opinions related to the topic or subject of discussion?
- foster the development of each student's self-esteem?
- create a safe, accessible learning environment for all students?

2.6 Employing classroom routines, procedures, norms, and supports for positive behavior to ensure a climate in which all students can learn

As teachers develop, they may ask, "How do I…" or "Why do I…"

- involve all students in the development of classroom procedures and routines?
- help students transition smoothly and efficiently from one instructional activity to the next?
- apply knowledge of students' physical, social, cognitive, and emotional development to ensure that adequate time and support are provided for students to complete learning activities?
- develop daily schedules, timelines, classroom routines, and norms that maximize learning?
- connect district, site, and classroom procedures to promote a climate of fairness and respect for all students?
- adapt routines, procedures, and norms to ensure the success of students with special needs?

Source: Commission on Teacher Credentialing (2009).

Chapter EIGHT

Educating the Whole School

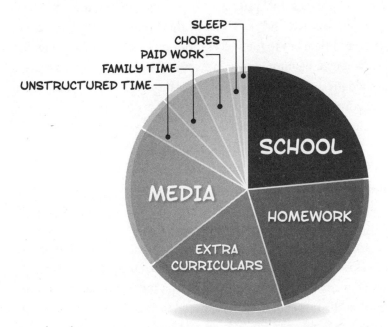

SLEEP
CHORES
PAID WORK
FAMILY TIME
UNSTRUCTURED TIME

SCHOOL

HOMEWORK

MEDIA

EXTRA
CURRICULARS

Over the years, working with various stakeholders, we have heard many common misunderstandings about kids, schools, and the learning process that can get in the way of effective school change. For instance, we often hear statements like: "I thought it was OK for high school kids to sleep five or six hours a night if they made up for it on the weekends"; "I am not assigning too much homework—the reasons kids take so long to complete it is because they are completely overscheduled with extracurriculars"; and "I never see my teenager these days because she is so busy, but it's better for her to be busy than bored." In this chapter, we'll discuss ways to clear up these misunderstandings and educate the whole school community on the fundamentals kids need to lead healthy, engaged lives. We'll also provide scenarios and tools that you can use at your school to achieve the widespread buy-in necessary for effective, "sticky" school change.

WHAT DO WE WANT EVERYONE IN THE COMMUNITY TO KNOW?

Even the best-laid plans will likely remain plans without effective communication and professional development for school faculty and staff, a mechanism for soliciting and truly hearing student voices, and extensive parent education on the goals you are trying to accomplish with your new policies and programs. It seems so obvious, but we've seen schools take this part for granted and watch all of their hard work go nowhere. Communication is often the ultimate key to the success and sustainability of a particular reform, and, as you have heard us say a number of times in this book, bringing the school community together to dialogue and solve problems, even though it will be difficult at times, is the best way to accomplish what you set out to do.

Research shows that including a variety of stakeholders—from parents to students to school teachers and staff—in the design and implementation of a school change is critical to its success (Mitra & Gross, 2009; Osberg, Pope, & Galloway, 2006; Rice, 2011). Will everyone buy into your plans for change? Most likely not, but being inclusive, communicating your plan honestly and effectively, and supporting it with data will give you the best chance for success. In order for students, parents, teachers, counselors, and administrators to work together toward effective school change, all parties need to have a basic understanding of what kids need for optimal health and school engagement. At Challenge Success we developed a mnemonic aid: PDF. It stands for playtime, downtime, and family time. We looked at the research for protective factors for kids—those things that every kid needs in order to thrive physically, mentally, and academically—and we boiled these down to three main categories for well-being. Our mantra is "every kid needs PDF every day."

Playtime

Play is really the work of kids. It helps them to solve problems, negotiate with others, try out new ideas and identities, and develop self-regulation, among other things. Playtime can include structured activities, such as Little League and an after-school art class, and it can include unstructured activities, such as playing with toys, going to the playground, and shooting the basketball with friends. For tweens and teens it can also include some time spent on social media. For all ages, research suggests that play—especially when it is freely chosen, unstructured, and kid-directed—is linked to a wide variety of positive outcomes including increased cognitive skills, physical health, self-regulation, language abilities, and social skills (Alliance for Childhood, 2010; Barker et al., 2014; Hofferth & Sandberg, 2001).

Experts agree that every child needs some time for play every day, but we know that many kids don't get this. One reason may be, as we noted in Chapter Two, that time spent in school has increased. Twenty years ago, the time spent in school ranged from five to six hours a day, but currently children in the United States spend at least six to seven hours a day in school (Juster, Ono, & Stafford, 2004). In our own research with Challenge Success schools, we have found that, on average, after you count hours in school and hours in structured extracurricular activities such as sports, drama, or debate, as well as hours for commuting and paid work, middle school students report that on a typical weekday they have approximately 1.5 hours of free time, and high school students report having approximately 1 hour (Conner & Pope, 2013a). Another nationwide study found that children under 12 years old have approximately two hours of free time during the day and that this decreases as they get older (Hofferth & Sandberg, 2001). In addition to differences between younger and older children, the amount of free time reported in the research varies depending on family income: Children from lower income households often have more free time than peers from households with higher incomes (Hofferth & Sandberg, 2001; Larson, 2001.) Of course, the benefits (or risks) associated with the amount of free time depends on what kids do with that free time. Watching TV for three hours each day may be detrimental to kids, but spending unstructured time playing with friends or family is associated with positive outcomes (Barnes, Hoffman, Welte, Farrell, & Dintcheff, 2007; Larson, 2001).

Unfortunately, time for free play within school hours has also declined. Many schools have reduced or even eliminated recess for elementary school children, and several have cut back on free play and play-based learning in the early grades such as kindergarten and first grade (Zygmunt-Fillwalk & Bilello, 2005). For instance, we used to see several hours of free play and free choice activities in the younger grades, where kids could build in the blocks corner or enact their own stories in the dress-up area, but more schools are focused on traditional, often worksheet-based, literacy and numeracy activities now. We recommend keeping ample time for recess in school, as well as carving out time for kids to have more choice in activities in the classroom so they are able to use their imagination, build and make things, interact with others, and have some ownership over what and how they are learning. As we mentioned in Chapter Four on project-based learning, these kinds of play-based projects and activities, in which students of all ages have a choice and voice, can lead to authentic motivation to learn and important lifelong skills.

Playtime for middle and high school kids looks a little different from playtime for younger kids, both at home and at school. For kids in middle school and high school, playtime often means spending time with friends as well as doing things they enjoy, such as extracurricular activities. Activities such as sports, visual and performing arts, community service, journalism, and academic clubs can be sources for positive playtime for teenagers (Mahoney, Cairns, & Farmer, 2003; Mahoney, Larson, & Eccles, 2005). In our research, the vast majority of our sample of almost 8,000 high school students reported that the main reason they participate in extracurriculars is because they enjoy them (Conner & Pope, 2013a). Other studies have also linked participation in extracurricular activities to positive social and academic outcomes (Mahoney et al., 2003). When kids participate in these activities, they have a chance to interact with peers, learn new skills, exercise, and challenge themselves in rewarding ways.

Research also shows that you need to find the right balance when it comes to extracurricular activities. We know that kids have many wonderful extracurricular choices these days, and parents tell us they don't want to disadvantage their children by restricting what they do. Unfortunately, over-scheduling students in too many hours of extracurricular activities and limiting free unstructured playtime may do more harm than good (Levine, 2006). How much is too much? In our survey results, we found that when high school students participated in very high amounts of extracurriculars during the week (over 15–20 hours), they had more emotional problems such as depression and anxiety, slept less, and experienced higher stress levels than those doing fewer hours of extracurricular activities (Conner & Pope, 2013a). Dr. David Elkind (2007), one of the country's most respected experts on play, recommends that kids have around the same amount of structured playtime, such as time for extracurricular activities, as unstructured playtime, such as time to shoot hoops or hang out with friends.

In fact, friends are of the utmost importance to tweens and teens and understandably so (Berscheid, 2003; Gifford-Smith & Brownell, 2003). Making and sustaining friendships is an important part of adolescents' overall social and emotional adjustment (Buhrmester, 1990); by interacting with peers, teens begin to form their own identities. Ideally, the majority of the time teens spend with their friends should be in person, but we know from recent research that some (or much) teen interaction may take place via mobile phones and social media. The Pew Research Project found that texting is now the most common form of communication teens have with their friends (Lenhart, Ling, Campbell, & Purcell, 2010). Pew researchers also found that the percentage of teens using social media rose from 55 percent in 2006 to 81 percent in 2012. Though it is clear that the use of social media and texting is on the rise, the research is not as well-developed concerning the right amount of time for kids to spend on social media and on the quality of the friendships that are formed and maintained online (Bargh & McKenna, 2004). What we do know is that teens are particularly susceptible to peer pressure and have lower abilities to self-regulate than adults; therefore, social media can pose real risks to teens, including cyberbullying, sexting, and the negative influences of online "friends" and advertisers (O'Keefe & Clarke-Pearson, 2011). Though many teens report that they feel less shy, more confident, and more popular when they use social media, most teens say that they prefer face-to-face communication and recognize some of the trade-offs when using social media (Common Sense Media, 2012).

With this in mind, we recommend that free playtime for this age group include time with friends, but parents and teachers should emphasize that the majority of this time should take place face-to-face rather than via social media. We recommend that teachers discuss the pros and cons of social media with kids as well as ask parents — especially those with preschool and elementary aged children, tweens, and young teens — to monitor online activities. One suggestion teachers might make is for parents and kids to remove all social media equipment (phones, tablets, computers, televisions, and so on) from bedrooms at nighttime, and to keep most social media activity in a public place, such as a living room or kitchen, where an adult can monitor more easily. And, of course, parents and kids need to be sure they are not overscheduling extracurricular activities. We offer the timewheel tool in Figure 8.1 as one way to track how much time each kid is spending on daily activities and where some balancing work needs to be done.

Finally, we encourage schools to build in time for play for kids of all ages. Along with creating more time for student-centered, project-based learning in which students

Figure 8.1 Timewheel

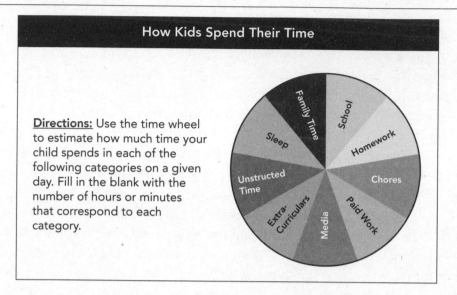

have some say over what they do, several schools are utilizing design labs or maker fairs where students can create and build projects of their choice in their free time. In addition, some of our Challenge Success schools have been planning specific times for joyful, unstructured activities that promote face-to-face interaction and playtime to help alleviate student stress at particularly intense moments during the year. For instance, some middle and high schools host spirit weeks or other fun traditions just before or after implementing standardized testing or after midterms or final exams.

Downtime

The "D" in our PDF stands for downtime. As we showed in Chapter Two on scheduling, running from class to class followed by running from activity to activity is exhausting for adults and kids alike. Kids especially need downtime throughout the day for general physical and emotional health and well-being (Larson & Kleiber, 1993). We define downtime as time that is not focused on structured play or academics; rather, it is time to reflect and to do nothing much—literally. That might mean listening to music, reading a book, watching a television show, or spending time outside in nature. As we discussed earlier in this chapter, we know there are good reasons to be concerned about screen time—both the quality and quantity—but a moderate amount of screen time, in which kids play a video game, watch a show, or check in on social media, may be a good way for kids (and adults) to relax before getting started on homework or heading out to the next activity.

Sleep is an obvious component of downtime for all ages, and as we have already noted, many kids just don't get enough of it. The American Academy of Pediatrics and other health organizations have documented the relationship between sleep deprivation and ADHD, headaches, depression, obesity, and other health problems across childhood and adolescence. According to the National Sleep Foundation (2015), children ages 6 to 13 years old need 9 to 11 hours a night of sleep, and over half don't get the recommended amount. Teens need at least 8 to 10 hours of sleep each night, and 80 percent don't get this much. In our research, students reported, on average, that they got between six and seven hours of sleep on a typical weeknight, well under the amount they need (Galloway et al., 2013; National Sleep Foundation, 2006).

A typical teen has a lot going on, both in and out of school, and particularly within his or her body as puberty takes place. Because of this busy time developmentally, teens need rest and downtime for physical and mental health as they mature and begin to form their own identities. They need time to reflect and seek answers to some big questions: Who am I? What kind of person do I want to be? In the busy hustle and bustle of six or seven classes, extracurricular activities, social lives, and family obligations, this important reflection time often gets overlooked. So the next time you see a high school student asleep at his desk or a middle school student staring into space, consider how exhausting it can be to be a teen today. Educate parents to enforce bedtime routines and to encourage enough downtime throughout the day. Sometimes when a teenager is lying on her bed after school, with earbuds in, singing at the top of her lungs—not looking like she is doing anything productive—that actually might be the best way for her to spend 20 to 30 minutes. And even though it might be torture for parents to watch this—knowing the kid has at least two hours of homework to do, a math test to study for, and a two-hour volleyball practice ahead (or a two-hour shift to fulfill at a paid job)—we urge them to resist interrupting this valuable time. After a brief respite, the teen will likely be more productive and, more important, will have found time to debrief and consolidate her thoughts (Carey, 2014).

We also urge schools to consider ways to build in more downtime throughout the school day. In Chapter Two we discuss late starts and longer breaks and lunch periods as important ways to increase downtime in school. Teachers can also schedule more time for reflection in their classes, and build in brief breaks before switching to new units or topics.

Family Time

Finally, it's important for adults and students to know that family time is a significant protective factor. When kids are part of a family unit that spends time together, they are more likely to feel supported, safe, and loved unconditionally (Hofferth & Sandberg, 2001). This holds true for kids of all ages and in all kinds of families. Recent research has shown that kids from preschool to twelfth grade benefit when they have regular family meals together (Fulkerson et al., 2006). Specifically, Fulkerson et al. found that the frequency of family dinners was associated with a variety of positive aspects of development, including an increase in cooperation and getting along with others, higher expectations, a more positive sense of family values, and a commitment to learning. These authors as well as others found that family time was associated with fewer high-risk behaviors such as substance abuse and delinquency, and lower rates of depression, eating disorders, and antisocial behavior. Other studies found that family rituals and traditions were associated with positive mental health outcomes as well as positive identity formation for adolescents and increased marital satisfaction for the parents within the family unit (for a review, see Fiese et al., 2002). Maybe it's a family movie or game night, a regular Saturday morning hike, or cheering your favorite sports team—traditions and rituals like these and regular family meals help to build the support and connection kids need. We know that juggling multiple work schedules and activities can be difficult, but when you make time for family members to be together and create a safe home base, you send a message that your child is loved and supported no matter what.

How can schools support family time? Teachers can limit homework assigned over vacations and holiday breaks to allow for more family time, and they can assign a few low-stakes, family-based projects each year, such as a biology assignment researching a family's medical history or genetic family tree, to help build family connections. Similarly, as we show in Chapter Seven, teachers can help promote a caring climate at school, similar to a safe home base, as a source of support for kids. When done well, advisories, tutorials, teacher-student conferences throughout the year, and informal times to build faculty-student relationships can all promote family-like relations at school and increase a student's feeling of belonging.

SPREADING THE WORD ABOUT PDF

We encourage schools to work with students, faculty, and parents to help spread the word about PDF and why it's important. For best results, schools will need a concerted, coordinated effort to make sure all stakeholders understand the importance of student health and well-being. We have helped schools design robust parent education programs, student wellness programs (described in the previous chapter), and professional development workshops for faculty. The remainder of this chapter will highlight strategies and tools you can use to make sure everyone in the school community is aware of the developmental needs of kids and that as many stakeholders as possible are on board to make the policy and program changes necessary to help students thrive.

When Kids Talk, We Should Listen: Tools to Promote Dialogue Between Adults and Kids

Since the inception of Challenge Success, we have put kids at the center of all that we do. They experience firsthand the stress of school and the pressure to achieve, yet we often forget to include them in our conversations about school improvement. Good CEOs take listening tours on factory floors to learn how to make processes work better, and good educators should do the same. That is the reasoning behind our requirement to have at least two student members on each Challenge Success school team, and that is why we recommend that schools survey their students at the beginning of their work with us and throughout the change process. We need to hear from the kids themselves about what is and isn't working at their schools, and then the kids need to have a say throughout the action planning process about the best ways to alleviate overload and increase engagement. The students often come up with ideas and suggestions that the adults might miss. In one school, for example, the adults were planning to change the schedule and build in more time for active learning. To do this, they planned to shorten lunchtime. The student members of the Challenge Success team immediately spoke up and warned the adults that most kids would not be able to make it through the cafeteria line if they allotted only 25 minutes for lunch. Together, the adults and kids worked on an alternate plan that would allow enough time for lunch but also allow for some longer academic periods.

In addition to soliciting advice from a few students on your team or task force and periodically surveying the entire student body, we have found a few other tools to be extremely effective for fostering communication between adults and students: Fishbowls and Dialogue Nights. We briefly summarize them here; you'll find step-by-step directions for both tools in the Appendix.

Fishbowls

The Fishbowl format offers a unique opportunity for faculty to listen in as a small group of thoughtful students share their experiences and feelings on a variety of topics, from college pressure to cheating to communicating with teachers. Students sit in the center of a circle and weigh in on the issues that concern them most at the school and ways to make effective changes, while faculty members or parents sit in the outer circle listening silently. Schools select students who represent different grade levels and come from diverse backgrounds to participate in the Fishbowl, and they hire or select a skilled facilitator to lead the process. Students typically meet with the facilitator in advance of the Fishbowl so that they fully understand the purpose of the event and are comfortable with the kinds of questions that they may be asked. After the session, the adults participate in debrief sessions to discuss reactions and work with the students to generate ideas for future school changes. As one faculty member noted after a Fishbowl at her school: "That was so powerful. We need more open, honest discussions like this."

Dialogue Nights

Another effective tool to help adults and students listen to one another is the Dialogue Night. Dialogue Nights bring adults and students together to participate in an open discussion about the issues related to teen stress and pressure. The discussion is prompted by a student-performed skit that depicts typical student-teacher or student-parent interactions. Schools can use some of the skits written by Challenge Success students (see the Appendix for sample skits), or they can have students create their own scenes to act out during the evening. After each short skit is performed, adults and students break into small groups to discuss the issues raised in the skit. Participants are asked: What hidden or unintended messages did you hear? What messages can we identify that can easily be misconstrued? Were there any healthy messages in the skit? If you were to rewind the skit, what suggestions do you have that would foster better communication?

Teachers, parents, and students all sit at tables to discuss the skits together—though to promote a more honest discussion, we suggest that parents and kids from the same family don't sit at the same table. After the last skit is performed, we usually separate the students from the adults and ask each group to brainstorm words, phrases, and actions that can be used to decrease stress and improve student life. As one student noted after a successful Dialogue Night:

> It was a really nice opportunity for us to come together and talk about the stress, which I think is the first step ... Even though it's always there, and we are complaining about it, we never actually dig into the topic and figure out why we are stressing to begin with. One of the cool things that we did during Dialogue Nights is we split up with parents and teachers in one room, and then all the students in the other, and

we just talked about coping strategies and like what we could try to do to eliminate [stress] and what we want to tell our parents, and vice versa. And then they [the adults] told us things they wanted us to know, things they thought would make it easier for us. I feel like if everyone did that sort of thing, it would be fantastic. It's not something that will be easy. I feel like if we start now with the groundwork—it'll be better in the next few years or so. (Yasmeen Sherman, Los Altos High School)

Another student added,

"There's a lot that I took away from [the Dialogue Night], and a lot I thought other people could possibly be taking away from it too. You don't have to be stressed all the time—which was not something that had ever occurred to me before I was involved in this program. To be honest, I never even thought of it that way—that you don't have to be stressed all the time to accomplish what you want to accomplish or to be happy". (Lauren Biglow, Los Altos High School)

Parents Are Our "Students" Too: Strategies for Successful Parent Education

As a teacher at a Challenge Success conference recently said: "Our job used to be teaching kids; now it is also teaching parents"—and like it or not, she's right. If we truly want to see healthier and more engaged kids, we need to get the parents on board. Parents need to understand the steps the school is taking to reduce stress and improve teaching and learning, and they need to learn how their actions at home can impact what is happening at school. We have helped schools create a series of parent education events throughout the year, team with other like-minded schools to bring in national level speakers, and provide intensive parenting classes and workshops. As researchers, we know that change is more likely to happen when ideas are consistently conveyed and reinforced. While single night, one-off parent education talks can be useful, we believe that schools do better when they offer regular, well-constructed parent education series and/or workshops (Fine, 1989). Admittedly, this can be expensive and resource intensive. Parent education groups, like Common Ground and Speakers for Parents Educators and Knowledge (SPEAK) in the Bay Area, link private schools together so that they can afford to bring in well-known speakers on a variety of topics throughout the year and divvy up the administrative volunteer efforts. We've also seen some large public schools, such as Menlo-Atherton High School, work to get grants to support a speaker series, and we've seen local parochial schools organize a "community of concern" by creating a theme-based grade-level curriculum with mandatory parental attendance. We describe these in detail in the following case studies.

Menlo-Atherton High School, Atherton, California

In 2004, when Charlene Margot was a parent at Menlo-Atherton High School (M-A) and a member of the Challenge Success school team (then known as SOS: Stressed-Out Students Project), she began a parent education series to address several concerns. She knew that local private schools often brought expert speakers in to present to their communities, but public schools such as hers, especially those with large numbers of low-income and non-English-speaking parents, did not have access to these speakers. Charlene's interest in and awareness of parent education had much to do with her background in teaching and education. She knew that several other parent groups in her district were working on various aspects of parent education, such as sleep education and drug and alcohol education, and she thought it was time to pull all these efforts together under a common "umbrella" organization. She sought approval from Principal Matt Zito and his administration to create a robust parent education series funded by the PTA.

During the first year of the program, the primary focus was on reducing student stress. Challenge Success Cofounder Denise Pope spoke to parents about the impact of stress on student health and engagement. Denise returned the following year to talk to parents about the results of the school-wide survey that Challenge Success conducted and to show parents the high levels of stress and sleep deprivation that students reported in the data. Talks on sleep, mental health, drug and alcohol use, suicide, college admission, and other issues related to the "whole child" rounded out the program. In addition, for each of the first six years, Charlene kicked off the school year with M-A 101, an icebreaker event where Principal Matt Zito met with parent groups in the morning or evening so that they could hear about the history of M-A and his plans for the year. This "nuts and bolts" discussion filled a need for early parent involvement and helped integrate new parents into the school. Charlene also offered Spanish translation services, childcare, and refreshments at her parent education events to encourage as many parents as possible to attend.

The now well-established parent education series has spread to each of the three high schools in the district and reflects the initiatives of each school. Prior to the start of the school year, Charlene meets with each principal to talk about themes and to generate a list of possible speakers. She works with principals to set dates for four or five programs at each school that fit with the overall school calendar, and she secures funding from each school's PTA/PTSA, school foundation, and a grant from a local health care district to cover speaker honoraria, expenses, and her salary as program director. From her first small program in 2004, the M-A series has grown over the years to reach over 10,000 parents at the three district high schools.

Keeping this program up and running takes a lot of hard work. The coordinator works many hours each week to ensure the program's success. As Charlene notes, "If you take your foot off the gas for two weeks, you've lost the promotion window." She promotes events and creates a buzz with heavy marketing efforts such as school e-newsletters, website blurbs, and email pushes, and spends time working closely with the speakers to ensure smooth logistics and successful presentations. Charlene also believes that the parent education coordinator must be a well-connected and respected school leader. She originally served as a parent member of the shared decision-making site council at M-A and was a former teacher, so parents, faculty, and administrators alike knew and trusted her. Charlene also highlights the importance of bringing in more of the parents' voice by regularly surveying the community about future topics and evaluating each speaker to learn parent reactions and suggestions to improve the program.

Junipero Serra High School, San Mateo, California

Mary Dowden, French teacher at the all-boys, Catholic Junipero Serra High School and member of the Serra High Challenge Success team, helped to develop the Community of Concern parent education program in 2002. The program began because faculty and community members at Serra felt the need to build better communication with parents and wanted to partner with parents on issues concerning adolescent behavior. They saw the mandatory parent education approach as a way to get all parents on the same page as the students and teachers concerning key topics such as stress, drugs and alcohol, and media use, and they knew that high school parents were especially difficult to reach without an established program that required all parents to attend.

(continued)

Originally, the program was set up to have a four-year curriculum where each year would be devoted to a particular theme: freshman year was devoted to drug and alcohol education, sophomore year focused on stress and mental health, junior year focused on media safety and the digital footprint, and senior year focused on the moral compass and transition to college. Each year, every student and faculty member would hear a presentation on the grade-level topic during a student assembly and faculty meeting during the day, and then parents would be required to attend the same lecture that evening. The idea was to educate all stakeholders and ask them to weigh in on specific ways the school could help to support healthy practices in each of the four areas of concern.

For each topic, a team of faculty members created a handout for parents and students and a discussion guide and signature page to track attendance. After each student assembly, students would typically meet with homeroom teachers to have small group discussions about the presentation. Through student surveys, the committee learned that the students greatly valued these opportunities to discuss real-world concerns in smaller, more intimate settings, and they appreciated having a voice in ways the schools could make changes to improve their education. Teachers would also meet together at a faculty meeting to discuss the presentations and find ways to integrate more information on these topics into their classroom curricula.

Initially, Serra partnered with two other Catholic schools in the area to pool resources, share costs for the speakers, build community between the schools, and, of primary importance, to allow parents a choice of three different dates each year to attend the lectures. Parents could attend a lecture at any of the three schools each year to fulfill the attendance requirement. Schools also videotaped lectures for parents who could not make any of the three dates, and they even offered an online component for the drug and alcohol lecture in freshman year. The schools sent email blasts, blurbs in the weekly school newsletters, and several reminders to alert parents of the events well ahead of time. At Serra, Mary was in charge of following up with families who failed to meet the requirement. She tried emailing and calling these families each year, but after a few years, the schools found it to be too time-consuming to track each family every year, and decided to make only two of the four presentations mandatory for parents (one during the freshman and sophomore years, and one during the junior and senior years).

The feedback from faculty, students, and parents on the evaluation forms was mostly positive. Parents appreciated hearing the same speakers that their students heard; they said they could use the information for family discussions. They also appreciated that the school was going above and beyond the standard academic curriculum to focus on student health and well-being, something that Serra makes a point of showing in their admission materials is a priority for the school. Mary affirmed that the program raised the level of awareness about these topics for the entire school community and led to further dialogue and knowledge. She noted that "The students and parents, especially right after [a speaker event], tend to be a lot more communicative about either the issues [from the presentation] or the problems that they are having [at home]," and that teachers and counselors received more questions from parents and students immediately after a presentation. "It's by raising the consciousness of the whole community that I feel like those students and parents feel like this is a safe place and [that they have the] opportunity to reach out and not feel judged."

Mary coordinated the entire program on top of her teaching load—which was not ideal and ultimately not sustainable. The logistics proved difficult for Mary to handle alone. She was a French teacher, not a school counselor or expert in these topic areas, and she felt underprepared to choose speakers and to write the handouts, even with the help of her faculty committee. Ultimately the school decided to assign an administrator to handle the parent education program and coordinate with the other schools. Mary recommended that the school spend much-needed time to vet new speakers and to work with faculty members to improve the quality of the post-speaker discussions with students. And she recommended that Serra find a dedicated time to host post-speaker discussions for students and parents. When Serra changed to a modified block schedule a few years later, the school included an activity period that is now used to accommodate the school assembly and small group discussion times, and the new coordinator continues to adapt the program in response to feedback from parents, students, and faculty members.

In both of these cases, it is clear that initiating and maintaining a successful parent education program at a school or district takes an enormous amount of time, resources, and hard work; however, we have seen the benefits to schools when they find ways to raise the money and find a champion or two to take this on. If starting a full program sounds a bit too daunting for your school, you can consider starting small with one or two evenings of discussion or distributing an interesting and provocative article before a back-to-school night to get folks talking. In the next section, we'll discuss other ways to help foster important community dialogue.

IT TAKES A VILLAGE: INTERACTIVE SCENARIOS AND SOCIAL MEDIA

In addition to working with schools to design their own parent education programs, we have developed several social media outlets and education scenarios that we use in our courses and workshops. As evidenced by the rapid growth of mommy- and daddy bloggers and social media advice columns for parents, we know that people want help when it comes to making key parenting decisions, and they crave community and safe venues for discussing these decisions. Parents and educators alike want easy-to-digest research—and they can turn to our white papers and "Do You Know" research fact sheets for this—but people also want specific advice and a place to share their divergent opinions on best practices concerning parenting.

Interactive Scenarios

At Challenge Success, we often rely on interactive scenarios in our work with parents, students, and faculty. Similar to the Dialogue Night skits mentioned earlier, we use interactive scenarios to pose sticky situations for folks to think through, weigh options, and practice resolving. We typically pose a scenario, let participants argue a bit about how best to handle it, and then offer different pieces of advice from experts in the area. We often say in these instances that there is no one right answer or one-size-fits-all response; thus we leave it to the parent or educator to weigh the different opinions heard along with the latest research, and then make a decision based on what might be best for a particular child in that particular situation at that particular time. As an example, we now have a tradition at our annual conference plenary sessions where we poll over 1,500 people on the spot via cell phones to weigh in on tough scenarios. This one is from our recent conference:

Question: Home Editor

Your sixth grader proudly shares with you a writing assignment into which she's put a lot of time and effort. The assignment also happens to be worth a lot of points. As you read it, you notice that it's very disjointed and lacking supporting evidence. What should you do?

We asked educators, parents, and middle and high school students to weigh in on the following options for what the parent ought to do in this situation:

1. Celebrate and offer positive feedback.
2. Have your child rewrite the essay.
3. Sit with your child and revise the essay together.
4. Revise the essay yourself.
5. Hire a writing tutor.

Figure 8.2 shows how the different audience members reacted. Interestingly, audience members disagreed on which answer might be the best in this scenario. The favored choice for educators (though by only a slim margin) was number 1: to have the parent offer praise and positive feedback. A large number of educators also selected answer number 3 (parent and child revise the essay together), but educators also selected the other answer choices as well, including hire a tutor. Parents and students both showed preferences for answer number 3 (revise the essay together), though parents and students also liked answers number 1 and 2, and a few chose number 5, to hire a tutor as

Figure 8.2 Conference Scenario Results

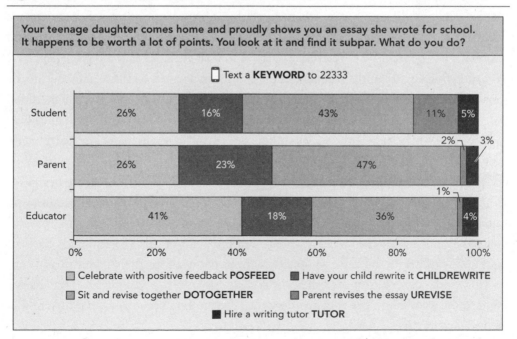

well. Finally, several students (and a few educators and parents) chose answer number 4, in which the parent revises the essay for the child.

In response to the audience poll, our panel of experts—including Dr. Madeline Levine, Dr. Denise Pope, Dr. Wendy Mogul, Dave Evans, and Harker School junior Naomi Molin—discussed the pros and cons of each reply. On the one hand, it was made clear that the student *proudly* shared the essay with the parent. That seems to be a key word, and if the parent criticizes the essay strongly, the student may be upset and possibly so hurt by the reaction that she may decide not to share any writing with the parent again. Worse yet, she could decide that she is a bad writer and lose motivation for future writing assignments. On the other hand, it was made clear that the assignment is worth a lot of points. Shouldn't the parent warn the student that the writing is subpar and save the student some embarrassment of turning in poor writing—especially when the student thinks that she has done well on the assignment? Also, if it is worth a lot of points, doesn't the parent have an obligation to help the student do her best possible work on the assignment? As the poll shows, there is no easy answer here.

In this case, we have heard teachers caution that too much criticism can lead to the negative results just described; this student may lose future motivation for writing if the parent critiques too harshly and demands a rewrite. Other writing teachers advocate that parents first ask the student what exactly she is proud of in the piece, and then ask if she thinks there are parts that can be improved. This may lead the student to decide on her own that she wants to revise some parts. And if she decides that the piece is perfect as is, then the parent should probably let the child turn it in and let the teacher decide the worth of the piece and whether further revision is needed. Other educators suggest that the parent ask the student to read the piece aloud. This may trigger the student to hear some of the errors and fix them. Still others argue that schoolwork—and particularly assignments like this—should really be assessed by the teacher and the student together, not the parents. They believe that parents should act as cheerleaders and advocates for kids, but that parents should leave the writing instruction (and the math instruction, and so on) to the educators. For instance, it may be that this is a rough draft of an assignment to be finished in class. It may also be that the focus of this assignment is on writing fluency or practicing topic sentences without the need for the student to add supporting evidence. Without the full knowledge of the purpose and intent of the assignment, the parent might actually be doing more harm than good by asking the child to go back and revise.

Surprisingly, as shown in Figure 8.2, when we give this scenario to teachers and ask what they want parents to do in this situation, their responses vary, even within the same department! If the teachers aren't clear on the right way to handle this scenario, then what are the parents to do? We suggest that before responding to student work at home in general, parents should ask the teacher about his or her expectation for parental feedback on homework. What does the teacher want the parents' role to be vis-à-vis homework? Ideally, teachers should provide this information in a handout at the beginning of the school year or back-to-school night to avoid potential mishaps at home.

As you can see, these scenarios are powerful ways to spark dialogue among stakeholders and educate parents (and student and teachers) about how to react to everyday situations in order to avoid or lessen unnecessary stress and tension. When you can predict, talk through, and resolve these kinds of issues ahead of time, you are more likely to build an informed community with more aligned actions between home and school.

Using Social Media

Another way to spark dialogue and build community buy-in is to utilize the power of social media at your school. At Challenge Success, we have active Facebook and Twitter followers who react to our daily articles and advice blogs. Cofounder Madeline Levine, author of *Teach Your Children Well* (2012), writes a regular blog on "Courageous Parenting" that educators can use to help teach parents about the many paths to success. In this sample from one of Madeline's recent posts, she encourages parents to keep the big picture in mind and recognize that sometimes their well-meaning actions may lead to the opposite results. Educators can send blogs like this one to parents via school newsletters or email and can use articles like this to help create a unified culture of parenting and educating for student health and well-being.

Regaining Gratitude This Thanksgiving: A Blog Post by Madeline Levine

Ever notice how ironic it is that the holiday that's designed to make us feel serenely grateful for all that we have — our family, our friends, our prosperous life here in the land of turkey and maize and cranberry salad — falls right in the middle of the most hectic, exhausting time of the year?

Think about it. Our kids are burned out from tests and endless pages of homework. One school project follows closely on the heels of another. Sports and other extracurricular events have left all of us exhausted. Meanwhile, Hanukkah and Christmas (with all their economic, social and familial obligations) loom forebodingly on the horizon.

So how can we pause for a day in the midst of all the chaos and stress—not to mention the weird family dynamics that must be navigated over the Thanksgiving table—and just feel *thankful*?

The complete answer to that question could fill a book! (And if you know a good one, I'd love the name of it!) But because parenting is my area of expertise, I will zero in on our (complicated, stressful, worry-filled) relationship with our children.

Twenty-first century parents fret. It's what we do. We wring our hands over our kids' grades, their social development, their performance on the playing field, their future.

Yet it's been proven again and again that all of our over-parenting behaviors—our bribes, our threats, our micromanagement, our insistence that kids do more, better, faster—not only don't work, they have the opposite effect. Our frantic efforts to give our kids "an edge" are harming rather than helping them.

And so, based on the knowledge that anxiety and gratitude can't co-exist, let's all just relax and trust the research. By research I mean the reams of solid scientific evidence that proves backing off a little is the best thing we can do for our kids.

Below are 10 resolutions that I originally wrote for the beginning of the school year. In the spirit of Thanksgiving I have repurposed them here. I think they speak to the mindset that keeps us from living in the moment and truly savoring the all-too-short time we really have with our kids.

Ten Resolutions for Becoming a More Grateful Parent

I will make sure my child gets a full night's sleep. Kids need between nine and 11 hours a night. Sleep deprivation impairs concentration, memory, and the ability to accurately read emotional cues. It makes kids crabby and compromises their ability to learn.

I will remember that I am a parent, not a CEO. Results are down the line, not at the end of the quarter. This means the occasional "B" or "C" will not break your child's future prospects. Stop catastrophizing. You won't see the final fruits of your parenting until your child is grown and gone.

I will remember the success trajectory is a squiggle ... not a straight line. Few of us become successful by simply putting one foot in front of the other. Most of us encounter a multitude of twists, turns, direction changes, and stops on the way to our goals.

I will love the child in front of me. Appreciate and be thankful for your child's unique gifts. Children are talented in a multitude of different ways. See your child's particular talents clearly.

I will not push my child to be perfect. Besides genetics, perfectionism is the strongest predictor of clinical depression. Life is full of mistakes, imperfect days, and human failings. Kids need to learn how to cope with these inevitabilities. They (and you) need to be able to feel happiness and gratitude in the face of imperfection.

I will not do for my child what he can do for himself. This kills motivation and the ability to innovate. Both are missing from too many young people in today's workforce.

I will not do for my child what she can *almost* do for herself. At one time your child could almost walk. Now she can walk. Enough said.

I will not confuse my needs with my child's needs. This is the most toxic manifestation of overparenting. Get a hobby or a therapist instead.

I will honor the importance of PDF (Playtime, Downtime, and Family Time). Don't overschedule. Kids need time to play, daydream, and just hang out. It's in these precious "between" times that crucial developmental tasks are accomplished.

I will value my own (adult) life. Being a happy, fulfilled, and yes, grateful adult makes you a better parent. It's one of the best gifts you can give your child. It makes adulthood look like something worth striving for.

When we observe Thanksgiving the way I believe we're meant to, we realize that life is truly rich and bountiful. As parents, we've been given life's greatest gift. Learning to appreciate and honor that gift may mean breaking the culturally sanctioned patterns that cause us to unknowingly damage our kids even as we seek to make life better for them.

Overparenting is about anxiously exerting control. Gratitude is about accepting what we've been given and noticing the joy that it brings. This Thanksgiving weekend, let's try to do less of the former and more of the latter. And from here out, let's try to guide and teach our kids without seeking to force them into the mold that we (and society) believe they should conform to. When you can master that balance you will become a perpetually grateful parent.

As more parents are educated about PDF and ways they can improve their parenting, educators find they have more partners than adversaries at home, and the students benefit from hearing more consistent messages at school and at home. Of course, there is only so much a school can do to teach parents better parenting habits, and vice versa; parents can serve as advocates for positive changes at school, but they can push only so hard. The more that all parties are educated about the developmental needs of kids and all parties strive for consistent communication and coplanning, the more likely it becomes that real, lasting changes will take place.

Chapter **NINE**

Keeping Momentum for Positive School Change

In this book we have cited specific research studies, depicted real-life cases, and offered lots of advice on the best ways to effect change at your school to improve student engagement and well-being. Our research and experience tell us that, whatever changes you pursue, your school will need to involve all stakeholders; develop a well thought-out plan of action; deliver high-quality comprehensive professional development and workshops to teachers, parents, and students; and practice patience. We know the time spent laying the foundation for the policy or practice changes and anticipating and carefully navigating the potential obstacles will pay off with a smoother implementation process. Now that you have read this book, you may be ready and raring to get started. Before you do, however, we offer one last chapter with advice on handling some of the naysayers and the negative reactions as well as the distractions and competing demands you may face.

DEALING WITH NAYSAYERS AND COMPETING DEMANDS

In our conference workshops we use a dramatic skit to help team members prepare for their community's reaction when they return to their school sites, all pumped up with exciting new ideas to explore and changes to pursue. In our skit, our motivated team leader, Principal Jim, returns to his high school after the Challenge Success Fall Conference. He is literally pumped up, with balloons stuffed into his shirt to represent his excitement. He enthusiastically begins sharing the new vision for the school with other stakeholders as he pulls out balloons that are labeled as follows:

- Survey?

- Homework policy?

- Parent education?

- Block schedule?

- Honor code?

- Wellness classes?

- Advisory?

- Eliminate final exams?

- Limit AP courses?

Then a series of school community members (other workshop participants) come to his office, give a "push back" statement, and burst a balloon each time they speak:

- Overwhelmed assistant principal says, "We just don't have time for this. We've got more pressing priorities, such as focusing on Common Core."

- Honors teacher says, "Your new plans sound 'anti-achievement.' We have high standards here, and we shouldn't apologize for them or water down our curriculum."

- Concerned college counselor says, "This all sounds nice in theory. But we may end up putting our kids at a disadvantage as they compete for admissions."

- Veteran school board member says, "Will our test scores go down because of this? We have our good reputation to maintain."

- Stressed student with demanding classes and a heavy extracurricular load says, "I'm not stressed!"

- New teacher says, "I am already stressed with everything else I need to do, including trying to flip my classroom and integrate the iPads, and now you are adding this to my plate?"

- Sympathetic teacher says, "I agree we need to change the school climate and that things are too stressful for kids and faculty here, but there are too many forces causing this that are beyond our control."

- Angry teacher says, "Your approach is wrong. Stress *is* a problem, but it's the parents' fault: they over-schedule their kids and focus on grades instead of learning."

- Angry parent says, "Your approach is wrong. Stress *is* a problem, but it's the school's fault: there is way too much homework and test pressure."

Alas, what is poor Principal Jim to do?

We then walk through a series of scenarios and role-plays to help address some of these naysayers and the distractions that can get in the way of making progress towards the school's action plan. Here are some of the suggestions from the workshop.

Make Time

Many of us have grand expectations for school improvement and then realize we never have time to implement our plans because we are too busy putting out fires day to day. Planning the kinds of long-lasting changes addressed in this book takes ample time and energy. Make sure you have a multistakeholder team to help you put a plan in place. Schedule team meetings well in advance, and make it a priority to stick to the schedule. Many teams benefit from meetings that occur once a month or at least once a quarter. And don't forget to include the students when you set the meeting times. For best results, aim for regular meetings at times that work for all of the team members.

Align and Combine Your Initiatives

When possible, fold your action plan into an existing school program or task force so as not to create one more thing on your growing to-do list. Some schools benefit from connecting this work to their accreditation processes; others align some of these changes with strategic plans. For instance, many of our schools are working on integrating new technology into the classroom, such as implementing one-to-one devices, flipped classroom models, and a host of other new applications. When used effectively, education technology has the potential to help level the playing field, increase motivation and engagement, and allow for a more learner-centered and self-paced environment; but for these outcomes to occur, schools need careful planning, stakeholder buy-in, professional development, and strong leadership (Bebell & O'Dwyer, 2014) — exactly what we suggest is necessary for all of the policy and practice changes we propose in this book. How do you implement a change to ensure that it truly adds value and will improve student learning and understanding instead of becoming yet another distraction? As you work on a new initiative, ask how it might impact and enhance the SPACE framework (introduced in Chapter One). Does this initiative help to increase student engagement?

Can it be used to foster more project-based learning and alternative assessment practices? Does it impact the school climate in a positive way? How does it affect the pace of the school day or students' workload? In short, you can use the SPACE framework as a guide as you decide which new policies and practices to pursue. When faculty, students, and parents see how your action plan aligns with other initiatives, they are more likely to buy into it and be supportive and are less likely to suffer from school reform fatigue and burnout.

Embrace the Curmudgeons and the Eeyores

Every school has a few folks on the faculty and in the community who are as pessimistic as the *Winnie-the-Pooh* character of Eeyore or are surly curmudgeons who want to simply close their classroom doors and be left alone. One of our principals decided to put one of her most outspoken and negative faculty members on her Challenge Success team. He was adamantly opposed to changing to a modified block schedule, and his negativity was spreading throughout his department. Once she convinced him to join the team, he began to hear other opinions from students, teachers, and parents who supported the change. Along with other team members, he educated himself by reading the research and visiting other schools that had adopted new schedules. At the end of the pilot year, he told his principal, "I was completely against this initiative from the start, but, you know, I was wrong. All of the things I worried about never came to fruition. I thought teaching the long blocks would be terrible for the kids and really hard on the teachers, but I see the benefits now. I can get a lot more done at a deeper level."

Sometimes the teachers, parents, or students are resisting for reasons you did not expect. A good leader must listen carefully to understand the real sources of resistance and pain points. For instance, the Menlo-Atherton principal was surprised to learn that some teachers opposed the late start because it would impact their commute times. He had not considered this concern when he proposed the time change. Once you learn some of the underlying reasons behind the negativity, you can validate stakeholders' feelings and work to address the issues openly and directly, as Matt was able to do at Menlo-Atherton. You may also want to enlist some of the more influential faculty, parent, and student leaders to help promote the change. They have built-in credibility and can be true assets to help tailor messages appropriately to the different stakeholders.

Take Advantage of Opt-in and Pilot Programs

As several of the cases here reveal, sometimes it can be advantageous to allow interested teachers to opt in as opposed to mandating a new policy or process school-wide. Carola at Forest Ridge started with just a few interested teachers who were willing to experiment with alternative assessments instead of final exams, and this eventually spread to the entire English department. Sharon at JLS had similar success when she allowed teachers to opt in to an alternative homework policy, and Notre Dame Belmont made sure that the first year of the new schedule was considered a pilot—not a permanent change—until the school had time to test it and tweak it sufficiently.

Of course, at some point, school leaders will need to take the plunge and implement a new policy or practice. One of our principals admitted that she never reached full approval and consensus for the schedule change, but eventually decided that she had "more teachers at the front end of the train than in the back…and at some point, you just have to decide that you have enough support to move forward."

Gather Data and Regular Feedback

Throughout this book we have urged team leaders to encourage dialogue through each step of the change process, to be transparent, and to be open to learning and hearing new ideas. Many stakeholders hold on tight to personal beliefs that may fly in the face of the research data you collect. The student who believes she can survive on six hours of sleep, the teacher who believes that all the stress and pressure is the fault of the helicopter parents, the parent who insists that homework rates are skyrocketing each year—each of these stakeholders needs further education on the issues and may experience a steep learning curve. Local and national data can help to convince folks of the depth of the problem and the benefits of different solutions. Use the research from this book, along with the information you gather from your own community via surveys, polls, dialogue nights, and shadow days to bolster support for your plan. Then be open to hearing that a new policy or initiative isn't working exactly as planned. Use this feedback to learn from mistakes and try a new approach.

Calm Fears about Colleges and Test Scores

A common theme in the "pumped up" skit described earlier and in our work with schools and families is a worry that the changes made in accordance with the SPACE framework will negatively impact student achievement. The arguments sound something like this: If we cut back on homework or reduce our AP offerings, or if we aim for depth over breadth in our curriculum, or if we eliminate final exams or take time doing mindfulness exercises or host advisories, aren't we going to see a drop in student test scores and college acceptances? The short answer is no. Throughout this book we cite research that shows the positive effects on student achievement for each component of the SPACE framework. We also have data from our Challenge Success schools that affirms these positive results. For instance, one Challenge Success school, after implementing a new bell schedule, advisory periods, and moving midterm exams to before winter break, tracked student grades, SAT/ACT results, and college admission rates and saw no drop in student achievement, college acceptances, or standardized test scores. Another school made substantial changes to homework and the AP curriculum, and reported that their students' scores on the AP exams went up in classes where teachers cut homework in half (Conner, Pope, & Galloway, 2009). And these schools and others in our program showed positive results in areas such as student health, sleep, academic integrity, and engagement in learning (Challenge Success, 2014).

As for fears regarding college admission, parents and students may be excited to learn about some recent "disruptions" in the higher education field. Over the past several years, we have seen the growth of massive open online courses (MOOCs) that offer students more accessible, flexible, and affordable opportunities for higher education, and we have seen some innovative changes in the college admission process. Many colleges and universities are exploring the possibilities for a different kind of undergraduate experience. They are asking, for example: Why is the undergraduate experience a four-year event? With student debt levels at historic rates, does a blended undergraduate and graduate school experience make sense? Should students take some basic courses online before they come to campus? How can students be better prepared for the world after graduation? Should internships and global programs be required for graduation? Should higher education take place over a series of many years, with times for stepping out and getting real-world experience, then looping back for more coursework to enhance this experience?

As colleges and universities explore what makes for a compelling and engaging undergraduate experience, they are starting to reexamine the kinds of applicants they hope to attract. Some universities are reconsidering how much weight they put on standardized test scores, since these are often biased or unreliable (Medina & Neill, 1988). Many are adopting test-optional policies, whereby students are not required to take standardized tests for admission. Other colleges and universities have stopped requiring students to submit high school transcripts and personal essays. Instead, they ask potential applicants to write college-level analytical essays based on a set of rigorous academic articles, or send in short video essays, or submit a portfolio of their high school work. This allows students who may be extremely motivated and bright, but for whatever reasons do not have a high GPA or do not score well on standardized tests (or prefer not to take them), to have a chance to be accepted to a selective school.

Parents and students are often relieved to hear that there is a college spot available for every student who wants to attend. Though experts measure "selectivity" differently, several agree that out of over 4,000 colleges and universities in the United States, there are at least 200 that can be considered "very competitive to most competitive," and they urge students to consider the full range of college opportunities when deciding where to apply (Hoxby, 2009). As universities continue to reduce their reliance on test scores and grade point averages and seek other ways to assess applicants, high school students can focus more on mastering important skills and content necessary to succeed in college and in life after college—content that we have emphasized in the SPACE framework presented here.

THE BOTTOM LINE

Though none of us knows what new innovations or disruptions may take place in the future, we are confident that the developmental needs of kids will remain constant. No matter what the latest technology may offer or what the next generation of school standards may cover, students still have some basic needs that must be fulfilled for learning to take place. The emerging field of "brain-based learning" confirms this. As we learn more from science about the human brain and the connection between the mind and the body, we understand the importance of focusing on strategies, such as those in the SPACE framework, that foster more intrinsic motivation and personalize the learning experience for students. Since learning depends in part on the student's physical state, personal comfort, emotional health, mindset, and preferred learning style (Carey, 2014; Dweck, 2006; Erlauer, 2003), schools need to focus more on educating students about health, stress management, and wellness, along with adapting curriculum and pedagogy that is engaging and relevant and that does not confuse rigor with load. What seems fundamental is that students need to feel safe and cared for in school; they need to be healthy, both physically and mentally, to be able to concentrate and focus in their classes; they need supportive teachers, mentors, parents, and peers who will cheer them on, encourage them to take risks, and help them learn from their mistakes; they need to see the value and relevance of what they are learning so that they are motivated and excited to work hard; and they need to learn the skills of communication, collaboration, adaptability, and critical thinking to be able to participate fully as active and ethical members of a global society.

We know that schools will pursue these goals in different ways, and that there is not one best way to achieve them. We hope that by sharing the SPACE framework, along with our research-based findings and lessons from case study schools, that we have motivated you to reflect on your own school policies and practices, and that you are inspired to begin the difficult but rewarding work needed to redesign your school so that every student can thrive.

Shadow Day, Fishbowls, and Dialogue Nights

SHADOW DAY

Contributions from Jane Lathrop Stanford Middle School, Palo Alto, California
Sharon Ofek, Principal

The following information is provided to support a school administrator, counselor, or teacher leader seeking to implement Shadow Day at their school. This information is offered as a recommended guideline and includes talking points for faculty and students about this process.

What Is a Shadow Day?

Shadow Day is an opportunity for teachers and administrators to shadow students to learn about the daily experience of attending school. Hosting a Shadow Day provides a snapshot of a student's school experience and a lens for teachers and administrators, enabling them to discuss potential variables contributing to student stress, such as homework, academic engagement, teacher care, and overall scheduling demands. The information collected helps to inform meaningful discussions among faculty members to address potential areas of concern.

Recommended Steps

1. Share with faculty information about and the protocol for Shadow Day. Facilitate a discussion about this suggested protocol (see "Recommended Talking Points — Faculty Meeting").

2. Ask teacher volunteers to participate as "shadow teachers." We encourage administrators to also shadow a student, so invite some of them as well.

3. Select students to be shadowed. These selected "shadow students" should reflect all grade levels, learning profiles, ethnicities, and genders.

4. Schedule a lunchtime meeting for selected students to learn about the process and rationale (see "Recommended Talking Points — Student Meeting").

5. Schedule Shadow Day — Have substitutes scheduled to provide release time for participating teachers.

6. Print selected student schedules to share with shadow teachers during a meeting.

7. Schedule a lunchtime or after-school meeting for shadow teachers and administrators and students to meet, review the student schedule, and determine a meeting place for Shadow Day. Ensure that all faculty and staff members are aware of the Shadow Day date.

8. Shadow Day! Confirm that substitutes are in place and all participating students and teachers meet prior to the starting bell.

9. At the end of the day, participating teachers and administrators receive the reflection sheet. An example of the reflection sheet, used by Jane Lathrop Stanford Middle School, is included here. You may use the worksheet provided or tailor your reflection worksheet based on specific areas on which you'd like teachers to focus.

10. Collect all completed reflection sheets and decide on a protocol (panel, summary of responses, open-ended discussion) to share learnings and reflections with the whole faculty. For instance, at your next faculty meeting you might want to have a panel of shadow teachers speak about their experiences.

11. Facilitate a discussion about the information learned from teachers and administrators who shadowed a student for the day. What are some of the themes that

surfaced? What did you learn? What do we now know about our students' daily experiences at school? What are areas the faculty can focus on to improve teacher care, engagement, homework, and so on?

12. Develop next steps to address a focus area.

Recommended Talking Points—Faculty Meeting
Introduction
Read "What Is a Shadow Day?" Explain that the purpose of this exercise is to gain a greater perspective of our students' daily experiences in school.

Details
In this protocol volunteer teachers are matched to shadow students for one day. Each teacher will be matched with a particular student, get a copy of the student's schedule, and spend the designated day attending the student's classes, breaks, lunch, and all school activities. Teachers who volunteer to shadow students will each have a substitute for the day. Selected students to be shadowed will reflect all grade levels, learning profiles, ethnicities, and genders. Participating faculty members will be asked to complete a reflection sheet and share observations and reflections at the next faculty meeting. All information is confidential and will not reflect student or teacher names.

Discussion
What are some of the themes that may surface in participating in Shadow Day? Faculty may brainstorm ideas as a whole group or in smaller groups. Ideas surfaced may include: learning about students' schedules, the pacing of the day, homework load, and academic engagement. Some faculty members might be concerned that the shadow experience is a way to assess or evaluate their teaching. Emphasize that the focus is on learning about the student's daily experience and not on teacher evaluation or assessment. Walking in the shoes of a student for a day may yield new information to help inform ways for us as a faculty and school community to better support our students.

Next Steps
Ask for questions and clarifications. Provide a sign-up sheet for teachers interested in volunteering on Shadow Day.

Recommended Talking Points—Student Meeting
Introduction

Welcome students and allow time for introductions. Read "What Is a Shadow Day?" The purpose of this exercise is to gain a greater perspective of our students' daily experiences in school. Explain that students were selected to represent all grade levels and this meeting is to inform them of what's involved with Shadow Day.

Details

Volunteer teachers will be matched to shadow students for one day, bell to bell. Your shadow teacher will have a copy of your schedule, meet you at a designated location on Shadow Day, and spend the day attending your classes, breaks, lunch, trips to your locker, and so on. The shadow teacher will write down your homework assignments and listen to class lectures but will not participate directly in class. Shadow teachers will be asked to complete a reflection sheet at the end of the day. All information collected is confidential and will not reveal student or teacher names.

Next Steps

Ask for questions and clarifications. Let students know there will be a follow-up meeting in advance of Shadow Day, where all participating teachers and students will have the opportunity to meet one another, review student schedules, and determine a meeting location for Shadow Day itself.

Student-Teacher Meeting

Schedule a meeting for all shadow teachers and students prior to Shadow Day. Prior to the meeting, match each teacher or administrator with a student. Print out each participating student's class schedule. At the meeting, review the process and allow time for teachers and students to get acquainted, review the student schedule, and determine a meeting place on Shadow Day.

Shadow Day—Suggested Guidelines for Teachers

Please read through the following information about today's scheduled Shadow Day.

- Meet your student 10 minutes prior to the first bell.

- Stay with your student for the entire day. Follow your student to each class, his or her locker, and to lunch. Wherever your student goes, you follow/shadow. On the way to each class ask the student what homework was assigned for today's class and how much time it took to complete.

- While in the classroom, remain a silent observer. Do take notes, take the quiz or test if applicable (don't worry – it won't be graded!), and engage in any written or reading assignments in each class. If your student is participating in a group project or partner activity, quietly sit beside and listen to the conversation. Find out about what homework is due the next time the class meets and any larger projects that may have been assigned.

- While walking to the student's classes, locker, lunch, or any other extracurricular activity, do be positive, interactive, friendly and talkative. Take this opportunity to ask about the student's daily experience at school.

- At the end of the school day, thank your student for the opportunity to shadow his/her day.

- Complete the reflection sheet and write any notes that will help you share your experience with the faculty at a later date. Turn in your reflection sheet to (person and room #) by (date).

Post–Shadow Day

After collecting the reflection sheets, meet with participating shadow teachers to discuss reflections and anecdotal experiences. Determine how to share this information with the faculty. Based on findings, determine possible next steps to address specific areas of concern.

SHADOW DAY REFLECTION
(TO BE COMPLETED BY SHADOW TEACHERS)

Thank you for participating in Shadow Day. Your reflections, representing a *typical student* experiencing a school day, are important in our continuing efforts to address what makes homework meaningful and to build evidence of teacher care to reduce student stress and increase student connectedness. Please answer these reflection questions through the lens of your student experience, keeping in mind that the intention is *not evaluative* of teachers but *is reflective of a student's perspective on learning.*

Circle the response that fits best:

1. Engagement in classroom lessons and activities:

   No Engagement   Little Engagement   Some Engagement   Very Engaged
   Comments or Reflections:

2. Directions in classroom lessons and activities:
   Unclear   Somewhat Clear   Mostly Clear   Very Clear
   Comments or Reflections:

3. Written directions and visual instruction in classroom lessons and activities:
   No Written/Visual   Few Written/Visual   Some Written/Visual
   Lots of Written/Visual
   Comments or Reflections:

4. Clarity and understanding of homework purpose:
   No Clarity/Understanding   Some Clarity/Understanding
   Full Clarity/Understanding
   Comments or Reflections:

5. I feel prepared by classroom lessons and directions to complete my homework:

Strongly Disagree   Disagree   Agree   Strongly Agree

Comments or Reflections:

6. I have this amount of homework to complete (per day / week):

0–15 min.   15–30 min.   30–60 min.   60–90 min.   90–120 min.   120 min. plus

Comments or Reflections:

7. My homework is meaningful to me (I am clear about purpose, I understand the connection to other lessons/units, and I understand how it will be used):

Not Very Meaningful   Some Meaningfulness   Very Meaningful

Comments or Reflections:

8. I feel I have enough time to manage my schoolwork:

No Time   Little Time   Some Time   Much Time

Comments or Reflections:

9. Regarding having time to interact socially with my peers, I feel there was:

No Time   Little Time   Some Time   Much Time

Comments or Reflections:

10. Regarding having time during passing periods to do what was needed and get to class on time, I feel there was:

Not Enough Time   Barely Adequate Time   Adequate Time   Too Much Time

Comments or Reflections:

11. What was your level of stress during the day?

No Stress   Little Stress   Some Stress   Much Stress

Comments or Reflections:

Other Comments or Reflections:

Did you find value in this activity? ____ YES ____ NO

Would you recommend colleagues to participate? ____ YES ____ NO

Name [OPTIONAL]

_____

Grade Level of student that I shadowed_____

FISHBOWL
How to Run a Student Fishbowl

Contributions to the following guidelines come from Jen Coté, Marin Academy, California, and Kristen Plant, Miramonte High School, California

A Fishbowl offers a unique opportunity for adults to listen in as a small group of thoughtful students share their experiences and feelings on a particular topic. A facilitator, such as a teacher or counselor, moderates this event. Fishbowl participants are asked a series of questions and share their ideas while a faculty or parent group listens in quietly. This is an effective way to share student perspectives on stress and high school pressures and to get the students' opinions on ways to improve school practices and policies.

Recommended Steps

1. Recommend a Fishbowl to spur dialogue between students and staff and/or students and parents, once there is agreement on the importance of student voice.

2. Hire or appoint an experienced facilitator to help prepare for, deliver, and debrief the Fishbowl, and agree on the format for carrying out the event and follow-up.

3. Consider forming a committee or Challenge Success group to take leadership of the Fishbowl. We suggest including a teacher, a counselor, and three seniors. This committee will work together to decide whom to invite to be a part of the Fishbowl, which questions to ask the students involved (see the following examples), and how to promote the activity.

4. Select students to participate in the Fishbowl. The number may vary based on the school size but should be representative of various grades and backgrounds. If you are a Challenge Success school, include the student members of your team.

5. Send out a formal letter providing background about why the Fishbowl is taking place and inviting the students to participate (see the following example). A teacher typically sends the invitations and hosts a lunchtime meeting with free pizza (or other favorite foods) to draw interested students to discuss the upcoming Fishbowl.

6. Hold the lunchtime meeting to help students to feel more comfortable with what's going to happen at the Fishbowl. Often upperclassmen can take a leadership role in the discussion. Rather than providing the actual fishbowl questions in advance, we suggest giving the students some sample questions. This way, the students can

have a sense of what might be asked during the Fishbowl, but their answers during the actual activity will not sound rehearsed. Students should also be told when and where to arrive for the Fishbowl.

7. Inform staff and faculty. Make sure to notify department chairs, established committees, and anyone else who can help get the word out. The principal should send an email informing the faculty and staff of the meeting date, time, and location. Create and post signs in the faculty room as reminders to attend the upcoming Fishbowl.

8. Coordinate the setup with the custodial staff, who should set up concentric circles of chairs to facilitate the discussion. Send reminder notes to the student participants and create nametags.

9. Conduct the Fishbowl. Once the faculty has assembled, the teacher introduces the Fishbowl by briefly describing the work of the committee and the purpose of this activity. The teacher should also explain that today the faculty will only be listening, not reacting or responding to the students. Explain that there will be an opportunity to discuss faculty stress and debrief their reactions to the Fishbowl during an upcoming faculty meeting. The facilitator should introduce the members of the committee, talk a bit about the purpose of Fishbowls, and set up some ground rules, such as ensuring the confidentiality of information shared during the Fishbowl and making sure that every student participant feels safe sharing honest opinions in front of the faculty.

10. Follow up with faculty. In the week following the Fishbowl, we suggest holding a faculty meeting to debrief their reactions to the Fishbowl and ideas for the future. Provide the staff with a copy of the questions and notes on the student comments at the Fishbowl to remind them of what was said (see the following example). The teachers should then be asked to join smaller discussion groups at tables. Each table should have handouts containing possible discussion topics (see the following example) and a large sheet of paper and marker for recording ideas. A note taker should be assigned to record all ideas shared by the faculty. Allow time for each table group to share main discussion points. Discuss possible ideas to address student stress and pressures at the school.

11. Meet with student participants for feedback sometime after the Fishbowl takes place. We suggest pulling the student participants together to give them an opportunity to provide feedback and to encourage them to remain involved, perhaps by creating or joining a committee tasked with implementing ideas.

12. Compile and distribute the notes from the debrief sessions to the faculty and committee.

Possible Fishbowl Questions

- When you are on your way to school on a Monday morning, what are three adjectives that describe your state of mind or how you are feeling?
- What is one of the most challenging aspects of performing well academically here?
- What do you wish the adults in this community really understood about the challenges of being a good student here?
- Picture yourself graduating from this school. How do you think you would describe your four years here?
- How would you describe this school's culture to someone who has never been to the school?
- Have you had to (or felt that you will have to) give up something you love in order to stay on top of the workload or handle the pressure here?
- What unspoken messages do you get from the adults in your life about their expectations and opinions of you?
- Are there any behaviors over which students have control that seem to increase stress?
- If you were a teacher, what is the number one thing you'd do to try to help alleviate student stress?
- If you were a parent, what is the number one thing you'd do to try to help alleviate student stress?
- What do you think our school teaches students about dealing with failures?
- How do you define success?

Sample Letter Inviting Students to Participate in Fishbowl

Dear _____,

I am writing on behalf of the [name your school] Challenge Success Committee to ask you to play a crucial part in sharing student perspectives on stress and high school pressures. Our committee, which includes students, parents, teachers, counselors, and administrators, feels that you would be a great participant in our upcoming fishbowl activity. We are reaching out to selected students who might be willing to share open and honest feedback on the topic of stress and high school pressures. Please read through the following information to learn about the committee and the Fishbowl.

Information about Challenge Success

Our school has partnered with Challenge Success (www.challengesuccess.org) to examine existing policies and practices and focus on ways to support student well-being. Our committee initially came together at the Challenge Success Fall Conference, where we had the opportunity to attend workshops on stress-related topics and openly discuss our perceptions of stress on our campus and in our community. Since that time, we have been meeting to try to come up with ideas as to how to spark dialogue on this issue and to begin to promote some healthy change at our school. To that end, we've been working hard to coordinate some activities this month, including a student Fishbowl at an upcoming faculty meeting.

What's a Fishbowl?

A Fishbowl offers a unique opportunity for adults to listen in as a small group of thoughtful students share their experiences and feelings on a particular topic. A facilitator, such as a teacher or counselor, moderates this event. Fishbowl participants will be asked a series of questions and share their ideas with the group while the faculty listens in quietly. This is an effective way to share student perspectives on stress and high school pressures and to get the students' opinions on ways to improve school practices and policies.

We Need Your Help!

We have scheduled this fishbowl discussion on [name, date, time, and location]. A group of about 15 students will have a discussion about stress. The facilitator, [name the teacher or counselor], will ask the students questions and give them an opportunity to respond. The teachers' job will be to silently listen and think about the various issues raised. You don't need to prepare anything—all that we are asking is that you come ready to share your honest opinions about how stress affects you.

Next steps

Please come to a mandatory meeting [name date, time, room #] for a pizza lunch to learn more about the fishbowl discussion. If you cannot make the lunchtime meeting but you are interested in participating, please contact [teacher and room #] no later than [date] to discuss this opportunity. Thanks so much for helping us make our school a place where we can work hard and feel happy, healthy, and proud of our successes.

Notes on Student Comments during Fishbowl

Be sure to have someone take notes during the fishbowl discussion. Share these notes during the faculty discussion. Do not list individual student names or comments. List each of the questions and the students' reflections or actual statements. Here is an excerpt of how a school transcribed their fishbowl notes.

What are the most challenging aspects of succeeding here?

- balancing school, sports, extracurriculars, and community service
- "if you aren't stressed-out, you aren't working hard enough"
- forgetting that there are other fulfilling aspects of life
- "whoever is the most stressed out must be the hardest worker"
- hard to stay motivated

What suggestions would you have for teachers or parents as to how they could help reduce stress?

- quality not quantity for homework
- lessen expectations for production
- test days don't help that much
- it's hard when everything builds up in one night
- there's a feeling that if you don't do all of your work you're flakey or lazy
- the week before a break or the end of a quarter all of the teachers pile on the work
- we're assigned lots of homework over breaks

Notes on Teacher Comments after Fishbowl

On a designated date, the school faculty met to debrief their reactions to the student fishbowl activity. During the debrief session, faculty members were asked to sit at eight tables and engage in an open and honest discussion. The following is a copy of the instructions they were given:

Please discuss the following questions with the other colleagues at your table. Select one person to record your responses on the large paper. We will reconvene toward the end of the session to share information as time permits. This information will be shared with the Challenge Success committee, and we will attempt to implement some of your ideas. Thank you!

1. Discuss your reactions to the Fishbowl. Sample topics include:
   - What was effective about the activity?
   - What could be improved next time?
   - Were you surprised by anything the students said?
2. Has the Fishbowl inspired you to
   - Discuss stress in class?
   - Adjust your expectations or routines somehow in response to the students' comments?
   - If so, how?
3. To what extent is the faculty responsible for helping to control student stress?
4. Which other school stakeholders should be involved in examining this issue? How could we make that happen?
5. Other suggestions about how we should continue to explore this topic…

Each group recorded their responses and shared one important idea from their group. All responses were recorded and later distributed to the Challenge Success committee and faculty.

Here is an excerpt of the feedback and reflections shared by the faculty:

Fishbowl

- need more open, honest discussions like this
- need student participants who more accurately represent our student body (Resource? Underachievers? Freshmen?)
- need a faculty fishbowl to educate students and parents
- have more fishbowls with smaller audiences
- need a fishbowl evening involving: students, parents, teachers, admin., and alumni (junior high and high school)

Teachers

- suffer from same stresses, but better able to cope as adults (setting bad example)
- more collaboration: master scheduling, school events, major projects
- AP classes add stress and limit elective options
- cut back on busy work (define "busywork") / make assignments as meaningful as possible

- need to educate kids as to time management
- provide a homework schedule in advance (1 week, must be on blackboard)
- give more notice as to tests and projects (at least 1 week, schedule by quarter, must be on blackboard)
- be flexible
- set clear expectations at start of the year
- efficient use of class time reduces outside stress
- no homework over long break
- include stress-relieving activities in class (meditation, relaxation exercises)

DIALOGUE NIGHT

Contributions to the following came from Dafna Adler and Judy Prothro, Los Altos High School, California, and Lauren Schryver, Castilleja School, California

The following information is provided to support a school administrator, counselor, teacher leader, or group of students interested in hosting a Dialogue Night at their school. Please read through the following guidelines to plan for the presentation. Resources are provided to support your planning and program facilitation.

Overview of Dialogue Night

Dialogue Night is an evening program for parents, students, and faculty members to participate in an open discussion about the issues related to teen stress and pressure. The evening includes a presentation of three skits (usually enacted by 11th graders), which are then discussed in small groups in order to tease out various areas of stress students are experiencing at school and home. Dialogue Night creates a space for students and parents to talk about homework, sleep, course load, college, and the everyday balancing act of being a student.

Recommended Steps:

1. Share information about Dialogue Night with the school faculty and/or parent groups. Provide an overview of the protocol and reasons why the community might benefit from this event.

2. The lead facilitator (counselor, teacher, administrator, student/peer leader) recruits four to six students to participate and help facilitate Dialogue Night. We recommend having at least one counselor and one administrator present at Dialogue Night to answer any questions that might surface from the dialogue.

3. Choose a date, time, and location for Dialogue Night. (Many schools use the library.)

4. Send Dialogue Night invitations to all parents (see Exhibit A.1).

5. Schedule a meeting with those students helping to facilitate Dialogue Night. Provide an overview of the program and talk through a proposed agenda (see Exhibit A.2). Provide a copy of each of the three skits to share with students (see Exhibit A.3).

6. Advertise Dialogue Night in the school and/or community newspaper and on the school/community website, and/or create posters for the school hallways, office, and other communal gathering spaces at the school.

7. Schedule a second student meeting to finalize the agenda and skits (see Exhibit A.4).

8. On Dialogue Night—Set up tables for groups of six to eight people. Review materials and technology list to ensure that you are prepared (see Exhibit A.5).

Exhibit A.1 Sample of Invite Letter to Parents/Students

Please join us for Dialogue Night!

[State the date, time, location]

[School name] is presenting a **Parent/Student Dialogue Night** on [date, time, location]. All parents and their teens are invited to join us and discuss the issues of stress and pressure in our school community.

This is an evening of student skits, honest discussion, and brainstorming ways to de-stress our students' lives. Light refreshments will be served beginning at [time]. Please reply to [contact name, email and/or phone] to reserve your spot as soon as possible. For questions regarding this event, please contact [contact name, email and/or phone]. We are very excited to offer this event to our families and hope you can join us!

Exhibit A.2 Recommended Talking Points—Student Meeting

Introduction

After you have recruited four to six students (11th and 12th graders recommended), schedule a meeting to review the Dialogue Night agenda. Share the description and purpose of Dialogue Night. Ask students to share what conversations or topics might surface during the evening.

Details

Share the process involved in hosting a Dialogue Night.

1. Introduction and welcome presented by a school counselor, teacher, or administrator.

2. Introductions made by all students and participants in the room.

3. Student skits performed, reflecting typical scenarios played out at home and in school.

4. Breakout discussion groups occur after each skit to allow time for parents and students to reflect and brainstorm answers to prompts. Parents and their teens sit at different tables throughout the program.

5. Whole group share and reflection time.

Talk through each of these components and ask for student input and questions. Distribute copies of the three skits to each student. Read through each skit together as a group. Discuss the messages in each skit. Have students self-select or assign roles for each of the skits. Allow time for students to practice each of the three skits and to tweak the language as needed to more accurately reflect your community.

Next Steps

Decide on next steps to prepare for Dialogue Night. What props do students need to bring for each skit? Cocreate an agenda to include student voice and facilitation help. Schedule a follow-up meeting a few days prior to the scheduled Dialogue Night to finalize the presentation, skits, and overall program.

Exhibit A.3 Skits #1 through 3

Skit #1: Stress, Homework, and Sleep Issues—Parent to Daughter

Scene: Parent checks in on daughter, while she is studying on her bed.

Parent: Sweetie, it's time to go to bed—it's almost midnight.

Student: I can't go to bed yet. I still have to finish studying for my history test, and I haven't even started studying for my bio quiz yet!

Parent: I know you want to do well, but your health is more important. You need to go to bed.

Student: But you said that I have to work harder in history in order to get that A.

Parent: I would never have said that. I've always told you to get your rest, or else you won't be able to concentrate on your test.

Student: I clearly remember the day when comment cards came in the mail, and you told me. (*Mimics parent.*) "If you just work a little harder, put in a little more effort, you will be able to get that A you have always wanted. That A will help you in the long run."

Parent: I never said that!

Student: Yes, you did. I remember it clearly.

Parent: I think you misunderstood me. What I meant to say was that you need to work harder, but I didn't mean working until 1:00 in the morning!

Student: Well, it's not my fault that we had a four-hour tennis match today!! You were the one who encouraged me to play tennis this season—you said that colleges love to see extracurricular activities on a transcript.

Parent: OK, well…(*Pause.*) Ask your teacher for an extension. This is not right for you to be stressed at this hour. I'm going to email Mr. Jones! You need an extension. Five more minutes, then lights out.

Skit #2: Hidden Messages Between Parents and Students

All family members wearing Stanford T-shirt or shirts from another prestigious college. Student comes home from school.

Mom: Hi, honey. How was school? (*No pause.*) How did your biology test go?

Daughter: I don't know, I just took it today…

Mom: Well, how do you feel you did?

Daughter: I don't know. OK, I guess.

Mom: Do you know when you'll get it back?

Daughter: I don't know; it depends on how fast the teacher grades it.
Daughter takes her backpack to go to her room.

Mom: (*in a cheery voice*) Be sure to tell me when you get it back.

Daughter: (*on her way out*) I always do…

… … … … … …

Someone holds up placard that says, "The Following Week"
Everybody still wearing same college T-shirt. Again, student comes in from school.

Mom: Hi, honey, did you get your bio test back yet?

Daughter: Yeah.

Mom: Well…

Daughter: Well what?

Mom: How did it go?

Daughter: Not great, but then the whole class did not do well.

Mom: How bad is "not well"?

Daughter: I don't know, I got a "C," but the average was a "C," so I did pretty well.

Mom: Hmmmm. (*Long pause*)…Did you meet with the teacher after school?

Daughter: No, Mom, it's OK. If I feel I don't understand something I'll talk to her.

Mom: Well, you need to take this a little more seriously. You're a junior now, after all, applying to college next year.

Dad, with other family members, stepping up and facing student and audience:

"And remember, honey, it doesn't matter what college you go to!"

Skit # 3: Hidden Messages Between Students

Lunchtime, after the clubs fair.

Leila: Omigosh, you know soooo many vocab words! How do you do it all?

Betty: Well, I started over the summer with my SAT tutor. After all, the SAT is coming up fast!

Leila: But it's in like four months!

Betty: Yeah, but I have to get at least a 2350 if I want to get into Princeton. Although obviously I should shoot for a 2400…

Leila: Wow. Yeah, well I'm concentrating on my extracurriculars. You know, three sports, club leadership, student government, peer tutoring, and then those five APs….

Gerdie: SPEAKING OF WHICH, how did you think that APUSH test went?

Betty: SO badly. I didn't get question 13, so I guessed…and last time I got a 90, so I really have to shape up my grade…

Leila: I stayed up really late studying again, so I think I got most of it. (*Yawns.*)

Gerdie: Betty, I would LOVE a 90. Honestly, that's really good!
Silence. Everyone stares at Gerdie.

Betty: Welllll, I should get back to studying.

Leila: Yeah. I have to go to my club. (*Leaves.*)

Betty: See you, Gerdie. It's been supercalafragilisticexpealidocious conversing with my amicable fellow scholars. (*Leaves.*)

Gerdie: (*Left alone.*) Uh. Bye, then…(*Looks around, bewildered and a bit sad.*)

Exhibit A.4 Dialogue Night—Recommended Program/Agenda

I. Welcome and Introductions (10 minutes)

- All members of the team stand up in front of the room.

- Opening remarks—Provide a brief overview of the evening's agenda and the purpose behind Dialogue Night; acknowledge student helpers for the evening. Have everyone sit in small groups; make sure parents are not at the same table as their own children.

- State: "Before we begin, please introduce yourself to the other small group members by saying your name; grade, if you are a student; child's name and grade, if you are a parent; and briefly say why you came tonight."

II. Student skit #1 is performed. Table debrief (10 to 15 minutes)

Post directions for participants (either on poster paper, PowerPoint, or whiteboard). Each group chooses a speaker representative to share the main discussion points from each table (or from a selection of tables, if the turnout is too large to share from each table). We recommend assigning a note taker to record group ideas.

Ask:

- What hidden or unintended messages did you hear?

- What messages can we identify that can easily be misconstrued?

- Were there any healthy messages in the skit?

- If you were to rewind the skit, what suggestions do you have that would foster better communication?

If time allows, groups can role-play the skit using healthier interactions.

III. Skit #2 plus table discussion (10 to 15 minutes)

Repeat the process from Skit #1.

List the prompts again and ask for a volunteer to share the main discussion points from each table.

IV. Skit #3 plus breakout discussions (10 to 15 minutes)

After Skit #3 is performed, separate students and parents into different groups. Instruct students to go into another room for their discussion. Each group will have a separate task. Be sure you have poster paper and a note taker assigned to each group to record ideas shared.

Post directions for participants (either on poster paper, PowerPoint, or whiteboard).

Parent Group Instructions: Brainstorm one list:

"Words, phrases, and actions that I can use to decrease stress for my daughter/son are…"

Student Group Instructions: Brainstorm two lists:

"Words, phrases, and actions parents can use that could help decrease my stress are…"

"Words, phrases, and actions that I can use to decrease stress for my classmates and myself are…"

Star the top three on each list. Students return to the main room for whole group to share and debrief ideas.

Allow the parent group and student group to each share their top three words, phrases, and actions that can be used to decrease stress.

V. Closing remarks, reflections, and appreciations

Exhibit A.5 Recommended Materials

- Copy of the agenda for each participant.
- PowerPoint slides or other visual display for group discussion questions.
- Computer or poster paper and markers for recording table conversations.
- Paper and pens for tables.
- Set up tables to accommodate six to eight people. Have students and their parents sit separately to promote openness in discussions.

References

Alliance for Childhood. (2010). The loss of children's play: A public health issue. *Policy Brief 1*. Retrieved from http://www.allianceforchildhood.org/sites/allianceforchildhood.org/files/file/Health_brief.pdf

Alpern, A. V. (2008). *Student engagement in high performing urban high schools: A case study*. (Doctoral dissertation). Retrieved from University of Southern California Digital Library. (File name: etd-Alpern-20080721).

American Academy of Pediatrics. (2013). The crucial role of recess in school. *Pediatrics, 131*(1), 183–188.

American College Health Association. (2012). Depression and college students. *National College Health Assessment II: Reference Group Executive Summary*. Retrieved from http://www.nimh.nih.gov/health/publications/depression-and-college-students/index.shtml

American Management Association (2010). *AMA 2010 Critical Skills Survey*. American Management Association: Washington, DC.

Amrein, A. L., & Berliner, D. C. (2002). High-stakes testing, uncertainty and student learning. *Education Policy Analysis Archives, 10*(18).

Babinet, L. (2013, October). *Round Table Discussion on Authentic Assessment*. Roundtable presentation at the Challenge Success Conference, Stanford, CA.

Baker, D. P., & LeTendre, G. K. (2005). *National differences, global similarities: World culture and the future of schooling*. Stanford, CA: Stanford University Press.

Bangert-Drowns, R. L., Kulik, J. A., & Kulik, C.-L. (1991). Effects of frequent classroom testing. *Journal of Educational Research, 85*(2), 89–99.

Bargh, J. A., & McKenna, K.Y.A. (2004). The internet and social life. *Annual Review of Psychology, 55*, 573–590.

Barker, J. E., Semenov, A. D., Michaelson, L., Provan, L. S., Snyder, H. R., & Munakata, Y. (2014). Less-structured time in children's daily lives predicts self-directed executive functioning. *Frontiers in Psychology, 5*(593).

Barnes, G. M., Hoffman, J. H., Welte, J. W., Farrell, M. P., & Dintcheff, B. A. (2007). Adolescents' time use: Effects on substance use, delinquency and sexual activity. *Journal of Youth and Adolescence, 36*(5), 697–710.

Barron, B. (2003). When smart groups fail. *Journal of Learning Sciences, 12*(3), 307–359.

Barron, B., & Darling-Hammond, L. (2008). Teaching for meaningful learning: A review of research on inquiry-based and cooperative learning. In Darling-Hammond et al. (Eds.), *Powerful learning: What we know about teaching for understanding*. San Francisco: Jossey-Bass.

Barrows, H. S., & Tamblyn, R. M. (1980). *Problem-based learning: An approach to medical education*. New York: Springer.

Barth, R. S. (1991). *Improving schools from within: Teachers, parents, and principals can make the difference*. San Francisco: Jossey-Bass.

Battistich, V., Watson, M., Solomon, D., Lewis, C., & Schaps, E. (1999). Beyond the three R's: A broader agenda for school reform. *Elementary School Journal, 99*(5).

Bebell, D., & O'Dwyer, L. M. (2014). Educational outcomes and research from 1:1 computing settings. *Journal of Technology, Learning and Assessment, 9*(1).

Bempechat, J., Li, J., Neier, S. M., Gillis, C. A., & Holloway, S. D. (2011). The homework experience: Perceptions of low-income youth. *Journal of Advanced Academics, 22*(2), 250–278.

Bennett, S., & Kalish, N. (2006). *The case against homework: How homework is hurting our children and what we can do about it*. New York: Crown.

Berscheid, E. (2003). The human's greatest strength: Other humans. In L. G. Aspinwall & U. M. Staudinger (Eds.), *Psychology of human strengths: Fundamental questions and future directions for a positive psychology* (pp. 37–47). Washington, DC: American Psychological Association.

Biesinger, K. D., Crippen, K. J., & Muis, K. R. (2008). The impact of block scheduling on student motivation and classroom practice in mathematics. *NASSP Bulletin, 92*(3), 191–208.

Black, D. S., Milam, J., & Sussman, S. (2009). Sitting-meditation interventions among youth: A review of treatment efficacy. *Pediatrics, 124*, 532–541.

Black, P., & Wiliam, D. (2012). Assessment for learning in the classroom. In J. Gardner (Ed.), *Assessment for learning: Practice, theory and policy* (2nd ed., pp. 11–32). London, UK: Sage.

Boaler, J. (1997). Equity, empowerment and different ways of knowing. *Mathematics Education Research Journal, 9*(3), 325–342.

Broad Foundation. (2013). *The Road to equity: Expanding AP access and success for African American students*. Retrieved from http://broadeducation.org/img/roadtoequity.pdf

Broderick, P. C., & Metz, S. (2009). Learning to BREATHE: A pilot trial of a mindfulness curriculum for adolescents. *Advances in School Mental Health Promotion, 2*(1), 35–46.

Buhrmester, D. (1990). Intimacy of friendship, interpersonal competence, and adjustment in preadolescence and adolescence. *Child Development, 61*(4)S, 1101–1111.

Burkett, E. (2002). *Another planet: A year in the life of a suburban high school*. New York: Harper Perennial.

Butler, D. L., & Nisan, M. (1986). Effects of no feedback, task-related comments, and grades on intrinsic motivation and performance. *Journal of Educational Psychology, 78*(3), 210–216.

Carey, B. (2014). *How we learn: The surprising truth about when, where, and why it happens*. New York: Random House, as cited in the *New York Times*, October 6, 2014. Retrieved from http://well.blogs.nytimes.com/2014/10/06/better-ways-to-learn/?module=BlogPost-Title&version=Blog%20Main&contentCollection=The%20Well%20Column&action=Click&pgtype=Blogs&region=Body

CASEL: Collaborative for Academic, Social and Emotional Learning, www.casel.org.

Casner-Lott, J., & Barrington, L. (2006). *Are they really ready to work? Employers' perspectives on the basic knowledge and applied skills of new entrants to the 21st century U.S. workforce.* New York: Conference Board.

Cercone, K. (2006). Chapter XIII: Brain-based learning. In E. K. Sorensen (Ed.), *Enhancing learning through technology* (pp. 293–322). Hershey, PA: Idea Group.

Chajewski, M., Mattern, K. D., & Shaw, E. J. (2011). Examining the role of Advanced Placement exam participation in 4-year college enrollment. *Educational Measurement: Issues and Practice, 30*(4), 16–27.

Challenge Success. (2012a). Cheat or be cheated? What we know about academic integrity in middle & high schools & what we can do about it. Retrieved from http://www.challenge success.org/Portals/0/Docs/ChallengeSuccess-AcademicIntegrity-WhitePaper.pdf

Challenge Success (Producer). (2012b, July 16). Challenge Success Vodcast – Academic Integrity. Podcast retrieved from https://www.youtube.com/watch?v=QTZ2Gv_46Qc

Challenge Success. (2013). The Advanced Placement program: Living up to its promise? Retrieved from: http://www.challengesuccess.org/Portals/0/Docs/ChallengeSuccess-AdvancedPlacement-WP.pdf

Challenge Success. (2014). Program impact study. Retrieved from http://www.challengesuccess .org/Research/ProgramImpactStudy.aspx

Chang, A., Aeschbach, D., Duffy, J. F., & Czeisler, C. A. (2014). Evening use of light-emitting eReaders negatively affects sleep, circadian timing, and next-morning alertness. Proceedings of the National Academy of Sciences of the United States of America. Retrieved from www.pnas.org/cgi/doi/10.1073/pnas.1418490112

Chang, C. (2001). Comparing the impacts of problem-based computer-assisted instruction and the direct interactive teaching method on student science achievement [Abstract]. *Journal of Science Education and Technology, 10*(2), 147–153.

Chua, A. (2011, Jan. 8). Why Chinese mothers are superior. *Wall Street Journal.* Retrieved from http://online.wsj.com/article/SB10001424052748704111504576059713528698754.html

Cizek, G. J., & Burg, S. S. (2006). *Addressing test anxiety in a high-stakes environment: Strategies for classrooms and schools.* Thousand Oaks, CA: Corwin Press.

Colarossi, L. G., & Eccles, J. S. (2003). Differential effects of support providers on adolescents' mental health. *Social Work Research, 27*(1), 19–30.

College Board. (2013). AP program size and increments (by year) [Table]. Retrieved from http://media.collegeboard.com/digitalServices/pdf/research/2013/2013-Size-and-Increment .pdf

College Board. (2014). AP Capstone. Retrieved from http://advancesinap.collegeboard.org/ap-capstone

Commission on Teacher Credentialing. (2009). *California Standards for the Teaching Profession (CSTP).* State of California: Sacramento.

Common Sense Media. (2012). *Social media, social life: How teens view their digital lives.* Retrieved from https://www.commonsensemedia.org/research/social-media-social-life-how -teens-view-their-digital-lives

Conboy, L. A., Noggle, J. J., Frey, J. L., Kudesia, R. S., & Khalsa, S.B.S. (2013). Qualitative evaluation of a high school yoga program: Feasibility and perceived benefits. *Journal of Science and Healing*, *9*(3), 171–180.

Connell, J. P. (1990). Context, self and action: A motivational analysis of self-system processes across the lifespan. In D. Cicchetti & M. Beeghly (Eds.), *The self in transition: From infancy to childhood* (pp. 61–97). Chicago: University of Chicago Press.

Connell, J. P., & Wellborn, J. G. (1991). Competence, autonomy, and relatedness: A motivational analysis of self-system processes. In R. Gunnar & L. A. Sroufe (Eds.), *Self processes in development: Minnesota Symposium on Child Psychology*, Volume 23 (Minnesota Symposia on Child Psychology Series) (pp. 43–77). Chicago: Chicago University Press.

Conner, J. O., & Pope, D. C. (2013a). *Extracurricular activity in high-performing school contexts: Stress buster, booster, or buffer?* Paper presented at the annual meeting of the American Educational Research Association, San Francisco, CA.

Conner, J. O., & Pope, D. C. (2013b). Not just robo-students: Why full engagement matters and how schools can promote it. *Journal of Youth and Adolescence*, *42*(9), 1426–1442. Retrieved from http://link.springer.com/article/10.1007%2Fs10964–013–9948-y

Conner, J. O., & Pope, D. C. (2014). Student engagement in high-performing schools: Relationships to mental and physical health. In D. Shernoff & J. Bempechat (Eds.), *Engaging youth in schools: Evidence based models to guide future innovations*. New York: NSSE Yearbook by Teachers College Record.

Conner, J. O., Pope, D. C., & Galloway, M. (2009). Success with less stress. *Educational Leadership*, *67*(4), 54–58.

Conner, J. O., Pope, D. C., & Miles, S. B. (2014). How many teachers does it take to support a student? Examining the relationship between teacher support and adverse health outcomes in high-performing, pressure-cooker high schools. *High School Journal*, *98*(1), 22–42.

Cooper, H. (1989). Synthesis of research on homework. *Educational Leadership*, *47*(3), 85–91.

Cooper, H. (2007). *The battle over homework: Common ground for administrators, teachers, and parents*. Thousand Oaks, CA: Corwin Press.

Cooper, H., & Valentine, J. C. (2001). Using research to answer practical questions about homework. *Educational Psychologist*, *36*(3), 143–153.

Crooks, T. J. (1988). The impact of classroom evaluation practices on students. *Review of Educational Research*, *58*(4), 438–481.

Crowley, S. J., & Carskadon, M. A. (2010). Modifications to weekend recovery sleep delay circadian phase in older adolescents. *Chronobiology International*, *27*(7), 1469–1492.

Csikszentmihalyi, M. (1990). *Flow: The psychology of optimal experience*. New York: Harper & Row.

Danner, F., & Phillips, B. (2008). Adolescent sleep, school start times, and teen motor vehicle crashes. *Journal of Clinical Sleep Medicine*, *4*(6), 533–535.

Darling-Hammond, L. (2001). *The right to learn: A blueprint for creating schools that work*. San Francisco: Jossey-Bass.

Darling-Hammond, L. (2002). *10 features of good, small schools: Redesigning schools: What matters and what works*. Stanford, CA: School Redesign Network, Stanford University.

Darling-Hammond, L., & Conley, D. T. (2015, February 3). What will ready today's students for their college and career futures? P21 Blog: College and career readiness and the Common Core, Volume 2, Issue 1, Number 2. Retrieved from http://www.p21.org/news-events/p21blog /1590-college-and-career-readiness-and-the-common-core

Darling-Hammond, L., & Ifill-Lynch, O. (2006). If they'd only do their work! *Educational Leadership, 63*(5), 8–13.

Desimone, L. (2002). How can comprehensive school reform models be successfully implemented? *Review of Educational Research, 72*(3), 433–479.

Deuel, L-L. S. (1999). Block scheduling in large, urban high schools: Effects on academic achievement, student behavior and staff perceptions. *High School Journal, 83*(1), 14–25.

Dewey, J. (1897). My pedagogic creed. *School Journal, LIV*(3), 77–80. Retrieved from http:// dewey.pragmatism.org/creed.htm

Dewey, J. (1902). *The child and the curriculum*. Chicago: University of Chicago Press.

Dewey, J. (1916). *Democracy and education: An introduction to the philosophy of education*. New York: Macmillan.

De Wit, D. J., Karioja, K., Rye, B. J., & Shain, M. (2011). Perceptions of declining classmate and teacher support following the transition to high school: Potential correlates of increasing student mental health difficulties. *Psychology in Schools, 48*(6), 556–572.

Dougherty, C., & Mellor, L. (2009). *Preparation matters*. Austin, TX: National Center for Educational Achievement. Retrieved from http://www.act.org/research/policymakers/pdf /Preparation-Matters.pdf

Durlak, J. A., Weissberg, R. P., Dymnicki, A. B., Taylor, R. D., & Schellinger, K. B. (2011). The impact of enhancing students' social and emotional learning: A meta-analysis of school-based universal interventions. *Child Development, 82*(1), 405–432.

Dweck, C. S. (2006). *Mindset: The new psychology of success*. New York: Random House.

Eaton, D. K., McKnight-Eily, L. R., Lowry, R., Perry, G. S., Presley-Cantrell, L., & Croft, J. B. (2010). Prevalence of insufficient, borderline, and optimal hours of sleep among high school students—United States, 2007. *Journal of Adolescent Health, 46*(4), 399–401.

Eineder, D. V., & Bishop, H. L. (1997). Block scheduling the high school: The effects on achievement, behavior, and student-teacher relationships. *NASSP Bulletin, 81*(589), 45–54. Retrieved from http://bul.sagepub.com/content/81/589/45.abstract

Elder, C., Nidich, S., Moriarty, F., & Nidich, R. (2014). Effect of transcendental meditation on employee stress, depression, and burnout: A randomized controlled study. *Permanente Journal, 18*(1), 19–23.

Elias, M. J., & Haynes, N. M. (2008). Social competence, social support, and academic achievement in minority, low-income, urban elementary school children. *School Psychology Quarterly, 23*(4), 474–495.

Elkind, D. (2007). *The power of play: Learning what comes naturally*. Philadelphia, PA: Da Capo Press.

Erlauer, L. (2003). *The brain-compatible classroom: Using what we know about learning to improve teaching*. Alexandria, VA: ASCD.

Ertmer, P. A., & Simons, K. D. (2005). Scaffolding teachers' efforts to implement problem-based learning. *International Journal of Learning, 12*(4), 319–328.

Farrington, C. A., Roderick, M., Allensworth, E., Nagaoka, J., Keyes, T. S., Johnson, D. W., & Beechum, N. O. (2012). *Teaching adolescents to become learners—The role of noncognitive factors in shaping school performance: A critical literature review*. Chicago: The University of Chicago Consortium on Chicago School Research.

Feliz, J. (2013). *Adderall increases among high school teenagers*. News Release, Partnership for Drug-Free Kids. Retrieved from https://www.drugfree.org/newsroom/adderall-abuse-increases-among-high-school-students

Fiese, B. H., Tomcho, T. J., Douglas, M., Josephs, K., Poltrock, S., & Baker, T. (2002). A review of 50 years of research on naturally occurring family routines and rituals: Cause for celebration? *Journal of Family Psychology, 16*(4), 381–390.

Fine, M. (1989). *The second handbook on parent education: Contemporary perspectives*. San Diego, CA: Academic Press.

Frank, J. L., Jennings, P. A., & Greenberg, M. T. (2013). Mindfulness-based interventions in school settings. *Research in Human Development, 10*(3), 205–210.

Fredericks, J. A., Blumenfeld, P. C., & Paris, A. H. (2004). School engagement: Potential of the concept, state of the evidence. *Review of Educational Research, 74*(1), 59–109.

Fredricks, J. A. (2011). Engagement in school and out-of-school contexts: A multidimensional view of engagement. *Theory into Practice, 50*(4), 327–335.

Friedlaender, D., Burns, D., Lewis-Charp, H., Cook-Harvey, C. M., & Darling-Hammond, L. (2014). *Student-centered schools: Closing the opportunity gap* (Research Brief). Stanford, CA: Stanford Center for Opportunity Policy in Education. Retrieved from https://edpolicy.stanford.edu/sites/default/files/scope-pub-student-centered-research-brief.pdf

Fuligni, A. J., & Hardway, C. (2006). Daily variation in adolescents' sleep, activities, and psychological well being. *Journal of Research on Adolescence, 16*(3), 353–378.

Fulkerson, J. A., Story, M., Mellin, A., Leffert, N., Neumark-Sztainer, D., & French, S. A. (2006). Family dinner meal frequency and adolescent development: Relationships with developmental assets and high-risk behaviors. *Journal of Adolescent Health, 39*(3), 337–345.

Furrer, C., & Skinner, E. (2003). Sense of relatedness as a factor in children's academic engagement and performance. *Journal of Educational Psychology, 95*(1), 148–162.

Galloway, M., Conner, J. O., & Pope, D. C. (2013). Nonacademic effects of homework in privileged, high performing high schools. *Journal of Experimental Education, 81*(4), 490–510.

Geier, R., Blumenfeld, P. C., Marx, R. W., Krajcik, J. S., Fishman, B., Soloway, E., & Clay-Chambers, J. (2008). Standardized test outcomes for students engaged in inquiry-based science curricula in the context of urban reform. *Journal of Research in Science Teaching, 45*(8), 922–939.

Geiser, S., & Santelices, V. (2004). *The role of Advanced Placement and honors courses in college admissions* (Research & Occasional Papers Series, CSHE 4.04). University of California,

Berkeley: Center for Studies in Higher Education. https://cshe.berkeley.edu/sites/default/files/shared/publications/docs/ROP.Geiser.4.04.pdf

Gewertz, C. (2007). An advisory advantage. *Education Week*, *26*(26), 22–25.

Gifford-Smith, M. E., & Brownell, C. A. (2003). Childhood peer relationships: Social acceptance, friendships, and peer networks. *Journal of School Psychology*, *41*(4), 235–284.

Gill, B. P., & Schlossman, S. L. (2003). A nation at rest: The American way of homework. *Educational Evaluation and Policy Analysis*, *25*(3), 319–337.

Gill, B. P., & Schlossman, S. L. (2004). Villain or savior? The American discourse on homework. *Theory into Practice*, *43*(3), 174.

Gill, W.W.A. (2011). Middle school A/B block and traditional scheduling: An analysis of math and reading performance by race. *NASSP Bulletin*, *95*(4), 281-301.

Goldberg, C. (2012). *National study: Teen misuse and abuse of prescription drugs up 33% since 2008, stimulants contributing to sustained RX epidemic*. News Release, Partnership for Drug-Free Kids. Retrieved from https://www.drugfree.org/newsroom/pats-2012

Grant, H., & Dweck, C. (2003). Clarifying achievement goals and their impact. *Journal of Personality and Social Psychology*, *85*(3), 541–553.

Greenberg, M. T., & Harris, A. R. (2011). Nurturing mindfulness in children and youth: Current state of the research. *Child Development Perspectives*, *6*(2), 161–166.

Greenland, S. K. (2010). *The mindful child: How to help your kid manage stress and become happier, kinder, and more compassionate*. New York: Free Press.

Hackmann, D. G. (1995). Ten guidelines for implementing block scheduling. *Educational Leadership*, *53*(3), 24–27.

Hammond, B. (2005, January 19). On dropping AP courses: A voice from the developing movement. *Education Week*. Retrieved from http://www.edweek.org/ew/articles/2005/01/19/19hammond.h24.html

Hardiman, M., & Whitman, G. (2014). Assessment and the learning brain. *Independent School*, *73*(2), 36–41.

Harlen, W., & Crick, R. D. (2003). Testing and motivation for learning. *Assessment in Education: Principles, Policy & Practice*, *10*(2).

Harmston, M. T., Pliska, A.-M., Ziomek, R. L., & Hackmann, D. G. (2001). *The relationship between schedule type and ACT assessment scores: A longitudinal study*. Paper presented at the meeting of the 2001 Convention of the University Council for Educational Administration, Cincinnati, OH. Retrieved from http://www.act.org/research/researchers/reports/pdf/ACT_RR2003-3.pdf

Hattie, J., & Timperley, H. (2007). The power of feedback. *Review of Educational Research*, *77*(1), 81–112.

Henry, K. L., Knight, K. E., & Thornberry, T. P. (2012). School disengagement as a predictor of dropout, delinquency, and problem substance use during adolescence and early adulthood. *Journal of Youth and Adolescence*, *41*(2), 156–166.

Hernandez-Ramos, P., & De La Paz, S. (2009). Learning history in middle school by designing multimedia in a project-based learning experience. *Journal of Research on Technology in Education*, *42*(2),151–173.

Hixson, N. K., Ravitz, J., & Whisman, A. (2012). *Extended professional development in project-based learning: Impacts on 21st century teaching and student achievement.* Charleston, WV: West Virginia Department of Education, Office of Research, Division of Curriculum and Instruction. Retrieved from http://bie.org/object/document/west_virginia_study_of_pbl_impacts

Hofferth, S. L., & Sandberg, J. F. (2001). Changes in American children's use of time, 1981–1997. In T. Owens & S. Hofferth (Eds.), *Advances in life course research series: Children at the millennium: Where have we come from, where are we going?* (pp. 193–229). New York: Elsevier Science.

Hoover-Dempsey, K. V., Battiato, A. C., Walker, J. M. T., Reed, R. P., DeJong, J. M., & Jones, K. P., (2001). Parental involvement in homework. *Educational Psychologist*, 36(3), 195–209.

Hoxby, C. (2009). *The changing selectivity of American colleges.* (Working Paper No. 15446). Cambridge, MA: National Bureau of Economic Research.

Hu, W. (2008, December 6). Scarsdale adjusts to life without Advanced Placement courses. *New York Times.* Retrieved from http://www.nytimes.com/2008/12/07/education/07advanced .html?scp=1&sq=%22Scarsdale+High+School%22+Advanced+Placement&st=nyt&_r=0

Isselhardt, E. (2013, Feb. 11). Creating schoolwide PBL aligned to common core [Web log post]. *Edutopia.* Retrieved from http://www.edutopia.org/blog/PBL-aligned-to-common-core-eric -isslehardt

Jenkins, E. D., Queen, J. A., & Algozzine, R. F. (2002). To block or not to block: That's not the question. *Journal of Educational Research*, 95(4), 196–202.

Jennings, P. A., Frank, J. L., Snowberg, K. E., Coccia, M. A., Greenberg, M. T. (2013). Improving classroom learning environments by Cultivating Awareness and Resilience in Education (CARE): Results of a randomized controlled trial. *School Psychology Quarterly*, 28(4), 374–390.

Jeong, D. W. (2009). Student participation and performance on Advanced Placement exams: Do state sponsored incentives make a difference? *Educational Evaluation and Policy Analysis*, 31(4), 346–366.

Juster, F. T., Ono, H., & Stafford, F. P. (2004). *Changing times of American youth: 1981–2003.* Ann Arbor, MI: Institute for Social Research, University of Michigan.

Kenrick, C. (2013, Apr. 8). School calendar survey: "Benefits outweigh tradeoffs." *Palo Alto Weekly.* Retrieved from http://www.paloaltoonline.com/news/2013/04/08/school-calendar -survey-benefits-outweigh-tradeoffs

Khalsa, S.B.S., Hickey-Schultz, L., Cohen, D., Steiner, N., & Cope, S. (2012). Evaluation of the mental health benefits of yoga in a secondary school: A preliminary randomized controlled trial. *Journal of Behavioral Health Services & Research*, 39(1), 80–90.

Kitsantas, A., Cheema, J., & Ware, H. W. (2011). Mathematics achievement: The role of homework and self efficacy beliefs. *Journal of Advanced Academics*, 22(2), 310–339.

Klem, A., & Connell, J. P. (2004). Relationships matter: Linking teacher support to student engagement and achievement. *Journal of School Health*, 74(7), 262–273.

Klopfenstein, K. (2010). Does the Advanced Placement program save taxpayers money? The effect of AP participation on time to college graduation. In P. M. Sadler, G. Sonnert, R. H.

Tai, & K. Klopfenstein (Eds.), *AP: A critical examination of the Advanced Placement Program* (pp. 189–218). Cambridge, MA: Harvard Education Press.

Klopfenstein, K., & Thomas, M. K. (2009). The link between advanced placement experience and early college success. *Southern Economic Journal, 75*(3), 873–891.

Klopfenstein, K., & Thomas, M. K. (2010). Evaluating the policies of states and colleges. In P. M. Sadler, G. Sonnert, R. H. Tai, & K. Klopfenstein (Eds.), *AP: A critical examination of the Advanced Placement Program* (pp. 167–188). Cambridge, MA: Harvard Education Press.

Klugman, J. (2013). The Advanced Placement arms race and the reproduction of educational inequality. *Teachers College Record, 115*(5), 1–34.

Knopf, D., Park, M. J., & Mulye, T. P. (2008). The mental health of adolescents: A national profile. Report from the National Adolescent Health Information Center, UCSF: San Francisco. http://nahic.ucsf.edu/wp-content/uploads/2008/02/2008-Mental-Health-Brief.pdf

Kohn, A. (2006). *The homework myth: Why our kids get too much of a bad thing*. Cambridge, MA: Da Capo Press.

Kralovec, E., & Buell, J. (2000). *The end of homework: How homework disrupts families, overburdens children, and limits learning*. Boston: Beacon Press.

Krashen, S. (2001). More smoke and mirrors: A critique of the national reading panel report on fluency. *Phi Delta Kappan, 83*(2), 119–123.

Lambert, A. L. (2007). *Student engagement in high-performing urban high schools*. (Unpublished doctoral dissertation). University of Southern California, Los Angeles, CA. Retrieved from http://digitallibrary.usc.edu/cdm/ref/collection/p15799coll127/id/524057

Larson, R. (2000). Toward a psychology of positive youth development. *American Psychologist, 55*(1), 170–183.

Larson, R. (2001). How U.S. children and adolescents spend time: What it does (and doesn't) tell us about their development. *Current Directions in Psychological Science, 10*(5), 170–183.

Larson, R., & Kleiber, D. (1993). Daily experience of adolescents. In P. H. Tolan & B. J. Cohler (Eds.), *Handbook of clinical research and practice with adolescents* (pp. 125–145). Wiley series on personality processes. Oxford, England: Wiley.

Lenhart, A., Ling, R., Campbell, S., & Purcell, K. (2010). *Teens and mobile phones*. Washington, DC: Pew Internet Project, Pew Research Center. Retrieved from http://www.pewinternet.org/2010/04/20/teens-and-mobile-phones/

Lepper, M. R. (1983). Extrinsic reward and intrinsic motivation: Implications for the classroom. In J. M. Levine & M. C. Wang (Eds.), *Teacher and student perceptions: Implications for learning* (pp. 281–317). Hillsdale, NJ: Erlbaum.

Levine, M. (2012). *Teach your children well: Why values and coping skills matter more than grades, trophies, or "Fat Envelopes"*. New York: Harper.

Levine, M. (2006). *The price of privilege: How parental pressure and material advantage are creating a generation of disconnected and unhappy kids*. New York: Harper.

Lewis, C. W., Winokur, M. A., Cobb, B. R., Gliner, G. S., & Schmidt, J. (2005). *Block scheduling in the high school setting: A synthesis of evidence-based research*. Office of Vocational and Adult Education: U.S. Department of Education. Retrieved from http://www.mprinc.com/products/pdf/Block_Scheduling_in_HS.pdf

Li, Y., & Lerner, R. M. (2011). Trajectories of school engagement during adolescence: Implications for grades, depression, delinquency, and substance use. *Developmental Psychology, 47*(1), 233–247.

Loveless, T. (2003). *The Brown Center Annual Report on American Education: Part II, Do students have too much homework?* Brookings Institution Press. Retrieved from http://www.brookings.edu/research/reports/2014/03/18-homework-loveless

Lythcott-Haims, J. (2015). *How to raise an adult.* New York: Holt.

Mac Iver, D. J. (1990). Meeting the needs of young adolescents: Advisory groups, interdisciplinary teaching teams, and school transition programs. *Phi Delta Kappan, 71*, 458–464.

Mac Iver, D. J., & Epstein, J. L. (1991). Responsive practices in the middle grades: Teacher teams, advisory groups, remedial instruction, and school transition programs. *American Journal of Education, 99*(4). Retrieved from www.jstor.org/stable/1085561

Mahoney, J. L., Cairns, B. D., & Farmer, T. W. (2003). Promoting interpersonal competence and educational success through extracurricular activity participation. *Journal of Educational Psychology, 95*(2), 409–418.

Mahoney, J., Larson, R., & Eccles, J. (Eds.). (2005). *Organized activities as contexts of development: Extracurricular activities, after-school and community programs.* Hillsdale, NJ: Erlbaum.

Maltese, A. V., Dexter, K. M., Tai, R. H., & Sadler, P. M. (2007). Breaking from tradition: Unfulfilled promises of block scheduling in science. *Science Educator, 16*(1), 1–7.

Marks, H. M. (2000). Student engagement in instructional activity: Patterns in the elementary, middle, and high school years. *American Educational Research Journal, 37*(1), 153–184.

Marzano, R. J. (2006). *Classroom assessment and grading that work.* Alexandria, VA: Association for Supervision and Curriculum Development.

Mass Insight Education. (2012). *Mass math + science initiative: Impact.* Retrieved from http://www.massinsight.org/mmsi/impact/

McClure, L., Yonezawa, S., & Jones, M. (2010). Can school structures improve teacher student relationships? The relationship between advisory programs, personalization and students' academic achievement. *Education Policy Analysis Archives, 18*(17). Retrieved from http://epaa.asu.edu/ojs/article/view/719/845

McHugh, R. M., Horner, C. G., Colditz, J. B., Wallace, T. L. (2013). Bridges and barriers: Adolescent perceptions of student-teacher relationships. *Urban Education, 48*(1), 9–43. Retrieved from http://uex.sagepub.com/content/48/1/9.full.pdf

McNeely, C., & Falci, C. (2004). School connectedness and the transition into and out of health-risk behavior among adolescents: A comparison of social belonging and teacher support. *Journal of School Health, 74*(7), 284–292. Retrieved from http://paa2004.princeton.edu/papers/42082

McTighe, J. & Ferrara, S. (1998). Assessing learning in the classroom. *Student Assessment Series.* Washington, DC: National Education Association.

Medina, N., & Neill, D. M. (1988). Fallout from the testing explosion: How 100 million standardized exams undermine equity and excellence in America's public schools. *A National Center for Fair and Open Testing Report.* Cambridge, MA: Fair Test.

Meiklejohn, J., Phillips, C., Freedman, M. L., Griffin, M. L., Biegel, G., Roach, A., … et al. (2012). Integrating mindfulness training into K–12 education: Fostering the resilience of teachers and students. *Mindfulness, 1*(1). Retrieved from http://www.mindfulnessinstitute.ca/Portals/15/pdf/Integrating_Mindfulness_Training_Into_K-12_Education.pdf

Mikki, J. (2006). Students' homework and TIMSS 2003 mathematics results. Paper presented at the International Conference, *Teaching Mathematics Retrospective and Perspective*, Tartu, Estonia. Retrieved from http://files.eric.ed.gov/fulltext/ED491866.pdf

Milewski, G. B., & Gillie, J. M. (2002). What are the characteristics of AP teachers? An examination of survey research. (College Board Research Report No. 2002–10.) New York: The College Board.

Mindful Schools (2013). Presentation at Bridging the Hearts and Minds of Youth conference. http://www.mindfulschools.org/about-mindfulness/research/

Mitra, D. L., & Gross, S. J. (2009). Increasing student voice in high school reform: Building partnerships, improving outcomes. *Educational Management, Administration, & Leadership, 37*(4), 522–543.

Murray, C., & Zvoch, K. (2011). Teacher-student relationships among behaviorally at-risk African American youth from low-income backgrounds: Student perceptions, teacher perceptions, and socioemotional adjustment correlates. *Journal of Emotional and Behavioral Disorders, 19*(1), 41–54.

National Association of Health Education Centers. (2005). Kids and stress, how do they handle it? *KidsHealth KidsPoll, October 12, 2005.* Retrieved from the National Association of Health Education Centers (NAHEC) database.

National Commission on Excellence in Education. (1983). *A nation at risk: The imperative for educational reform.* Washington, DC: U.S. Department of Education. Retrieved from http://www2.ed.gov/pubs/NatAtRisk/index.html

National Education Commission on Time and Learning. (2005). *Prisoners of time.* Washington, DC: Education Commission of the States. (Reprint of the 1994 Report of the National Education Commission on Time and Learning). Retrieved from http://www.ecs.org/clearinghouse/64/52/6452.pdf

National Research Council. (1999). *Myths and tradeoffs: The role of tests in undergraduate admissions.* Washington, DC: The National Academies Press. Retrieved from http://www.nap.edu/openbook.php?record_id=9632&page=14

National Research Council. (2002). *Learning and understanding: Improving advanced study of mathematics and science in U.S. high schools.* Committee on Programs for Advanced Study of Mathematics and Science in American High Schools. J. P. Gollub, M. W. Bertenthal, J. B. Labov, and P. C. Curtis (Eds.). Center for Education, Division of Behavioral and Social Sciences and Education. Washington, DC: National Academy Press.

National Research Council. (2004). *Engaging schools: Fostering high school students' motivation to learn.* Washington, DC: The National Academies Press.

National Sleep Foundation. (2006). *Stick to routines* [Press release].

National Sleep Foundation. (2011). *Sleepy connected Americans: National sleep foundation releases annual sleep in America poll exploring connections with communications technology use and sleep* [Press release]. Retrieved from http://sleepfoundation.org/media-center/press-release/annual-sleep-america-poll-exploring-connections-communications-technology-use-

National Sleep Foundation (2015). *National Sleep Foundation 2015 Poll*. Retrieved from http://www.sleephealthjournal.org/article/S2352-7218(15)00053-4/pdf

Nidich, S. I., Rainforth, M.V., Haaga, D.A.F., Hagelin, J., Salerno, J. W., Travis, F., … Schneider, R. H. (2009). A randomized controlled trial on effects of the Transcendental Meditation Program on blood pressure, psychological distress, and coping in young adults. *American Journal of Hypertension*, *22*(12), 1326–1331.

Noddings, N. (1992). *The challenge to care in schools: An alternative approach to education*. New York: Teachers College Press.

O'Connor, K. B. (2009). *How to grade for learning, K-12*. Thousand Oaks, CA: Corwin Press.

O'Keeffe, G. S., & Clarke-Pearson, K. (2011). The impact of social media on children, adolescents, and families. *Pediatrics*, *127*(4), 800–804.

Olsson, E. (2009). The role of relations: Do disadvantaged adolescents benefit more from high-quality social relations? *Acta Sociologica*, *52*(3), 263–286.

Osberg, J., Pope, D., & Galloway, M. (2006). Students matter in school reform: Leaving fingerprints and becoming leaders. *International Journal of School Leadership*, *9*(4), 329–343.

Osterman, K. F. (2000). Students' need for belonging in the school community. *Review of Educational Research*, *70*(3), 323–367.

Owens, J. A., Belon, K., & Moss, P. (2010). Impact of delaying school start time on adolescent sleep, mood, and behavior. *Journal of Pediatric & Adolescent Medicine*, *164*(7).

Paek, P. L., Ponte, E., Sigel, I., Braun, H., & Powers, D. (2005). *A portrait of Advanced Placement teachers' practices* (College Board Research Report No. 2005–7). New York: The College Board. Retrieved from http://research.collegeboard.org/sites/default/files/publications/2012/7/researchreport-2005–7-portrait-advanced-placement-teachers-practices.pdf

Palo Alto Unified School District. (2013). *2013 calendar survey results*. Retrieved from http://pausd.org/community/Committees/Calendar/index.shtml

Parker, W., Mosborg, S., Bransford, J., Vye, N., Wilkerson, J., & Abbott, R. (2011). Rethinking advanced high school coursework: Tackling the depth/breadth tension in the *AP U.S. Government and Politics* course. *Journal of Curriculum Studies*, *43*(4), 533–559.

Partnership for 21st Century Skills (2009). P21 framework definitions. Retrieved from http://www.p21.org/storage/documents/P21_Framework_Definitions.pdf

Partnership for Drug-Free Kids (Join Together Staff). (2008). *PDFA: Teens using drugs to cope with stress, parents underestimating pressures*. Retrieved from http://www.drugfree.org/join-together/pdfateens-using drugs-to-cope-with-stress-parents-underestimating-pressures/

Phillippo, K. (2012). "You're trying to know me": Students from nondominant groups respond to teacher personalism. *Urban Review*, *44*(4), 441–467.

Phillippo, K. (2013). *Advisory in urban high schools: A study of expanded teacher roles*. New York: Palgrave MacMillan.

Piedmont Middle School (2014, April 21). PMS Bulletin for the week of April 21, 2014, www.piedmont.k12.ca.us/phs/campus-life/wellness-center.php

Poliner, R. A., & Miller Lieber, C. (2004). *The advisory guide: Designing and implementing effective advisory programs in secondary schools*. Cambridge, MA: Educators for Social Responsibility.

Pope, D. C. (2001). *Doing school: How we are creating a generation of stressed-out, materialistic, and miseducated students*. New Haven, CT: Yale University Press.

Pope, D. & Galloway, M. (2006, April). *Hazardous homework? The relationship between homework, goal orientation, and well-being in adolescence*. Paper presented at the annual meeting of the American Educational Research Association, Chicago, IL.

Prince, A. (2005). Using the principles of brain-based learning in the classroom: How to help a child learn. *Super Duper Publications*. Retrieved July 30, 2014, from http://www.superduperinc.com/handouts/pdf/81_brain.pdf

Queen, A., Algozzine, R. F., & Eaddy, M. A. (1997). The road we traveled: Scheduling in the 4X4 block. *NASSP Bulletin, 81*, 88–99.

Queen, J. A. (2000). Block scheduling revisited. *Phi Delta Kappan, 82*(3), 1–16.

Queen, J. A. (2009). *The block scheduling handbook* (2nd ed.). Thousand Oaks, CA: Corwin Press.

Ramstetter, C. L., Murray, R., & Garner, A. S. (2010). The crucial role of recess in schools. *Journal of School Health, 80*(11), 517–526.

Reddy, R., Rhodes, J. E., & Mulhall, P. (2003). The influence of teacher support on student adjustment in the middle school years: A latent growth curve study. *Development and Psychopathology, 15*(01), 119–138.

Reeve, J., Jang, H., Carrell, D., Jeon, S., & Barch, J. (2004). Enhancing students' engagement by increasing teachers' autonomy support. *Motivation and Emotion, 28*(2), 147.

Reeves, D. B. (2004). The case against the zero. *Phi Delta Kappan, 86*(4), 324–325.

Rice, E. (2011). *Design thinking: A process for developing and implementing district reform*. Stanford, CA: Stanford Center for Opportunity Policy in Education. Retrieved from https://edpolicy.stanford.edu/publications/pubs/260

Rivkin, S. G., Hanushek, E. A., & Kain, J. F. (2005). Teachers, schools, and academic achievement. *Econometrica, 73*(2), 417–458.

Roediger, H. L., & Karpicke, J. D. (2006). Test-enhanced learning: Taking memory tests improves long-term retention. *Psychological Science, 17*(3), 249–255.

Rosaen, C., & Benn, R. (2006). The experience of transcendental meditation in middle school students: A qualitative report. *Journal of Science and Healing, 2*(5), 422–425.

Sadler, P. M., & Sonnert, G. (2010). High school Advanced Placement and success in college in the sciences. In P. M. Sadler, G. Sonnert, R. H. Tai, & K. Klopfenstein (Eds.), *AP: A critical examination of the Advanced Placement program* (pp. 119–137). Cambridge, MA: Harvard Education Press.

Sadler, P. M., Sonnert, G., Tai, R. H., & Klopfenstein, K. (Eds.). (2010). *AP: A critical examination of the Advanced Placement program*. Cambridge, MA: Harvard Education Press.

Sagor, R. (2002). Lessons from skateboarders. *Educational Leadership*, *60*(1), 34–38.

Sanchez, B., Colon, Y., & Esparza, P. (2005). The role of sense of school belonging and gender in the academic adjustment of Latino adolescents. *Journal of Youth and Adolescence*, *34*(6), 619–628.

Sax, L. J., Hurtado, S., Lindholm, J. A., Astin, A. W., Korn, W. S., & Mahoney, K. M. (2004). *The American freshman: National norms for fall 2004*. University of Los Angeles, CA: Higher Education Research Institute. Retrieved from http://www.heri.ucla.edu/PDFs/pubs/TFS/Norms/Monographs/TheAmericanFreshman2004.pdf

Schonert-Reichl, K. A., & Lawlor, M. S. (2010). The effects of a mindfulness-based education program on pre- and early adolescents' well-being and social and emotional competence. *Mindfulness*, *1*(3), 137–151. Retrieved from http://thehawnfoundation.org/wp-content/uploads/2012/12/KSR-MSL_Mindfulness_2010-copy.pdf

Shepard, L. A. (2010). What the marketplace has brought us: Item-by-item teaching with little instructional insight. *Peabody Journal of Education*, *85*(2), 246–257.

Shernoff, D. J. (2010). *The experience of student engagement in high school classrooms: Influences and effects on long-term outcomes*. Saarbrücken, Germany: Lambert Academic Publishing.

Shernoff, D. J., Csikszentmihalyi, M., Schneider, B., & Shernoff, E. (2003). Student engagement in high school classrooms from the perspective of flow theory. *School Psychology Quarterly*, *18*(2), 158–176.

Shochet, I. M., Dadds, M. R., Ham, D., & Montague, R. (2006). School connectedness is an underemphasized parameter in adolescent mental health: Results of a community prediction study. *Journal of Clinical Child and Adolescent Psychology*, *35*(2), 170–179.

Sklad, M., Diekstra, R., De Ritter, M., Ben, J., & Gravesteijn, C. (2012). Effectiveness of school-based universal social, emotional, and behavioral programs: Do they enhance students' development in the area of skill, behavior, and adjustment? *Psychology in the Schools*, *49*(9), 892–909.

Stanford Sleep and Dreams. (2010). The Menlo-Atherton teen sleep program. Retrieved from http://www.end-your-sleep-deprivation.com/m-a-teen-sleep.html

Stewart, T., & Suldo, S. (2011). Relationships between social support sources and early adolescents' mental health: The moderating effect of student achievement level. *Psychology in Schools*, *48*(10), 1016–1033.

Strobel, J., & van Barneveld, A. (2009). When is PBL more effective? A meta-synthesis of meta-analyses comparing PBL to conventional classrooms. *Interdisciplinary Journal of Problem-based Learning*, *3*(1).

Topping, K. J., Samuels, J., & Paul, T. (2007). Does practice make perfect? Independent reading quantity, quality and student achievement. *Learning and Instruction*, *17*(3), 253–264.

Totten, S., & Nielson, W. (1994). Middle level students' perceptions of their advisor/advisee program: A preliminary study. *Current Issues in Middle Level Education*, *3*(2), 8–33.

Trautwein, U., Koller, O., Schmitz, B., & Baumert, J. (2002). Do homework assignments enhance achievement? A multilevel analysis in 7th-grade mathematics. *Contemporary Educational Psychology, 27*, 26–50.

Ullrich, W. J., & Yeaman, J. T. (1999). Using a modified block schedule to create a positive learning environment. *Middle School Journal, 31*(1), 14–20.

The University of Chicago Consortium on Chicago School Research (CCSR), http://ccsr.uchicago.edu

Vatterott, C. (2009). *Rethinking homework: Best practices that support diverse needs.* Alexandria, VA: Association for Supervision and Curriculum Development.

Wahlstrom, K. L. (2002). Changing times: Findings from the first longitudinal study of later high school start times. *NASSP Bulletin, 86*(633), 3–21.

Wahlstrom, K. L. (2014). *Examining the impact of later high school start times on the health and academic performance of high school students: A multi-site study.* Center for Applied Research and Educational Improvement: University of Minnesota.

Weissberg, R. P., & Cascarino, J. (2013, October). Academic learning + social-emotional learning = national priority. *Phi Delta Kappan, 95*(2), 8–13.

Wentzel, K. R. (1997). Student motivation in middle school: The role of perceived pedagogical caring. *Journal of Educational Psychology, 89*(3), 411–419.

The Whole Child Initiative, http://www.wholechildeducation.org

Wigfield, W., Eccles, J. S., & Rodriguez, D. (1998). The development of children's motivation in school contexts. *Review of Research in Education, 23*(1998), 73–118.

Wiggins, G. (1989). Teaching to the (authentic) test. *Educational Leadership, 46*(7), 41–47.

Wiggins, G. (2012). Seven keys to effective feedback. *Feedback for Learning, 70*(1), 10–16.

Wiggins, G., & McTighe, J. (1998). *Understanding by design.* Alexandria, VA: Association for Supervision and Curriculum Development.

Wiggins, G., & McTighe, J. (2005). *Understanding by design.* (Expanded 2nd ed.). Association for Supervision and Curriculum Development.

Yankelovich. (2006). *Kids and family reading report.* Scholastic Books. Retrieved from http://www.scholastic.com/aboutscholastic/news/KFRR_0207.pdf

Yazzie-Mintz, E. (2010). *Charting the path from engagement to achievement: A report on the 2009 high school survey of student engagement.* Bloomington, IN: Indiana University Center for Evaluation and Education Policy.

Yeager, D., & Dweck, C. (2012). Mindsets that promote resilience: When students believe that personal characteristics can be developed. *Educational Psychologist, 47*(4), 302–314.

Yonezawa, S., McClure, L., & Jones, M. (2012). *Personalization in schools. Students at the center: Teaching and learning in the era of the common core.* Boston, MA: Jobs for the Future.

Zepeda, S. J., & Mayers, R. S. (2006). An analysis of research on block scheduling. *Review of Educational Research, 76*(1), 137–170.

Zhao, Y. (2002, February 1). High school drops its A.P. courses, and colleges don't seem to mind. *New York Times.* Retrieved from http://www.nytimes.com/2002/02/01/nyregion/high-school-drops-its-ap-courses-and-colleges-don-t-seem-to-mind.html

Ziegler, S., & Mulhall, L. (1994). Establishing and evaluating a successful advisory program in a middle school. *Middle School Journal, 25*(4), 42–46.

Zins, M. J., & Elias, J. E. (2007). Social and emotional learning: Promoting the development of all students. *Journal of Educational and Psychological Consultation, 17*(2–3), 233–255.

Zygmunt-Fillwalk, E., & Bilello, T. E. (2005). Parents' victory in reclaiming recess for their children. *Childhood Education, 82*(1), 19–23.

Index

Page references followed by *fig* indicate an illustrated figure; followed by *e* indicate an exhibit; followed by *t* indicates a table.

National Education Association, 55

National Education Commission on Time and Learning (NECTL), 25

National Math and Science Initiative (NMSI), 124

National Parent Teacher Association, 55

National Research Council, 62, 125

National Resource Council, 123

National Sleep Foundation, 30, 169

Neier, S. M., 44

Nella, J., 148

Neumark-Sztainer, D., 170

Newsweek magazine, 126

Nidich, R., 153

Nidich, S. I., 153

Nielson, W., 140

Nisan, M., 114

No Child Left Behind (2001), 40

Noddings, N., 138

Noggle, J. J., 153

Notre Dame High School case study, 26–28

The Nueva School and the Institute for Social and Emotional Learning case study, 148–152

O

O'Connor, K. B., 114

O'Dwyer, L. M., 187

Ofek, S., 49

Olsson, E., 137

Ono, H., 41, 165

The Open Session (SEL program), 150–152, 156

Opt-in programs, 188–189

Osberg, J., 164

Osterman, K. F., 136

Otten, D., 83, 85

Owen, J. A., 31

P

Pack, P. L., 124

Palo Alto Unified School District, 35, 36

Parent education: Community of Concern parent education program (Junmipero Serra High School), 175–177; interactive scenarios used for, 178–181; Menlo-Atherton High school program on, 174–175; social media and blogs used for, 181–183; strategies for effective, 173–174. *See also* Educating faculty, parents, and students

Parents: concerns over student engagement by, 62; culture of integrity action plan for, 15–16; educating them on on PDF (playtime, downtime, and family time), 164–174; involving them in implementing school schedule changes, 28; JLS Middle School policy on homework responsibilities of, 53*e*; preparing them for project-based learning (PBL), 85; recommendations on homework for teachers to suggest to, 55–56; responding to objections to moving semester exams by, 35–36; Tiger mom syndrome of, 43

Paris, A. H., 63

Park, M. J., 137

Parker, W., 69

Partnership for 21st Century Assessment, 108, 112, 113

Partnership for Drug-Free Kids, 2

Paul, T., 55

PDF (playtime, downtime, and family time): description of, 164–165; downtime component of, 168–169; family time component of, 170; playtime component of, 165–168; strategies for spreading the word about, 170–183; timewheel on how kids spend their time, 168*fig*

Peer pressure, 167

Performance-based assessments: description of, 94–95; framework of approaches and methods, 95, 96*fig*; process-focused, 95; of student understanding, 95, 97

The Pew Research Project, 167

Phillippo, K., 138, 140

Phillips, B., 31

Piedmont High Campus Life Wellness Center, 146

Piedmont Middle School survey (2014), 25–26

Piedmont Unified School District, 145–146

Pilot programs, 188–189

Playtime: PDF (playtime, downtime, and family time) component of, 164–165; physical, social, and mental benefits of, 165–168

Pliska, A.-M., 24

Poliner, R. A., 140

Ponte, E., 124

Pope, D. C., 1, 2, 34, 42, 62, 63, 65, 68, 90, 97, 113, 125, 137, 164, 165, 166, 174, 180, 190

Powers, D., 124

Pressure, identifying causes of unhealthy stress and, 12–14

Prince, A., 20

Prisoners of Time report (1994, 2005), 24–25

Process-focused assessment, 95, 96*fig*

Product-based performance assessment, 96*fig*

Project-based learning (PBL): backward planning role in, 83–84; description and two examples of, 68–69; getting started with, 83–86; Laura Docter's Classroom case study on, 71–82; origins of, 67–68; as requiring teacher flexibility, 82–83; research findings on, 69–71; Sample Materials from Laura Docter's Rome Project, 76*e*–82; school initiatives addressing, 5*t*; SPACE framework on, 17*fig*; Waldorf School of the Peninsula case study on, 86–87

Purcell, K., 167